REGIONAL DEVELOPMENT
Problems and Policy Measures

About the Editors

Abdul Aziz is a Professor of Economics at the Institute for Social and Economic Change, Bangalore. He holds a Chair in Micro-level Planning at the Institute and guides research students.

Prior to joining the Institute in 1975, Dr. Aziz worked at the Shri Ram Centre for Industrial Relations and Human Resources, New Delhi and taught economics at Mysore University. Besides directing several research projects, he has published several books and research papers.

Sudhir Krishna is currently Divisional Commissioner, Gulbarga Division (Karnataka). Earlier, he served as Assistant Commissioner of Chikamangalur, Director of Sugar, Deputy Commissioner of Dakshin Kannada District and Chief Secretary of Dharwad Zilla Parishad. In between, he served as Deputy Director/Deputy Secretary to the Government of Uttar Pradesh in its Institutional Finance Department.

He did his Master of Science in Physics from Banaras Hindu University in 1974. Later, he did a Master's Degree Programme in Public Management in the John Heinz III School of Public Policy and Management, Carnegie Mellon University, Pittsburgh (USA).

For about four years (1990-93) he worked in the LBS National Academy of Administration, Mussoorie as member of the Faculty of Public Administration and Social Management. During this stay, he took interest in Decentralised Administration, Panchayati Raj and Programme Evaluation. He has published some articles on the same issues.

REGIONAL DEVELOPMENT
Problems and Policy Measures

Editors

ABDUL AZIZ
Professor,
Economics Unit, Institute for
Social and Economic Change
Bangalore-560072

SUDHIR KRISHNA
I.A.S.
Divisional Commissioner
Gulbarga Division,
Gulbarga-585102

Published by

CONCEPT PUBLISHING COMPANY, NEW DELHI - 110059

for

INSTITUTE FOR SOCIAL AND ECONOMIC CHANGE
BANGALORE - 560072

ISBN 81-7022-581-7

First Published 1996

Abdul **Aziz** (*b.* 1937)
Sudhir **Krishna** (*b.* 1954)

Published and Printed by
Ashok Kumar Mittal
Concept Publishing Company
A/15-16, Mohan Garden,
New Delhi - 110 059
Phones : 5554042, 5504042

PREFACE

The papers included in this volume are those presented in a seminar held at Gulbarga during September 19-21,1994. The seminar was sponsored by the Hyderabad-Karnataka Area Development Board (HKADB), Gulbarga and organised by the Institute for Social and Economic Change (ISEC), Bangalore. The HKADB desired that a detailed study of the H-K region economy covering its problems and prospects for development should be undertaken by social science researchers with a view to getting inputs on future course of action to be followed. The region had remained economically and socially backward in spite of conscious efforts made by the Government of Karnataka to accelerate development. The weak response of the region to conscious efforts had remained a paradox. Further attempt to accelerate development ought to be preceded by resolving this paradox. This meant that the constraints operating in the H-K region economy should be identified and released, and that the opportunities available for promoting development in this region should also be identified and exploited. The seminar had kept this broad perspective both when the papers were commissioned and the discussion was directed.

The papers for the seminar were invited from scholars working in the various fields of regional development and the latter were provided with a brief framework of analysis for their use. To get appropriate feed-back and field insights, a brain-storming session was held in Gulbarga to which local leaders, scholars, administrators and NGOs had been invited. Two consultation sessions were held in ISEC to identify research issues, data sources and to discuss the tentative findings. The final version of the papers was presented in five technical sessions and the discussion was recorded by professors P H Rayappa, M Prahladachar, Nimbur and M R Narayana who acted as rapporteurs. Based on the findings of the papers and the seminar discussion, Sudhir Krishna prepared the seminar recommendations and presented them to the Government of Karnataka for necessary action. For want of space and other constraints we could not include in this volume all the papers presented in the seminar. We wish to thank all the paper writers and the participants of the seminar for their valuable time and effort.

The seminar was inaugurated by Dr P V Shenoi, Director, Institute for Social and Economic Change, Prof. G Thimmaiah presented the key-note address and Prof. N Rudriah, Vice-Chancellor, Gulbarga University, gave the presidential remarks. The valedictory address was delivered by Prof. D M Nanjundappa, Vice-Chairman, State Planning Board, Government of Karnataka under the Chairmanship of Shri S K Ghosal IAS, Additional Chief Secretary, Government of Karnataka. We wish to record our deep sense of gratitude to all of them for giving us their time.

The seminar was funded by the HKADB, and support in various forms came from ISEC, Gulbarga University, Hyderabad-Karnataka Chamber of Commerce and Industries, Gulbarga and the local Development Departments to whom we are extremely grateful. We wish to specifically remember the hard work put in by Messers. Paramesh Pande IAS, Pattana Shetty KAS, at Gulbarga and back at Bangalore by Messrs H S Sadananda, H K Govinda Rao and Muniyappa to make the seminar a success. The several drafts of the manuscript were typed by Ms. M S Nagavalli. To them all we are much beholden.

Bangalore, ABDUL AZIZ
October 24, 1994 SUDHIR KRISHNA

CONTENTS

CONTENTS

LIST OF CONTRIBUTORS

Abdul Aziz, Professor, Economics Unit, ISEC, Bangalore

A. S. Seetharamu, Professor and Head, Education Unit, ISEC, Bangalore

C. Charles Nelson, Technical Assistant, Economics Unit, ISEC, Bangalore

G. Thimmaiah, Professor and Head, Economics Unit, ISEC, Bangalore

Hemlata Rao, Professor, Economics Unit, ISEC, Bangalore

M. Johnson Samuel, Assistant Professor, Population Research Centre, ISEC, Bangalore

M. Devendra Babu, Technical Assistant, Economics Unit, ISEC, Bangalore

M. Prahladachar, Professor and Head, Rural Economics Unit, ISEC, Bangalore

M. R. Narayana, Associate Professor, Population Research Center, ISEC, Bangalore

M. Venkata Reddy, Associate Professor, Ecology Economics Unit, ISEC, Bangalore

M. Vivekananda, Assistant Professor, Agriculture Development and Rural Transformation Unit, ISEC, Bangalore

N. Sivanna, Assistant Professor, Development Administration Unit, ISEC, Bangalore

P. H. Rayappa, Professor and Head, Population Research Center, ISEC, Bangalore

S. N. Sangita, Associate Professor, Development Administration Unit, ISEC, Bangalore

Sudhir Krishna, Divisional Commissioner, Gulbarga Division, Government of Karnataka, Gulbarga

Syed Ajmal Pasha, Assistant Professor, Ecology Economics Unit, ISEC, Bangalore

V. S. Satyapriya, Associate Professor, Agriculture Development and Rural Transformation Unit, ISEC, Bangalore

1

EXECUTIVE SUMMARY AND RECOMMENDATIONS

Sudhir Krishna

In this Chapter an attempt is made to summarise the findings of the papers and the recommendations that emerged from the papers presented in the seminar and the discussion that followed. The presentation in this chapter is rather non-conventional and mechanical. Nevertheless, care is taken to capture, as far as possible, the main points of the papers and the discussion that is of interest to the policy makers.

While the sequencing of the points more or less follows the sequencing of the papers in the present volume, the findings and recommendations presented do not strictly follow the same order. The presentation of findings and recommendations is done under the theme of discussion than under each of the papers. This procedure is resorted to keeping in view the necessity of listing out the recommendations under different heads of development departments so that the policy making body could easily choose and pick up that set of recommendations which is of direct interest to it.

The summary of findings and the recommendations following therefrom are presented under 15 broad headings. The subjects covered are natural and human resources, infrastructure including irrigation, politico-administrative institutions, intra-regional disparities, regional development strategies, development of agriculture, industry, education and health, and development of various economic and social classes of people.

I. Sustainable Utilisation and Management of Land Resources

1. The common property resources available for marginal farmers and landless labourers have declined over the years due to increase in encroachment and grants of such lands.
2. The forests are getting severely degraded over the years.
3. The net cropped area has gone up over the years but only at the cost of uncultivated common lands.

   To overcome these problems, the following policy interventions are recommended:

   a. Further encroachment of uncultivated common lands should be checked forthwith by all means.
   b. Uncultivated common lands should be developed under Joint Forest Planning and Management (JFPM) for fodder, fuelwood, timber, grass and fruit yielding trees, with the active participation of the local people.
   c. Agro-forestry and silvi-pasture should be encouraged on these lands, so that higher levels of stall feeding of animals could be encouraged.

II. Human Resources

The human resources scenario of Hyderabad-Karnataka region is characterised by the following features:

a. A large proportion of rural population is engaged as agricultural labourers.
b. A significant out migration of work force, especially the male population, every year; and
c. An increasing work participation rate among women in the rural areas.

In the circumstances, the following recommendations are made for optimal utilisation of human resources in the rural areas of this region:

a. Promote stability of agriculture by providing irrigation facilities, which would reduce the need for migration of rural workforce.
b. Emphasise on dryland agriculture development.
c. Formulate an employment guarantee programme.

III. Development of Animal Husbandry

1. The indigenous variety of cattle dominate in the total livestock population of the region (being 41.6%) followed by goats and sheep (37.6%).
2. The yield of milk, meat and eggs is lower in this region as compared to rest of the State.
3. The rural economy of the region depends to a large extent on the livestock resources for draught power, manure, milk and even cash.
4. The cattle population is facing scarcity of fodder and water, and lack of medical attention.

To take care of the above problems, the following policy interventions are recommended:

a. Qualitative improvement in livestock should be taken up as a massive programme.
b. The local indigenous breed of livestock should be upgraded into more productive animals.
c. Veterinary staff should be properly trained.
d. Fodder and feed development should be given more attention.
e. Suitable animal husbandry programmes such as dairy development with good marketing facilities should be formulated and implemented.

IV. Infrastructure

A. Roads, Railways and Transport

1. The average length of all roads per 100 sq km of area is far less in this region as compared to the State average.
2. The quality of the road network is also not good, largely due to the black cotton soil terrain.
3. The rail network is strong but only in a limited area.
4. The road and rail networks are not fairly well interconnected.

The following recommendations are made on this sector of infrastructure:

a. The road development, including National and State highways, should be given special attention. A master plan should be prepared and implemented in a time-bound fashion to bring the road network on par with the State average and with the requirement of the economy.

b. The road and rail network should be developed in an inter-dependent and inter-linked fashion.

c. Gaps in rail network should be identified and bridged. For instance, rail link between Gulbarga and Bidar, and Gulbarga-Raichur and Bellary should be established. Hospet-Kottur railway line should be extended upto Harihar.

d. Maintenance of road network should be given special attention.

e. Bus connections should be provided to all the villages. If required, private sector should also be utilised along with KSRTC for the purpose.

B. Power

1. The per capita consumption of power in agriculture sector is far less in this region (5 kWh, 1993-94) as compared to the State average (137 kWh).
2. The number of energised electric pumpsets per 1000 ha of gross cropped area (March 1989) was 2.45 in H-K region as against the State average of 5.28. The consumption of power for agriculture per hec. of gross cropped area was only 12 kWh (1983-94) as compared to the State average of 512.

The reason for such low consumption of power for agriculture sector needs to be investigated further.

C. Credit Institutions

Although the network of credit institutions is adequate, atleast in comparison with the state situation, there is a lack of banking habit among the people as reflected in lower deposit and credit accounts per thousand of population in the region.

The recovery of cooperative dues is very poor, with the overdues of outstanding being as high as 73 per cent among agricultural cooperatives. The situation in Bidar district is better but the overdues and default plague the cooperatives of Gulbarga and Raichur districts. This has retarded the flow of credit especially for agricultural development.

In this scenario, the following recommendations are made:

a. A programme for credit awareness among the people to utilise credit facilities, and to save and invest money in a productive manner should be taken up.
b. The agricultural cooperative institutions should be activated to recover the outstanding dues and more funds be channelled into the area to promote economic activities.

V. Irrigation Development

1. In the existing major and medium irrigation projects in this region, particularly in the Tunga Bhadra project area, drainage is totally neglected. As a result, thousands of acres of highly fertile lands are turning saline and uncultivable. Therefore, such projects should be brought under a special programme for providing drainage.
2. The large availability of flow water through rivers—big and small—and canals of irrigation projects should also be harnessed for irrigation through lift irrigation systems. This should be of two types viz., individual lift irrigation and group or cooperative lift irrigation.
3. The on-going irrigation projects in the region, which are lingering for decades, should be provided with sufficient funds to complete them in the next five years' time so that the money spent on the project could be put to productive use.
4. Warabandi and localisation of command should be rigorously enforced. The system of reaching water to tail-enders in the canal systems should be given prompt and full attention.
5. A series of balancing reservoirs should be constructed in the command areas. This would provide better utilisation of water during the flood seasons and also help reach water to the tail-enders.
6. Funds under employment oriented schemes such as the Jawahar Rozgar Yojana and Nemmadi should also be utilised for irrigation projects as well.
7. The development of command area should be taken up on the basis of an integrated approach which would consist of water management, land development, drainage, appropriate cropping pattern and the required inputs.
8. The potential created under various irrigation projects is not being fully utilised due to inadequate land development. This

needs to be attended to immediately.

9. The canal system of Tungabhadra is suffering from frequent breaches and breakdowns. The patch work approach to their repairs is not leading us any further. A system of long-term remedial approach should be adopted to solve this problem.
10. The villages situated close to the river beds in irrigation project areas suffer from various problems including health hazard due to mosquito breeding. Such villages should be shifted sufficiently away.
11. The ground-water potential, which forms a significant part of irrigation in the region, deserves special attention for its harvesting as well as recharge. A careful development strategy should be designed and implemented for the purpose.
12. Water is a scarce commodity in this region. To use it with optimal economy, the sprinkler and drip systems should be encouraged, particularly for horticultural crops.

VI. Politico-Administrative Institutions

1. The Hyderabad-Karnataka Area Development Board should be promoted as an institution for preparing perspective plans not only for the region but for its sub-regions as well. It should also be capable of analysing and integrating the development programmes implemented through various other agencies such as Zilla Panchayats, CADA, State and Central sector agencies and NGOs. To perform such leadership roles, the politico administrative set up of the HKADB needs attention in the following ways:

a. The data base for regional and micro planning should be strengthened.
b. The membership of the Board being 52 is too large to make it effective. A smaller Executive Committee should be constituted, with representation to all the districts.
c. The Governing Body of the Board and its Implementation Committee should meet regularly with the prescribed periodicity of three months and one month respectively. This would help better planning and monitoring.
d. The Board should be in a position to interact with the Gram Panchayats also so as to identify the felt needs of the people in a more realistic fashion.
e. The technical and extension staff of the Board should be

strengthened so that the Board could provide effective leadership to the Zilla Panchayats and other institutions in making objective and qualitatively better micro and regional plans.

g. Training programmes for officials and non-officials should be organised to make their participation effective.

VII. Intra-Regional Disparities

1. Though the H-K region is backward as compared to the rest of Karnataka, yet within this region itself there are strong intra-regional variations.

a. There have to be structural indicators relating such as to agriculture, industry, finance, transport, communication, education, health etc., to measure the levels of development of different talukas from various perspectives. Such indicators should form the basis for allocation of funds among talukas and identification of thrust areas for development among them.

b. The concept of growth centres should be adopted to plan for the growth of different geographical/demographic conglomerations. For instance, a highly dense conglomeration, such as a municipal corporation, should be identified and development for each one of them should be uniquely defined.

VIII. Development Planning Strategy

The various development indicators such as the per capita income, persons working in industrial enterprises, number of non-agricultural enterprises, road length per 100 sq km area, telephones per lakh of population, literacy rate, hospital beds per lakh of population etc., are far less in the districts of this region as compared to the rest of Karnataka. Cryptically speaking, the following scenario emerges :

1. Though Bellary district is somewhat better in respect of a few of these indicators, yet, in the majority of development indicators, this region is certainly underdeveloped.
2. Planning for sectoral development attempted by the HKAD Board from 1990-94 has not been commensurate with the regional framework recommended by the Dharam Singh Committee in the year 1981. Further, the "MLA sector" of works, euphemistically described as the Rural Development and Panchayat Raj Sector, has also accentuated this problem viz.,

improper sectoral allocation of the scarce resources of the HKAD Board.

3. The funds provided to the HKAD Board amounted to Rs.50 to Rs. 60 crore per annum which are grossly inadequate for leaving any significant impact on the development of infrastructure situation in the region. This situation has further deteriorated on account of the so-called "MLA quota" in the annual plans of HKAD Board which took away as much as 40 per cent of the funds available with the Board.
4. The HKAD Board, instead of paying attention to regional and sectoral planning, has confined largely to monitoring projects and disbursing funds.
5. The HKAD Board has not been able to integrate its plan with the plans of other developmental agencies such as Zilla Panchayats, CADA, DLDB etc. Moreover, it has not yet involved Zilla Panchayats and Gram Panchayats in identifying the felt needs of each area and the people.

In the above background, the following recommendations are made for policy intervention:

1. The HKAD Board should focus its attention on more effective and qualitative regional planning by involving other institutions such as ZP, CADA, DLDB etc., in the process.
2. It should focus on the sub-regional planning at block/taluk level for making sub-regional plans effective.
3. The concept of "MLA quota" works should be reviewed and all people's representatives belonging to the H-K region should be involved in the process of planning. However, the technical element in preparing development plan should remain the main stay of planning.
4. The Board should not depend only on State for its financial resources; it should also examine the feasibility of raising loans, subventions, donations and gifts from central and state governments. It should invest money in productive lines also so that its activities could be sustained without total dependence on State Plan.
5. The Board should identify thrust and priority areas of development of the region, integrate them in a systematic manner among the sub-regions and then prepare development plans.
6. There should be more and more micro and macro studies to

analyse and highlight the basic issues relating to development of this area.

IX. Agricultural Development

1. Considering the scarcity of water and frequent spells of droughts in this region, proper cost-effective technology for dryland agriculture is very much required in this area.
2. Presently 45 per cent of the gross cropped area in the region is under pulses and oil seeds which are raised under largely rainfed conditions. This structure of agriculture needs greater attention by way of research and extension services.
3. The dependence of farmers on agricultural research programmes is very high in this region. The reason is that land is highly fertile but the current yields are fairly poor. The agricultural extension and the research institutions should work in close cooperation to improve the productivity of agriculture sector.
4. Side by side, the effectiveness of the existing extension departments should be enhanced by way of reorientation and constant upgradation of their knowledge and skills through training.
5. Large extent of command created under Upper Krishna Project is actually not utilised largely due to inadequate land development. Land development activities have come to a complete stand-still due to poor recovery of loans by CADA. These problems need to be solved expeditiously.
6. Marketing arrangements for the agricultural and allied sector produce need to be strengthened.
7. Value addition of the agricultural produce by way of agro-processing units deserves to be given prompt attention.
8. Instead of mono-crop, inter-cropping should be encouraged so that the failure of one crop due to diseases etc., does not hit the farmers too hard.
9. Sericulture needs to be encouraged. At the same time, coordination between extension departments such as Sericulture, Agriculture and Horticulture needs to be streamlined so that they work in a synergetic fashion and not at cross purposes.
10. Except for rice, jowar and wheat, productivity of all other agricultural crops in this region is lower than the State average. This calls for a closer study and more active research and extension work for all such crops, particularly sunflower, cotton,

groundnut and sugarcane.

X. Industrial Development

1. The resource inventory of the region, including at micro levels, needs to be prepared urgently. Assistance of professional/research organisations can be taken for this purpose.
2. Closer links need to be established between entrepreneurs/ industries and research/educational institutions.
3. The delays involved in implementing the schemes of incentives and concessions for industrial investments has discouraged entrepreneurs coming to this area. Such red-tapism needs to be removed promptly.
4. Infrastructural development such as industrial estates, roads and power/water supply, conducive for industrial development should be taken up as a significant programme in this area.
5. The normal provision of incentives and concessions for industrial investments available in the State do not provide any special attention to this region. Therefore, this region has been unable to match areas such as Bangalore and Mysore in attracting investment. Special incentives should be announced for industrial investment in this region.
6. Small-scale industrial units help in dispersal of industries, remove intra-regional disparities and provide better employment potential. Therefore, more and more small-scale industrial units should be encouraged to be established in this region.
7. Rural industrialisation is a significant possibility in this region, considering its natural resources. These include mineral-based industries, forest-based industries, agro-based industries, engineering and non-conventional energy, textile and khadi and chemical-based industries and service industries.
8. Cooperative credit societies should be established in each village to provide finances for village and cottage industries.
9. Cooperative marketing network should be strengthened in rural areas.
10. Entrepreneurship Development Programmes (EDPs) should be organised periodically and frequently. The quality of this programme needs to be assured as well as carefully monitored.
11. The District Industries Centres should be made more active in making inventory of industrial, natural and human resources and other data base required for these districts.

12. The District Industries Centres should give equal attention to all the talukas in the districts and not confine only to District Headquarters.
13. Sickness in industry should be closely monitored and corrective action taken from time to time.

XI. Education Development

1. The literacy levels in these four districts is the poorest in the whole of the State. The literacy ratio of women is still poorer. Therefore, the Total Literacy Mission (TLM) programme going on in all the four districts should be implemented in right earnest.
2. TLM should be implemented as a multi-disciplinary functional programme involving not only the departments of Adult Education but also those of welfare including Health, Women and Child Development, Rural Development, Social Welfare etc.
3. Involvement of non-governmental organisations should be promoted and encouraged for running non-formal education and adult education programmes.
4. Higher education in this region has focussed more on arts and social sciences. Now this should be reversed by giving greater attention and priority to science education, keeping the overall development of the region in view.
5. Women's education needs special attention in this region as their participation in higher education is extremely low.
6. More hostel facilities at taluka levels and sanitary facilities at higher primary and upward levels for girls should be provided. Maintenance of toilet facilities in girls' high schools should also be given attention.
7. In-service training programmes for teachers, particularly for primary and high school levels, should be taken. This is specially required because until 1984 many untrained teachers had been appointed and they have remained untrained even till now.
8. Periodical and continuous monitoring of educational development is most essential. The Zilla Panchayats and the Office of the Joint Director of Public Instructions (JDPI) should work in closer coordination for this purpose.
9. Intra-region and inter-taluka disparities in educational development need to be bridged on priority basis.
10. Transfer of teachers from this region to outside areas should be checked.

11. Physical education and vocational education should be encouraged in the area.

XII. Health, Family Welfare and Population

1. Low female age at marriage, very low female literacy and low proportion of eligible couples' protection by different methods of family planning are leading to high growth of population in this region. In addition, the social value of preferring son to daughter has also accentuated population growth. Proper social involvement and awareness needs to be created in this regard.
2. The vacancy position of staff in the Department of Health and Family Welfare also hampers the health and family welfare programmes. The vacancies of health staff in this region should be filled by way of a carefully drafted policy and not by the general policy being followed so far.
3. Involvement of private and voluntary organisations for health-care sector should be encouraged.
4. Intra-regional disparities in health sector need to be identified. For this purpose, the health sub-centres should be taken as the level for preparing action plans for this sector.
5. The concept of 'Sulabh Shouchalaya' should be encouraged particularly in urban areas to promote health and hygiene awareness.

XIII. Implementation of Poverty Alleviation Programmes (PAPs)

1. The PRIs and NGOs should be involved in micro planning, implementation, monitoring and evaluation of the rural developement programmes.
2. Grama Sabhas should be empowered and encouraged to get involved effectively in identification of the socio-economic strengths and weaknesses of the villages, and in selection of the beneficiaries/sites for rural development programmes.
3. The rules for implementation of Rural Development Programmes should be made transparent and widely publicised among beneficiary population.
4. Monitoring of assets and utilisation and recovery of loans need special attention, with a view to promoting sustainability of the projects.
5. The PRI officials and non-official members should be provided

with proper training to effectively plan and implement the PAPs.

6. Gram Sabha meetings should be properly structured and well attended by government of officials also.

XIV. Women's Development

The socio-economic status of women in this region is charecterised by some specific features, namely:

a. An increasing participation in work force, especially in rural areas.
b. Pretty low literacy rate.
c. Adverse discrimination at home and in society.

The situation needs to be taken on by the following strategic efforts:

a. A well-defined programme for self-employment for women needs to be designed. In this context, the success of women's participation in dairy cooperatives, particularly in Bidar district, should be taken note of;
b. Enforcement of compulsory primary education for girls;
c. Vocationalisation of higher education to a good degree;
d. Improvement of health and a nutrition infrastructure for women;
e. Training of the women members of the PRIs in the various issues connected with the functions of PRIs should bc organised; and
f. Legal awareness camps should be organised for the benefit of women.

XV. Development of Scheduled Castes and Scheduled Tribes

The charecteristics of the socio-economic conditions of the SCs/STs in this region are:

a. Below par literacy rate
b. Below par share in work-force, leading to higher unemployment
c. Inadequate capacity to hold on to their own agricultural lands
d. Weak influence of SCs/STs in Gram Sabhas.

The following strategy is recommended for the development of this section of the society:

a. A survey of the socio-economic conditions of SCs/STs should be undertaken.
b. A mechanism to improve co-ordination among various agencies which are working for the welfare of SCs/STs.
c. A well-defined mechanism to evaluate the programmes being implemented for the welfare and development of SCs/STs.
d. Effective programme for creating social and economic awareness among the SCs/STs should be designed.
e. Hostel facilities for SCs/STs students, especially girls, should be improved.

The politico-administrative system that existed in this region so far, has not been able to reach several weaker sections of the society and area. This gap has been filled up fairly successfully by the NGOs in many cases. This encourages us to make the following recommendations:

a. Participation of NGOs in the welfare of SCs, STs and women should be encouraged. Yet, it should not lead to any dependency syndrome. Thus, people should be kept aware and prepared that the NGOs are only catalyst and would withdraw after a defined time.
b. NGOs should particularly be used to create social and economic awareness among people and also to implement development programmes for the purpose.
c. The beneficiary group of different programmes should organise themselves into NGOs. For instance, the Watershed Sanghas, IRDP Beneficiary Sanghas, etc.
d. There is a need to have a coordinating body of NGOs.
e. NGOs, which are working at micro level, should be encouraged.
f. There should be a State Policy on participation of NGOs in development programmes.

2

REGIONAL DEVELOPMENT
Some Issues*

G. Thimmaiah

1. The development experience of various countries, including that of India, provides certain valuable lessons for formulating the development strategies for backward regions. Geographers define "region" in terms of the location of natural resources like minerals, rainfall, soil, etc., which are the gift of nature. These natural resources are given in quantum and many of them are non-renewable. It has been the experience of countries all over the world that economic activities tended to emerge near the location of natural resources, particularly minerals. This is how mining activity like gold mining, coal mining, and production activity like iron and steel, textile and cement manufacturing emerged near the sources of raw materials. Market forces motivated and guided the entrepreneurs to exploit these resources and fostered production activities. Such natural resource regions, no doubt, attracted capital and labour from neighboring areas. The latter also experienced some degree of economic prosperity not necessarily by design but as a consequence of the growth of the natural regions. But once the natural resources got exhausted, the mines were closed, the industries began to face shortage of raw materials and workers were thrown out of job. Towns where such activities had emerged became shanty towns. The natural resource regions eventually became depressed regions. It was not possible for the government to revive these activities or even to bring new economic activities into such depressed areas. This has been the story of the development pattern of the natural resource

* Key-note address presented at the seminar inauguration function.

regions all over the world.

2. Another historical experience is equally interesting. When the industrial revolution opened up the new world, the economies of the western countries came to be integrated with the economies of their colonies which were converted into sources of raw materials and markets for manufactured goods. Since sea transport was the common mode at that time and also cheap, manufacturing and distribution activities got located in port cities and towns. They became centre places and interacted with their hinterlands through the blind market forces. This was how most of the port cities of the world have developed including Bombay, Madras and Calcutta in India. Once these cities developed as manufacturing centres, they began to attract other production, distribution and infrastructure activities like banking, insurance etc. Though these cities have managed to remain as developing centres, their hinterlands on which they flourished in the beginning did not. The pace of development which flowed from hinterlands to the port cities was much more than that which originated from port cities. Therefore, the hinterland regions remained undeveloped. This has continued to be a problem even to this day. This is another experience of regional development pattern which we have before us.

3. The above mentioned experiences of regional development are historical in nature. Development took place in response to the economic stimuli provided by natural resources and the manufacturing activity. Consequently, all cities and regions could not benefit from such development process. Regional disparities, therefore, have been the consequential outcome of the development which was guided by free market forces. Market forces would leave even resource-rich regions underdeveloped if the monetary incentive was inadequate. In many countries, there were regions which were endowed with many natural resources but still they remained underdeveloped. Therefore, during the post-war era of government-sponsored planning for economic development, it was recognised that government intervention was necessary to utilise the natural resources in underdeveloped regions for their development. This was how the role of government in development of not only the economy as a whole but also of different regions within the economy came to be accepted as an integral part of the national development plan. What is more, it was realised that even under the government sponsored planning regime, there was a tendency to formulate development strategies for the country as a whole without paying adequate attention to the developmental needs of disparate regions. Such macro development strategies naturally depended upon the market forces to take developmental

stimuli to all regions of the economy through the trickle down process. But this did not work in many countries including India.

4. We are aware of the fact that Indian planners overemphasized the role of big push strategy and established the huge public sector steel mills in places like Durgapur in West Bengal, Bhilai in Madhya Pradesh and Rourkela in Orissa which have a huge stock of raw materials. But the evaluation and impact studies have shown that the big push strategy did not develop those resource regions. Only the steel towns emerged. Nothing else happened in those resource regions. The regional planners at this juncture drew the attention of the planners to the need for formulating appropriate macro level and micro level planning strategies for achieving a uniform level of regional development. Accordingly, during the period of Fourth Five-year Plan Indian planners recognised the need for regional planning and specific strategies for the development of backward regions. Several committees were appointed to make recommendations on the strategies, programmes and even schemes for promoting balanced regional development. Based on their recommendations, the Government of India have been formulating and implementing several types of regional development strategies and programmes. They include Hill Area Development Programme, Western Ghats Development Programme, Border Area Development Programme and Desert Development Programme. Thus, because of the failure of the big push strategy, various types of regional development programmes were conceived and implemented.

5. It was under these circumstances that the H-K region received the attention of the Planning Commission. Though the issue of the relative backwardness of the HK region has been kept alive at the state level by the political leaders, it did not get the approval of the national planning authority until recently. Now specific development schemes for development of the H-K region have come to be formulated by the planning department in consultation with the Hyderabad-Karnataka Area Development Board (HKADB).

6. Against the foregoing background, let us examine the nature and causes for the backwardness of the H-K region and the extent of development which has taken place so far and throw up some ideas for future strategies for accelerating the development of the HK region. Historically the HK region, consisting of the districts of Gulbarga, Raichur, and Bidar, came from the former Hyderabad State. The Government of Karnataka added the adjoining Bellary district to this region for the purpose of formulating and implementing the HK region development programme. However, it would be more appropriate to

examine the development of the HK region with and without Bellary district. When the HK region was integrated into the erstwhile Mysore region to form the State of Karnataka, the three districts of the HK region were really backward though they constituted small area and population. For example, the erstwhile Mysore region had tėn districts whereas the HK region had only three districts. The erstwhile Mysore region had 52 per cent of the population of the State of Karnataka whereas the HK region had only 13.4 per cent of the State population. Similarly, while the erstwhile Mysore region had 45.4 per cent of the geographical area of the State of Karnataka, the HK region had only 19 per cent of the State area. Today, the area has remained more are less the same in all the regions. However, the proportion of population of erstwhile Mysore region has increased to 55 per cent, whereas that of the HK region has experienced very negligible increase in this regard. In the case of Bombay-Karnataka and Madras-Karnataka regions the proportions of their population have actually declined from 27% to 25% and from 6.6% to 5.7% respectively. Given these two important indices, if we compare what has happened over the past 35 year period, we find that considerable development, particularly in the field of social and economic infrastructure facilities, has taken place in the HK region thanks to the plan programmes implemented by the successive governments of Karnataka. One may argue that this was made possible by the political pressure wielded by the people's representatives of the region. Even so, we should not belittle the efforts made by the successive state governments to bring the economy of this region to the present level. Before we go to present the extent of development that has taken place after integration of the HK region into greater Karṇataka, it may be useful to briefly recollect the main reasons why the HK region remained so backward and for so long.

7. Historically, the H-K region which was a part of the former Hyderabad state was ruled by a government which did not have development perspective. Naturally, that government left the development process to the free play of market forces. The blind market forces did not smile on the HK region partly because the region was not endowed with valuable natural resources and partly because the people of the region probably lacked enterprising spirit. The latter is, no doubt, a common problem of the people of the state of Karnataka in general. But it is much more so in the case of the people of the HK region. It may not be a far fetched imagination to say that the feudal rule of the former Nizam probably killed whatever enterprising spirit which the people of that region had. The Nizam government could have provided certain essential economic and social infrastructural facilities like good roads, primary education, and

health facilities. But these probably did not fit into the priorities of Nizam's government. So the people remained illiterate, unhealthy, poor and, therefore, unenterprising. They were naturally longing for freedom and after the achievement of independence, they were eager to join the reorganised State of Karnataka.

8. Immediately after joining Karnataka, the political leaders of this region started asking for more developmental projects to be located in the HK region. This was only natural and was evident from a special fact-finding committee which was appointed to collect relevant data and to present it to the state legislature. The fact-finding committee submitted a report indicating the extent of backwardness of HK region vis-a-vis other regions of Karnataka. The committee also collected data about the magnitude of public expenditure incurred by the state government over a period of ten years from 1957-58 to 1967-68. It is clear from these data that the proportion of expenditure was lower in the HK region. But it can also be looked at from another angle. The HK region stands third in area and population of the state of Karnataka. Accordingly, the proportion of expenditure was in tune with the proportion of area and population of the region. Therefore, we do not see any injustice having been meted out to the HK region in particular. Even so, these data on expenditure give an aggregate picture of the total amount spent in the region. What we are interested in is the location of necessary social and economic infrastructure facilities and also some public sector investment projects for initiating development activities in the region.

9. If we examine the available data relating to the development indicators of the HK region presented by Abdul Aziz and Johnson Samuel in their papers it becomes very clear that after the integration of the HK region into the State of Karnataka, remarkable development has taken place in infrastructure facilities. Even in the development of industrial activity the region has turned the corner. This is further evident from the taluk-wise data presented by Hemlata Rao in her paper included in the present volume. It may be observed that the HK region is lagging only in literacy rate, roads, health facilities and area under forest. Excepting these, the HK region has experienced considerable improvement in terms of the regional rankings. Even so, it can not be held that these outcomes are the result of any deliberate government policies. They are the result of the choice of the farmers and their efficient use of the inputs. One of the specific infrastructures in which the HK region is lagging behind is the location of Chawki rearing centers. Thus, while 78.5% of the chawki rearing centers were located in the erstwhile Mysore region in 1991-92, the corresponding figures for the Bombay-Karnataka region, the H-K

region and the Madras-Karnataka region are respectively 22.7%, 8.8% and 6.9%. Here again, the HK region is a new area as far as mulberry cultivation and cocoon rearing is concerned. Unless these activities take roots firmly in the region the state government cannot invest in establishing chawki rearing centers. However, if we take financial infrastructure facilities like commercial banks, cooperative banks and telephone exchanges, we find that the HK region is still lagging behind (Johnson Samuel). But then the state government cannot be held responsible for this as commercial banks and telephone facilities come under central government responsibility.

10. The decision for creating a separate Hyderabad-Karnataka Area Development Board for formulating special area development programme needs scrutiny from another angle, viz., "Will it not result in waste of scarce financial and manpower resources"? This is an issue which should be thoroughly examined because consequent on the creation of the HKADB, the Malnad Area Development Board was created and subsequently the Maidan Area Development Board has also been created. It is difficult to understand the justification for separate development boards for all the regions of Karnataka. Does it then mean that there is no need for one development plan for the state as a whole? This is a serious issue which should be examined because scarce financial resources are proposed to be spent on the administrative personnel manning these various boards. Apart from these boards, there are programmes for border area development and a national programme for western ghat development. It appears that we are allocating plan outlay not only sectorally but also in terms of several regions in addition to already existing district sector schemes. All these will involve duplication and the resultant wastage which will give more scope for leakage. On top of all these programmes, individual members of the state legislature (MLA/MLC) are likely to be given Rs. 50 lakh each by state government out of the HKADB Plan funds and an MP is given Rs 1 crore by the central government to be spent in his constituency on the development projects of his priority (choice?). This may appear perfectly legitimate from the point of view of participation of people's representatives in choosing the development priorities for their political constituencies. But if their priorities either clash or overlap with the state sector, district sector and regional development board's priorities, how will that be resolved? Will it not further increase duplication and leakage? One would strongly feel that the people of Karnataka, as tax payers, have a right to have a satisfactory answer to these questions and issues.

11. It may not be out of place to mention that during the past 35 years the HK region would have developed much more than what it has if only all the funds which were allotted for the developmental activities of the region were utilised productively and without leakages. One may argue that even if funds which were allocated for the development of the region had leaked out, the impact should have been reflected in the development of private economic activity like housing, small business etc. But this is very difficult to identify and what is surmised is that a lot of leaked out funds might have gone out of the HK region and even out of the state of Karnataka. This issue needs to be discussed in the light of the opinions expressed by the political leaders and the people of the HK region in the course of their interview with the ISEC Scholars (See N Sivanna and C Charles Nelson's paper included in this volume).

12. Paradoxically, the available data show that the other regions, particularly the erstwhile Mysore region, are losing in the development share over the years. It may be recalled here that the erstwhile State of Mysore was far ahead of other regions in social and economic infrastructure development, industrial development and even social sectors like health and education. After the reorganization of the States the development priorities of the reorganised State of Karnataka shifted to irrigation and power development. As a result, the net area irrigated has been increasing phenomenally in other regions much more than in the erstwhile Mysore region. Consequently, the proportion of net area irrigated in the erstwhile Mysore region declined from 64 per cent in 1957-58 to 45 per cent in 1991-92, whereas the proportion in the HK region increased from 6 per cent in 1957-58 to 19 per cent 1991-92. Even in absolute terms the total area more than doubled in the erstwhile Mysore region, whereas it increased by five times in the Bombay-Karnataka region, and by more than 100 per cent in the HK region. This may be the result of starting of the Upper Krishna Project. In fact, this single project has diverted huge amount of development funds of the State to the HK region. This is so even in the case of power sector consequent on locating of a thermal unit in Raichur district.

13. If we analyse the aggregate commonly accepted indicator of development, that is the per capita income, certain interesting trends emerge. The region-wise per capita income figures of 1990-91 at current prices show that Coorg region is having the highest per capita income (Rs.10,583) followed by ex-Madras region (Rs.5350), ex-Bombay-Karnataka region (Rs.4243). The erstwhile Mysore region and the HK region coming at the end with Rs.4164 and Rs.3642, respectively. It is also interesting to note that in terms of ranking of the per capita incomes, the HK region remained at the bottom both in 1960-61 and in 1990-91. This

was so in the case of ex-Madras region which retained its second position. Coorg region also retained its first position. But in the case of Bombay-Karnataka region its rank improved from fourth to third position and the rank of the erstwhile Mysore region slipped from third to fourth place (See Table 1). While examining these data on per capita income figures we should not forget the fact that Coorg is a plantation district where high level of income is generated but the whole of that income does not accrue to the people living in that region. The plantation income is transferred to the head offices of the plantation companies which are located outside Coorg district. Even in regard to the ex-Madras region (notably the Dakshina Kannada District), we should not forget the well-known fact that a lot of income flows into the region from outside through money orders and bank transfers. In other words, the per capita incomes of these regions do not reflect the income accrued to the people of those regions locally, but rather it suggests how part of the incomes originating in those regions comes in from other regions or goes out of the region. However, our conclusion is that in terms of this overall indicator of development the erstwhile Mysore region has experienced deterioration, the Bombay-Karnataka region has experienced improvement, whereas the HK region has not experienced any change in its rank. Even so, there is convergence of the levels of this development indicator of various regions in the State thanks to the fair development efforts of the successive state governments. Therefore, it is wrong to say that the HK region has remained backward even after integration with Karnataka state. It is also wrong to say that other regions, particularly erstwhile Mysore region, have gained disproportionately. These allegations are politically motivated and have no empirical basis. In fact, the administrative personnel of the erstwhile Mysore region lost many benefits in terms of their salary structure, promotional opportunities etc., whereas those from the HK region gained

TABLE 2.1: Region-wise Distribution of Per-capita Income at Current Prices, 1960-61 and 1990-91.

(in Rs.)

	Region	1960-61	Rank	1990-91	Per Capita Income Rank
1.	Erstwhile Mysore Region	306	III	4164	IV
2.	Bombay-Karnataka Region	293	IV	4243	III
3.	Madras-Karnataka Region	341	II	5350	II
4.	H-K Region	249	V	3642	V
5.	Coorg State	558	I	10583	I
	State Average	289		4631	

much immediately after integration. But those losses were tolerated by treating them as small sacrifices for bringing all the Kannada speaking people together.

14. The people of the HK region should also own some responsibility for not keeping a watch on how the public funds in the name of developmental activities have been spent in the region. The HK region cannot blame the State Government for not giving enough political opportunities for the people of their region. The people of Karnataka gave two opportunities for a person hailing from that region to become the Chief Minister - once in the 1960's and again in the 1990's. The state cabinet has been represented by many distinguished ministers from that region. All of them have rendered memorable service to the people of Karnataka in general and to the people of the HK region in particular. Because of their presence and perseverence, the HK region has developed after integration. Probably, it could have developed much more if the leakages in the funds spent in the name of developmental activities were plugged completely. Now there is a fear that in the name of special grant of Rs. 50 lakh (from HKADB budget) for each MLA and Rs. 1 crore for each MP, we may be heading for another period of wastage of public funds. This is a serious issue which every citizen has got a right to deliberate on.

15. After arriving at the conclusion that the HK region has developed over the past 35 years commensurate with its area and population, the question is: what more should be done to further hasten the pace of development in the region? It may be appropriate here to suggest that the state sector, district sector and the HKADB should complement their development schemes in such a way as to avoid duplication, overlapping and wastage. First priority should be given for improvement of literacy rate in the HK region. Primary education facilities should be expanded as well as improved in terms of its quality. If the state sector schemes provide funds for school buildings, the district sector schemes should provide funds for appointment of school teachers. The HKADB should provide funds for books, black-boards and other teaching aids. Similar complementarity should be promoted to expand and improve primary health facilities. The third priority should be given to road development in the HK region. Finally, there should be a scheme for the expansion of the area under forest as the HK region does not have adequate area under forest.

16. It is necessary to mention in this context that the structural reforms and the new economic policies formulated by the Narasimha Rao government have opened up new opportunities as well as challenges to the state governments. The states which have got farsighted development

leadership have begun to exploit these opportunities. Notable among them are Maharashtra, Gujarat, Punjab and Haryana. Even West Bengal is competing for opportunities. In the South, Karnataka, Andhra Pradesh and Tamilnadu are alive to the challenges as well as threats posed by the new economic policies. But the required policy changes for fully exploiting these opportunities have not yet been initiated in Karnataka. Therefore, the HK region may not benefit from these new opportunities if the state government remains indifferent to the required changes in the existing policics. No doubt, the state government has announced a new industrial policy. But the changes effected therein arc only cosmetic and not structural. It is hoped that all concerned will deliberate on the required structural reforms at the state and the regional levels to exploit the development opportunities thrown up by the economic liberalisation and the GATT agreement.

3

PROBLEMS AND PROSPECTS OF UNCULTIVATED LANDS AND THE LIVESTOCK ECONOMY OF HYDERABAD-KARNATAKA REGION

Syed Ajmal Pasha

Introduction

Uncultivated lands such as forests, pastures, tank foreshores, barren, cultivable and uncultivable wastes and permanent fallows, greatly supports the livelihoods of rural communities. When these lands are maintained properly, the symbiotic relationships between uncultivated lands and the cultivated lands ensures the overall sustainability of an eco-system. Uncultivated lands meet the basic requirements like fodder, fuelwood, small timber etc., of the rural communities, apart from checking soil erosion, siltation, and the depletion of water table. These lands are more useful and important when an economy depends, apart from agriculture, also on animal husbandry. There exist strong complementarities and supplementarities between crop cultivation and ruminant livestock keeping. The former provides fodder (crop residues and stubble grazing) to the latter and the latter enhances the productivity of the former through its manure and draught power. Particularly in regions where the potential of irrigation and rural industries are weak, uncultivated lands along with animal husbandry (ruminant livestock keeping) play a very important role. Animal husbandry supports the livelihoods and adds to the income of the rural communities to a considerable extent. Sustainable use and management of uncultivated lands and the development of livestock sector are essential for the overall economic development of the rural economies particularly the economies of arid and semi-arid regions.

Magnitude and the Role of uncultivated lands

Apart from constant efforts and investments, the Hyderabad Karnataka (HK) region is far behind in its overall economic development as compared with the other districts of the state. It, thus, becomes essential to identify the constraints as well as the potentialities of economic development of this region. An attempt has been made in this article to:

(a) investigate into the magnitude, physical condition and importance of and the role played by uncultivated lands as well as the livestock sector in the economy of Hyderabad -Karnataka region;

(b) understand/evaluate programmes/schemes being implemented by different agencies for the maintenance and development of both uncultivated lands and the livestock resources;

(c) identify the constraints in the sustainable use and management of these resources and their potential for development; and

(d) suggest policy measures for the sustainable use and management of these resources.

The article is based both on secondary and primary data. Secondary data were collected from official records whereas the primary data were built on information and insights collected from the rural areas of H-K region using rapid rural appraisal methods and on the basis of discussions with the officials of different departments.

Table 3.1 shows that in the region as a whole net area sown has increased by more than one hundred thousand hectares during the period 1976-77 to 1991-92. Net sown area constitutes more than 78 per cent of the total geographical area during 1991-92, which is much above the state average of 56.2 per cent. This shows that in the region more and more uncultivated lands (including the marginal lands) are being brought under cultivation. Even then the contribution of agriculture to the gross income of the region's economy is not satisfactory. This may be due to uneconomic and non-viable agricultural holdings, particularly those marginal lands which have been brought under the plough. Within the region, Gulbarga district shows the highest proportion of net sown area (85.1 per cent) followed by Raichur (80.8 per cent), Bidar (72.3 per cent) and Bellary (68.2 per cent) during 1991-92 (see Table 3.1). As for the net irrigated area is concerned, Bellary district ranks first (17.6 per cent) followed by Raichur (17 per cent), Gulbarga (10.1 per cent) and the last rank is that

TABLE 3.1 : Land Utilisation Pattern (thousand hectares) in Hyderabad Karnataka (HK) Region

Districts	Year	Total Geographical area	Forests	Land under non-agrl. uses	Barren & unculti-vable waste	Culti-vable waste	Permanent pastures & other grazing lands	Land under miscellaneous tree crops & groves	Other fallows	Net area sown*	Net irrigated area	Net irrigated area as % to net sown area
Bellary	1976-77	956	117	80	62	36	7	4	15	635	93	14.6
			(12.3)	(8.3)	(6.4)	(3.7)	(0.7)	(0.5)	(1.6)	(66.4)	(9.7)	
	1991-92	956	119	80	60	30	7	4	5	652	168	25.8
			(12.5)	(8.3)	(6.2)	(3.1)	(0.7)	(0.5)	(0.5)	(68.2)	(17.6)	
Bidar	1976-77	545	12	24.	22	16	21	24	56	369	21	5.7
			(2.3)	(4.5)	(4.1)	(2.9)	(3.9)	(4.4)	(10.2)	(67.7)	(3.9)	
	1991-92	542	25	20	22	19	14	12	38	392	43	11.0
			(4.6)	(3.7)	(4.1)	(3.5)	(2.6)	(2.2)	(7.0)	(72.3)	(7.9)	
Gulbarga	1976-77	1610	70	48	74	17	52	1	40	1307	22	1.7
			(4.4)	(3.0)	(4.6)	(1.1)	(3.2)	(0.07)	(2.5)	(81.2)	(1.4)	
	1991-92	1610	68	-	118	54	-	-	-	1370	163	11.9
			(4.2)		(7.3)	(3.4)				(85.1)	(10.1)	
Raichur	1976-77	1393	32	52	51	15	44	13	68	1117	149	13.3
			(2.3)	(3.8)	(3.6)	(1.1)	(3.2)	(0.9)	(4.9)	(80.2)	(10.7)	
	1991-92	1388	48	59	37	14	33	14	63	1121	236	21.0
			(3.4)	(4.3)	(2.7)	(1.0)	(2.4)	(1.0)	(4.5)	(80.8)	(17.0)	
H-K Region	1976-77	4505	232	204	209	84	124	43	179	3428	285	8.3
			(5.2)	(4.5)	(4.6)	(1.9)	(2.8)	(1.0)	(4.0)	(76.1)	(6.3)	
	1991-92	4497	260	159	236	117	55	30	106	3534	610	17.3
			(5.8)	(3.5)	(5.2)	(2.6)	(1.2)	(0.7)	(2.4)	(78.6)	(13.6)	

Note :Figures in the brackets are percentages to total geographical area. * : Net area sown includes current fallows.

Sources : (1) Directorate of Economics and Statistics, Bangalore. (2) District at a Glance of Gulbarga, Raichur, Bellary and Bidar Districts.

of Bidar district with 7.9 per cent during the same period. In all the districts of the region, except Gulbarga, the proportion of net irrigated area to total geographical area has more or less doubled during 1976-77 to 1991-92 whereas in Gulbarga district it has increased from 1.4 per cent to 10.1 per cent during the same period.

Further, it can be seen from Table 3.1 that in the region as a whole around 774 thousand hectares (17.2 per cent of the total geographical area) of uncultivated lands* are available. If we exclude forests, still we find around 514 thousand hectares of uncultivated lands which support the farming systems and livelihoods of the rural families of the region. But the actual figure could be different since a large proportion of these lands could have been illegally encroached upon as private property by the rural communities. Assuming that 50 per cent of these lands as being encroached by the rural people, still we have large quantities of public uncultivated lands which need proper care and development. Our field visit showed that the available uncultivated lands had already been degraded and there was severe pressure on them for fodder, fuel wood, and small timber etc.,from the rural communities. In fact, the rural population depends on these lands for their biomass requirements to a considerable extent.

The Forest Department of Karnataka has developed some of these lands both under social and territorial forestry**. But if we look at Table 3.2, the proportion of uncultivated lands developed under these programmes is very low, being 1.9 per cent of the available (estimated) uncultivated lands in the region. Further, the Forest Department has concentrated mostly on the development of degraded forests and paid little attention towards the development of other uncultivated lands. In fact, the Forest Department ought to concentrate more on increasing the area under forests since the current proportion of area under forest to total geographical area of the region is very much low, being 5.8 per cent (see Table 3.2). We may recall here that the policy makers/conservationists suggest that a minimum of 33 per cent of the total geographical area should be under forests or tree cover if we were to meet the basic biomass requirements of the local people and the environmental norms.

Livestock Population and its Role

As we have mentioned earlier, uncultivated lands support the ruminant

---

* Uncultivated lands include forests, barren and uncultivable waste, cultivable waste, permanent pastures and other grazing lands and other (permanent) fallows.

** The Dry Land Development Board in Gulbarga has also developed some of these lands in the watershed areas, which, however, is negligible.

TABLE 3.2: Plantations Raised by the Forest Department of Karnataka on Uncultivated Lands During 1990-91 to 1993-94 (in hundred hectares)

Districts	Plantations (00 hectares)	Proportion (%) of Planted Area to Total Available Uncultivated Lands
Bellary	14	0.6
Bidar	34	2.9
Gulbarga	63	2.6
Raichur	35	1.8
HK Region	146	1.9

Source: Office of the Conservator of Forests, Social Forestry, Gulbarga.

livestock, in the absence (decline or degradation) of which the latter cannot be sustained unless stall feeding is practised on a large scale based on commercial fodder. For under developed regions like H.K., ensuring complete stall feeding could be an uphill task. From Table 3.3, it can be seen that the ruminant livestock population (cattle, buffaloes, goats and sheep) has increased considerably between 1961 and 1990. This increase could exert greater pressure on the available uncultivated lands, resulting in their further degradation. In the region as a whole the cattle population has increased by 17 per cent, buffaloes by 40 per cent, goats by 53 per cent and sheep by 26 per cent between 1961 and 1990 (see Table 3.3). Poultry has also increased by about 150 per cent during the same period. In Bidar district both cattle and sheep population has declined whereas buffaloe and goat's population has increased during this period.

Numerically, indigenous cattle dominate in the total livestock population of the region (being 41.1 per cent) followed by goats and sheep (37.6 per cent). Buffaloes constitute 14.3 per cent (see Table 3.4). The impact/adaptability of crossbred animals appears to be very low. It can be seen from Table 3.4 that in the region the share of crossbred cattle to total livestock population is much less (0.6 per cent) as compared with the state figure of 2.9 per cent. The low proportion could be due to the poor adaptability of crossbred cattle by the farmers of the region. Further, Table 3.5 shows that the density of ruminant livestock population per sq.km. of total geographical area in the region is much less as compared with the state figures. But the pressure of ruminant livestock on uncultivated lands is much higher. Table 3.6 shows that in the region as a whole during 1991-92 around 3 cattle, 1 buffalo and 3 goats and sheep units are to be maintained on one hectare of uncultivated lands.

Rural communities depend to a considerable extent on livestock for draught power, manure, milk and cash. Livestock is an integral part of the

TABLE 3.3: Livestock Population (in thousands) in Hyderbad Karnataka Region

Districts	Year	Cattle (CB + ind-igenous)	Buff-aloes	Sheep	Goats	Horses and ponies	Donkeys mules & camels	Pigs	Total lives tock	Poul-try
Bellary	1961	379	125	205	140	· 1	2	5	857	165
		(100)	(100)	(100)	(100)	(100)	(100)	(100)	(100)	(100)
	1972	400	128	222	204	1	2	5	962	231
		(106)	(102)	(108)	(145)	(100)	(100)	(100)	(112)	(140)
	1983	476	140	241	240	neg	2	10	1109	468
		(126)	(112)	(118)	(171)	—	(100)	(200)	(129)	(284)
	1990	485	181	279	233	neg	2	6	1186	635
		(128)	(145)	(136)	(166)	—	(100)	(120)	(138)	(385)
Bidar	1961	318	106	79	67	4	4	6	584	845
		(100)	(100)	(100)	(100)	(100)	(100)	(100)	(100)	(100)
	1972	272	110	57	54	5	3	8	509	101
		(86)	(104)	(72)	(88)	(125)	(75)	(133)	(87)	(12)
	1983	334	140	77	97	2	4	9	663	112
		(105)	(132)	(97)	(145)	(50)	(100)	(150)	(114)	(13)
	1990	273	149	73	95	1	3	15	609	341
		(86)	(141)	(92)	(142)	(25)	(75)	(250)	(104)	(40)
Gulbarga	1961	659	166	279	217	10	5	7	1343	326
		(100)	(100)	(100)	(100)	(100)	(100)	(100)	(100)	(100)
	1972	626	137	248	278	6	4	10	1309	369
		(95)	(83)	(89)	(128)	(60)	(80)	(143)	(97)	(113)
	1983	803	170	321	402	3	5	20	1724	457
		(122)	(102)	(115)	(185)	(30)	(100)	(286)	(128)	(140)
	1990	769	194	308	315	2	4	24	1616	537
		(117)	(117)	(110)	(145)	(20)	(80)	(343)	(120)	(165)
Raichur	1961	467	130	246	172	3	4	9	1031	190
		(100)	(100)	(100)	(100)	(100)	(100)	(100).	(100)	(100)
	1972	501	157	216	214	4	3	6	1101	230
		(107)	(121)	(88)	(124)	(133)	(75)	(67)	(107)	(121)
	1983	640	172	325	319	1	3	13	1473	313
		(137)	(132)	(132)	(185)	(33)	(75)	(144)	(143)	(165)
	1990	611	211	364	267	1	2	15	1471	403
		(131)	(162)	(148)	(155)	(33)	(50)	(167)	(143)	(212)
H.K. Region	1961	1822	526	809	596	18	15	26	3812	766
		(100)	(100)	(100)	(100)	(100)	(100)	(100)	(100)	(100)
	1972	1798	532	743	750	15	13	29	3880	931
		(99)	(101)	(92)	(126)	(83)	(87)	(112)	(102)	(122)
	1983	2253	621	964	1058	6	14	51	4967	1350
		(124)	(118)	(119)	(178)	(33)	(93)	(196)	(130)	(176)
	1990	2138	735	1023	911	4	11	59	4881	1916
		(117)	(140)	(126)	(153)	(22)	(73)	(227)	(128)	(250)

Note : Figures in the brackets are index numbers.

Source : 14th Quinquennial Livestock Census 1990, Department of Animal Husbandry and Veterinary Sciences, Bangalore.

farming and livelihood systems of the people of the region which are maintained on crop residues and uncultivated lands. But the paradox is the increase in the population of ruminant livestock on the one hand and the decline/degradation of uncultivated lands on the other. This has affected both the farming and the livelihood systems as well as the ecology of the region. One could see cattle, buffaloes, goats and sheep scavenging on the available degraded uncultivated lands for their requirements of fodder.

Livestock Development Programmes

There are about 508 veterinary institutions (veterinary hospitals, dispensaries, mobile veterinary clinics, and artificial insemination centres) in the region. Apart from this there are two Livestock Development and Training Centres—one at Munirabad and the other at Kurikuppe. At Munirabad pure jercy is crossed with Krishna valley to produce the

TABLE 3.4 : Proportion (per cent) of Different Species of Livestock to Total Livestock Population in Hyderabad Karnataka Region as per 1990 Census

Districts	Cattle		Buffaloes	Sheep	Goats	Pigs	Other live-stock	Total live-stock
	Cross-Bred	Indi-genous						
Bellary	0.7	38.3	14.6	22.4	18.7	0.5	4.8	100
Bidar	0.8	41.9	23.2	11.3	14.9	2.3	5.7	100
Gulbarga	0.5	44.7	11.4	18.1	18.5	1.4	5.3	100
Raichur	0.5	39	13.7	23.5	17.3	1.0	5.1	100
H.K. Region	0.6	41.1	14.3	19.9	17.7	1.2	5.2	100
State (Karnataka)	2.9	37.9	16.2	18.9	15.6	1.2	7.3	100

Source : As in Table 3.3

TABLE 3.5 : Density of Livestock Population Per Sq.Km. of Total Geographical Area in the Hyderabad Karnataka Region as per 1990 Census

Districts	Cattle	Buffaloes	Goats	Sheep	Total Livestock*
Bellary	49	18	24	28	126
Bidar	50	27	17	13	117
Gulbarga	47	12	19	19	105
Raichur	44	15	19	26	111
H.K. Region	47	16	20	22	107
State (Karnataka)	56	22	21	26	137

* Total livestock includes camels, horses, ponies, pigs and dogs.

Source : As in Tables 3.1 & 3.3.

TABLE 3.6 : Ruminant Livestock Per Hectare of Uncultivated Lands (UCLs) in Hyderabad Karnataka Region

Districts	Year	Cattle per hectare of forests	Cattle per hectare of other UCLs*	Buffaloes per hectare of forests	Buffaloes per hectare of other UCLs*	Goats & sheep per hectare of forests	Goats & sheep per hectare of UCLs*	Cattle per hectare of forest & other UCLs*	Buffaloes per hectare of forest & other UCLs*	Goats & sheep per hectare of forests and UCLs*
Bellary	1976-77	3.2	3.1	1.0	1.0	2.7	2.7	1.6	0.5	1.3
	1991-92	4.1	4.7	1.5	1.8	4.3	5.0	2.2	0.8	2.3
Bidar	1976-77	19.7	2.1	7.9	0.8	11.4	1.2	1.9	0.8	1.1
	1991-92	10.9	2.9	5.9	1.6	6.7	1.8	2.3	1.3	1.4
Gulbarga	1976-77	8.2	3.2	1.8	0.7	8.2	3.1	2.3	0.5	2.3
	1991-92	11.3	4.5	2.9	1.1	9.1	3.6	3.2	0.8	2.6
Raichur	1976-77	16.1	2.9	4.6	0.8	14.1	2.6	2.5	0.7	2.2
	1991-92	12.8	4.2	4.4	1.4	13.3	4.3	3.1	1.1	3.3
H.K. Reg.	1976-77	7.4	2.9	7.4	2.9	6.4	2.5	2.1	0.6	1.8
	1991-92	8.2	4.2	2.8	1.4	7.4	3.8	2.8	1.0	2.5

* UCLs = Uncultivated lands include barren, uncultivable waste, cultivable waste, permanent pastures and other grazing lands and other (permanent) fallows.

Source : As in Tables 3.1 and 3.3.

improved varieties of cattle. Also, improved varieties of fodder species, fodder seeds and fodder stems are produced for dissemination among the local farmers. Further, there are two Livestock Inspectors' Training Centres-one at Bidar and the other at Gulbarga. The students, after completing pre-university classes in science, are selected for a one year training course in livestock sciences. Though there are milk marketing cooperative societies in the region, most of them are either defunct or lingering. The major constraint which hinders the smooth functioning of dairy cooperatives appears to be the assured supply of milk, which again depends on the productivity and production of milk from rural areas. Apart from this there are other programmes like special livestock breeding programme for the small and marginal farmers.

Thus, there are quite a few developmental programmes in operation for the development of livestock in the region—but their impact/dissemination is not satisfactory. There could be many reasons of this. For instance, it can be seen from Table 3.7 that a large number of villages are to be covered per unit of different veterinary institutions. In the region as a whole around 115 villages are to be covered per unit of veterinary

TABLE 3.7: No. of Villages covered per unit of Different Veterinary Institutions

Districts	VH	VD	PVC	MVC	AIC
Bidar	120	24	15	120	60
Gulbarga	119	36	12	130	59
Raichur	140	78	21	156	82
Bellary	74	25	10	74	54
H.K. Region	115	38	14	122	66

Note: VH : Veterinary Hospitals
VD : Veterinary Dispensaries
PVC : Primary Veterinary Centres
MVC : Mobile Veterinary Clinics
AIC : Artificial Insemination Centres

Source : Office of the Joint Director, Department of Animal Husbundry and Veterinary Sciences, Gulbarga

hospital and about 122 villages per unit of mobile veterinary clinic. Within the region, Bellary is much better off as far as the number of institutions is concerned; the coverage of villages by different veterinary centres is much better in Bellary district as compared with the other districts (see Table 3.7 for more details).

Husbandry and Veterinary Services, Gulbarga

Further, It has been reported by the officials of the animal husbandry department that the government's policy with regard to crossbred animals is not appropriate to the region; the policy-makers suggest that only jercy crossbred cattle with 60 per cent exotic blood should be encouraged in the region. But it is found that Bidar district has the potentiality of improving the indigenous 'Deoni' breed of cattle. This breed mixes well with HF (Holstein Fresien) even upto 66 per cent exotic blood level. In fact, the demand and the adaptability of HF crossbred cattle in Bidar district, particularly around Bhalki and Aurad talukas, is quite impressive. The local 'Deoni' breed is used for both milching and draught power. If the exotic blood level is maintained upto 50 per cent, the HF cross with Deoni breed suits well to Bidar district as a dual purpose (milk as well as draught power) improved variety of cattle.

In other areas of the HK region though jercy cross is quite satisfactory, its adaptability by the farmers is quite low. Generally it is those farmers with 4-5 acres of land with some assured source of irrigation who have maintained crossbred animals. The crossbred cattle need an assured supply of green fodder, particularly during summer. It has been reported that complete stall feeding of crossbred cattle in the region is very low (not even 0.1 per cent). Further, the adaptability of crossbred cattle in general is quite satisfactory only in Bidar district when compared with other districts of the region. This is due to the favorable weather condition, availability of ground water, irrigation, sugarcane crop and relatively small holdings in Bidar district as compared with the other districts of the region.

In the case of buffaloes the 'surti' breed suits well to the region. The department of animal husbandry is concentrating on the propagation of this high yielding breed of buffaloes. But it is reported that the conception rate is 20 per cent among surti buffaloes as compared with crossbred cattle (30-35 per cent). Also, the mortality rate among surti buffalo calves is much higher (25 per cent) as compared with crossbred cattle (5-10 per cent). Unlike crossbred cattle, buffaloes are also maintained on crop residues and common property land resources.

Though small ruminants play a very important role in terms of income and employment potential in the region, no concrete efforts are made, nor programmes are undertaken for their development. The local breed of goats is more adaptable to the region with low mortality rate and high prolificacy. Goats are maintained fully on free grazing on common property land resources. Recently the Department of Animal Husbandry in Gulbarga has imported high yielding (milk as well as meat) varieties of 'Jamnapari' goats from Uttar Pradesh and would like to propagate them in the rural areas of the region. Farmers can maintain these goats (a few animals) on stall feeding.

The population of sheep is showing a declining trend. This could be largely due to the shrinkage and degradation of grazing lands. The local 'black deccany' breed are poor quality animals. The quantity and quality of wool as well as meat yield is very poor from them. The animal husbandry department has a plan to upgrade the local breed of sheep. Further, the marketing of goats and sheep and their products is very poorly organised. Recently, the wool marketing board has been established to meet the marketing problem but its effectiveness is yet to be seen. Poultry has flourished in Bellary and Raichur districts but its marketing is still poor. The environment of these two districts has helped the rich entrepreneurs to invest in poultry on a large scale. But this has displaced the small and medium poultry farmers. It is reported that only large units (of above 1000 birds) can compete in the market and that has affected the middle class poultry farmers having small units.

Piggery is very poor in the region with very low potentialities. Majority of the population in the region are vegetarians. Those who eat meat have a taboo against piggery. In other words, there are social constraints for large scale development of piggery.

Further, though livestock plays an important role in the livelihoods and farming system of the people, the efforts and programmes for their development are inadequate. The existing veterinary institutions are not functioning properly to achieve the desired goals of development. This may be attributed to the following reasons:

(a) Inefficiency in the department, particularly among the implementing agencies and hence under-utilisation of the available infrastructure.
(b) Lack of motivation among the implementing officers/workers.
(c) Lack of sufficient manpower/infrastructure.
(e) Absence of T & V system.
(d) Lack of extension.
(f) Inappropriate technologies, institutions and breed of animals.
(g) Farmers have lost faith in the government machinery.

Conclusions and Suggested Policy Interventions

Both uncultivated lands and the livestock play a very important role in the rural economy of H K Region. Although the quantity and quality of public uncultivated lands has declined over time, still one can find vast areas of these lands which support the farming, livestock and livelihood systems of the region. Though the Forest Department of Karnataka has developed some of these lands under various programmes, still one can find vast areas under severe degradation. The net cropped area has, no doubt, increased over a period of time but it has been done so at the cost of public uncultivated lands. The contribution of agriculture to the region's economy is not satisfactory.

The rural economy of the region depends on the livestock resources for draught power, manure, milk and cash. The increase in the ruminant livestock population, on the one hand, and the decline and degradation of uncultivated lands, on the other, has affected both the livestock economy and the uncultivated lands. This is a paradoxical situation. The existing programmes and institutions for the development of both uncultivated lands and the livestock resources are not satisfactory. Either they are inappropriate/inefficient or defunct and lingering.

For the sustainable use and management of public uncultivated lands and the livestock resources the following policy interventions are required:

1. Protection and development of uncultivated lands. Furth-

er encroachments of these lands should be stopped forthwith.

2. Uncultivated lands need to be developed particularly under watersheds with appropriate fodder species of plants and trees.
3. Uncultivated lands could be developed under Joint Forest Planning and Management (JFPM) with fodder, fuelwood, grass and fruit yielding trees with the active participation of the local people.
4. Uncultivated lands may be leased out exclusively for fodder cultivation.
5. Agro-forestry and silvi-pasture may be encouraged on these lands, so that higher level of stall feeding of animals could be facilitated.
6. Uncultivated lands should be developed as common property resources (CPRs) so that the locals can graze their animals and collect fodder, fuelwood and small timber.
7. Appropriate species of livestock should be developed.
8. The local indigenous breed of livestock should be upgraded into more productive animals.
9. Efficient veterinary institutions with the required infrastructural facilities should be established and strengthened so as to provide adequate breeding and health cover facilities to the livestock population.
10. Veterinary officials should be suitably trained.
11. Appropriate livestock development programmes like dairy development with good marketing facilities should be implemented.

4

ANALYSIS OF HUMAN RESOURCES IN HYDERABAD-KARNATAKA REGION

M. Vivekananda

Introduction

Human resource is an important factor in economic development and its size has a relationship, though complex, with the identified natural resources in a region. The weak natural resource base of a region either due to untapped resources or lack of resources is generally reflected in low per capita income. The imbalance between population size and resources results in migration and a change in the occupational structure of population. In this paper, an attempt is made to highlight certain major issues concerning the stock and use of human resources in a backward region, namely, Hyderabad-Karnataka. The scope of the paper is restricted only to an examination of rural settlement pattern, population growth and migration, rural work participation rates, occupational pattern and urbanisation. An attempt is also made in a restricted way to associate the demographic factors with the agricultural development of the region. The development of human resources through education and health are not covered in this paper as there are separate papers on these themes.

Rural Settlement Pattern

The Hyderabad-Karnataka region comprising of Bidar, Gulbarga, Bellary and Raichur districts shares 23.8 per cent of geographical area, 29 per cent of cropped area and 17.9 per cent of population of the State. The region has low density of population with 185 persons per sq. km. as against 235 in the State (Table 4.1). Within the region, Gulbarga and Raichur districts have low population density (159 and 165 respectively) compared to

Bellary and Bidar districts (191 and 231 respectively). The region is predominantly rural in character as 76.4 per cent of its population lives in villages compared to the state average of 69.1.

The region accounts for 14.4 per cent of inhabited villages and 17.9 per cent of State's rural population in the year 1981. The average

TABLE 4.1: Density of population per Sq.Km.

Districts	1961	1971	1981	1991
Bellary	93	114	151	191
Bidar	122	151	183	231
Gulbarga	86	107	128	159
Raichur	78	101	127	165
Region	94	117	146	185
State	123	153	194	235

population per village works out to 1248 in the region and 977 in the state. The big villages with more than 2000 population account for 16.7 per cent of inhabited villages and 47 per cent of rural population in the region whereas in the state they account for 11.7 per cent of villages and 41.7 per cent of population (Table 4.2). These proportions show that the region has comparatively big villages. However, within the region there is wide difference between districts of Bellary and Raichur, though they are neighbouring districts. In Bellary, the big villages (with more than 2000 population) account for 31.4 per cent of total inhabited villages and 61.2 per cent of the total rural population; in Raichur these villages account for 10.1 per cent of inhabited villages and 38 per cent of population.

The low population density of the region suggests that the distance between villages is more in the region and it further gives an impression that provision of rural amenities and services required for development of human resources may pose a problem in the region. But relatively big size

TABLE 4.2: Percentage Distribution of Villages Classified by Population - 1981

	Less than 1000		1000 - 1999		2000 - 4999		5000 and above	
Districts	No.	Population	No.	Population	No.	Population	No.	Population
Bellary	35.59	10.99	33.05	27.76	28.14	48.07	3.22	13.18
Bidar	47.83	21.03	32.61	33.04	17.22	34.49	2.34	11.44
Gulbarga	57.39	19.29	26.74	33.91	14.10	36.79	1.76	10.01
Raichur	67.88	32.61	21.98	29.34	7.99	22.65	2.14	15.40
Region	56.39	21.91	26.89	31.06	14.51	34.45	2.21	12.58
State	68.93	30.48	19.38	27.79	10.07	30.12	1.61	11.62

villages in the region, excepting in Raichur, are conducive for the provision of rural amenities and services as many of the villages have the required threshold size for many rural amenities and services. Thus the low population density may not pose a problem for provision of amenities and services for most villages in the region.

Population Growth and Migration

The decennial population growth rate of the region during 1961-71 was 25.12 per cent (Table 4.3) which was a little higher than the state average (24.22 per cent). This relatively higher growth rate of the region was contributed by Raichur (28.6 per cent). In the following decade (1971-81), the population growth of the region was 24.46 per cent and it was less than the state growth rate (26.74 per cent) though Bellary district showed a growth rate of 32.65 per cent (introduction of irrigation attracted in-migration). The low growth rates in Bidar (20.83 per cent) and Gulbarga (19.63 per cent) affected the population growth rate of the region. In the latest decade (1981-91), the population growth in the region was 26.59 as against 21.11 per cent growth in state. All the four districts of the region have shown higher growth rates in the latest decade compared to the state.

The differential population growth rates in the districts of the region in different periods suggest that some districts of the region are losing population while other districts are gaining population through migration in different periods. An estimate of migration (P.J.Bhattacharjee, Dec. 1993, p.15) shows that there was net out-migration from Bidar and

TABLE 4.3: Decennial Population Growth Rates

Districts	1961-71	1971-81	1981-91
Bellary	22.66	32.65	26.92
Bidar	24.26	20.83	26.12
Gulbarga	24.28	19.63	24.10
Raichur	28.60	26.00	29.49
Region	25.12	24.46	26.59
State	24.22	26.74	21.22

Gulbarga districts to the tune of 16.2 thousand people during 1961-71 though the region had a net in-migration of the order of 35 thousand persons (Table 4.4). These two districts during 1971-81 accounted for a net out-migration of 117.1 thousand persons and the region as such lost 15.6 thousand persons due to migration. All the four districts showed net in-migration during 1981-91 and the region gained 253.7 thousand population by migration. The two districts—Bellary and Raichur - had net in-migration in all the three decades. Looking to the migration pattern over time, the region was not a net loser of population but on the other hand it was a net gainer particularly after 1981.

The above migratory trends were also in conformity with the growth rates of rural population of the region. (The rural population growth is calculated by taking the population of villages that were existing in 1961 and tracing their population in later decades irrespective of their classification in terms of villages or towns. This is attempted to remove distortions arising out of reclassification of villages from census to census). The region experienced 23.08 per cent growth rate during 1961-71, 19.5 per cent during 1971-81 and 26.1 per cent during 1981-91 (Table 4.5). The low rural population growth in the region during 1971-81 is an indication of net out-migration during that period and the high population growth during 1981-91 suggests net in-migration during eighties. Within the region, Bidar and Gulbarga have shown low growth rates during 1971-81 (17.2 and 14.2 respectively) and the growth rates of these districts were higher than the state average during 1981-91. These figures suggest that the out-migration from the region is of temporary nature and that there is a tendency for the migrating population to come back.

TABLE 4.4: Estimated Volume of Net Migration

(Figures in 000's)

Districts	1961-71	1971-81	1981-91
Bellary	13.0	79.2	50.3
Bidar	-3.0	-31.5	45.2
Gulbarga	-13.2	-85.6	58.4
Raichur	38.2	22.3	99.8
Region	35.0	-15.6	253.7

Looking at the migratory behaviour along with the agricultural development of the region, it appears that irrigation was an obvious factor for net in-migration in Raichur and Bellary districts. Bidar and Gulbarga districts with low level of irrigation showed better performance of growth

TABLE 4.5: Decennial Rural Population Growth Rates (Based on 1961 villages)

Districts	1961-71	1971-81	1981-91
Bellary	20.53	27.02	29.44
Bidar	21.13	17.21	22.25
Gulbarga	21.97	14.26	23.93
Raichur	27.61	21.64	28.14
Region	23.08	19.47	26.08

in production of cereals and pulses during 1956-57 to 1970-71 and during 1970-71 to 1980-81. In the period 1980-81 to 1990-91, the two districts exhibited stagnation in cereal production and a shift in cropping pattern in favour of non- cereal crops though there was no productivity gain in those crops. However, 'the cighties were marked with stagnation in productivity and lower instability in crop production in the State compared to the earlier periods (M. Vivekananda and V.S. Satyapriya, March, 1994, p.140). Bidar and Gulbarga districts might not be an exception to the State pattern. The migratory pattern and agricultural growth in these two districts show that out-migration was taking place when there was growth in production and in-migration was taking place when there was stagnation in production. This pattern is indeed contrary to the normal behaviour. These districts have low level of irrigation and are faced with many drought years during 1970's. The droughts brought in high instability in crop production though there was growth during that period. Further, these districts have high proportion of agricultural labourers. The lack of continuous employment for agricultural labourers in bad agricultural years probably compelled them to out-migrate. The reduction of instability in agricultural production coupled with the introduction of various government sponsored employment generation programmes during eighties to mitigate poverty might have been responsible for the home coming of the migrated people.

The migratory character of the region's population can also be viewed from the change in the sex ratio. In the context of migration that has taken place from a region, a reduction in sex ratio indicates that the migration that has taken place in that region was partial, and that the return migration has taken place in the later period by the migrated male members. Looking from this, the reduction in sex ratio in Gulbarga district from 981 in 1981 to 962 in 1991 and in the region from 984 to 967 (Table 4.6) provides an indication that the migration was partial and home coming has taken place for male population in the region after eighties.

From the data relating to population growth rates, migration pattern, changes in sex ratio and the nature of agricultural development in the region, it appears that the population in the region does not have a tendency to migrate from the region on a permanent basis.

Rural Work Participation Rates

The work participation rates presented in population census represent the stock concept of work force and it does not reflect the work intensity. Hence the stock concept of work force is used in this analysis. The work

TABLE 4.6: Sex ratio of rural population

Districts	1981	1991
Bellary	973	966
Bidar	968	954
Gulbarga	981	962
Raichur	988	980
Region	984	967
State	963	961

participation rates for male workers have declined over time from census to census and the decline has come mainly from the age groups of 0-14 and 60 plus. In the case of female work participation rates, such a decreasing trend is not observed in the State and their participation rates were lower than male participation rates. The increase in the female work participation rates might arise on account of deterioration in economic conditions of households due to drought conditions as well as due to job opportunities arising in areas of work which require female participation. So, to analyse the changes in female work participation rates, it require a proper understanding of changes that have taken place in the region.

The definition of worker has changed from census to census. However, work participation rates presented in 1961 census can be compared with work participation rates arrived at by considering both main and marginal workers presented in 1981 and 1991 census. These comparable figures (Table 4.7) show that the male work participation rate has declined in the region from 61.3 to 54.1 over the three decades and the corresponding decline in the state was from 60.4 to 55.9. The decline in the male work participation rates can be observed in all the districts in the region over time and there were no significant inter district variations in the region.

The female work participation rate in the region in the year 1961 was

TABLE 4.7: Rural Work Participation Rates

	Males			Females			Total		
Districts	1961	1981	1991	1961	1981	1991	1961	1981	1991
Bellary	60.35	57.65	55.46	37.41	37.21	43.91	49.04	47.31	49.76
Bidar	60.68	55.67	50.62	36.62	30.90	35.75	48.79	43.43	43.31
Gulbarga	62.30	58.62	53.85	37.16	41.57	41.98	49.75	50.11	47.99
Raichur	61.07	58.70	55.25	34.82	34.34	40.44	48.00	46.54	47.89
Region	61.27	57.94	54.07	36.47	36.75	40.91	48.96	47.40	47.57
State	60.40	57.18	55.91	36.79	30.66	36.33	48.76	44.07	46.24

36.5 and it remained more or less at the same level (36.7) in the year 1981. Among the districts in the region the work participation rate has increased in Gulbarga from 37.2 to 41.6 and this increase can be attributed to the economic compulsions of households in Gulbarga district during that period. The female work participation rate increased to 40.9 in the region in the year 1991. The increase can be attributed to the availability of work in agriculture in Bellary and Raichur districts arising out of increased area under irrigated crops like rice.

Rural Occupational Pattern

Data on marginal workers by occupational category are not yet made available for 1991 census. Hence occupational pattern of workers of 1961, workers and main workers of 1981 and main workers of 1991 are considered for comparison over time. The occupations considered for the present analysis are cultivators, agricultural labourers and the rest of categories classified as other workers. Workers in these categories are expressed as percentage to total population.

The proportion of male cultivator in the region declined from 35.4 per cent in 1961 to 24.82 per cent in 1991 and the decline in the proportion can be seen in all the districts within the region as well as in the state (Table 4.8). In the state, the decline was from 38.6 per cent to 28.1 per cent. These percentages show that cultivators form a low proportion in the region. In the case of agricultural labourers, their proportion has increased from 12.7 per cent in 1961 to 18.6 per cent in 1991 and the increase has come only during 1961-81. Bidar and Gulbarga have high proportion of agricultural labourers compared to Bellary and Raichur in 1961 and their proportions increased at a low rate and approached the proportions of Bellary and Raichur by 1981. This can be ascribed to the out-migration of agricultural labourers from Gulbarga and Bidar during that period. The four districts of the region have high proportion of agricultural labourers and this might be due to the big size of land holdings and the skewed distribution of land in the region. Coming to other workers, the region has slightly higher proportion of other workers (13.2 per cent) than in the state (12.8 per cent) in the year 1961 and by 1991 this proportion has gone down in the region (10.2 per cent) even below the state proportion (12.7 per cent). This has happened in all the four districts of the region. However, across the districts, Bidar and Gulbarga have higher proportion of other workers compared to Bellary and Raichur. The decline in the proportion of other workers over time shows that the desired diversification from agriculture has not taken place in the region.

TABLE 4.8: Occupational Pattern of Male Workers

(Percentage to Male Population)

Districts	Cultivators				Agricultural labourers				Other occupations			
	1961	1981	1981	1991	1961	1981	1981	1991	1961	1981	1981	1991
			(Main workers)				(Main workers)				(Main workers)	
Bellary	36.98	29.74	29.54	26.48	11.19	18.13	17.93	18.78	12.19	9.77	9.68	9.48
Bidar	28.66	24.54	24.40	20.02	16.90	19.12	18.85	19.03	15.12	12.01	11.92	11.29
Gulbarga	34.46	26.76	26.47	24.25	13.73	18.31	17.83	18.73	14.11	13.54	13.38	10.43
Raichur	39.6	29.72	29.61	26.90	9.98	19.63	19.47	18.21	11.48	9.35	9.28	9.86
Region	35.41	27.87	27.68	24.82	12.71	18.80	18.51	18.64	13.16	11.27	11.16	10.20
State	38.64	31.54	31.21	28.06	8.91	13.61	13.32	14.48	12.85	12.03	11.88	12.67

The occupational structure of females also shows low proportion in cultivators and high proportion in agricultural labourers (Table 4.9). The reduction in the proportion of cultivators between 1961 and 1991 was much drastic for females in the region as well as in the state. In the region it has come down from 16.7 per cent to 7.5 per cent and in the state it has declined from 22.1 per cent to 8.3 per cent—much of the reduction having taken place during 1961-81. The reverse trend can be seen in the proportion of agricultural labourers—their proportion having increased from 14 per cent in 1961 to 25.2 per cent in 1981; and the corresponding increase in the state was from 9.2 per cent and 15.3 per cent. The high proportion of female agricultural labourers in the region, though is in line with male agricultural labourers, the increase was much faster compared to the male agricultural labourers in the region. The marginal female workers in agricultural labour were about 6 per cent in Bidar and 8 per cent in Gulbarga as against 3 per cent in Bellary and 4 per cent in Raichur in 1981. The high proportion of female marginal workers in agricultural labour also suggests the economic compulsions in the two districts. Coming to the proportion of female other workers, it was lower and its decline over time was much faster compared to male workers in the region. Thus relatively high proportion of females participate in economic activity in the region and their occupation was mainly agricultural labour.

Urbanisation

The Hyderabad-Karnataka region has a low level of urbanisation (23.6 per cent) compared to the state (30.9 per cent) as per 1971 population census (Table 4.10). Among the districts in the region, Bellary has high urbanisation level (29.9 per cent) followed by Gulbarga (23.6 per cent), Raichur (20.8 per cent) and Bidar (19.6 per cent). The region had 31 towns in 1961 and the number of towns has increased to 45 by 1991. Among these towns, apart from the four district headquarters, only Hospet (Bellary district) has the status of a city (population exceeding 100,000). The region has only two Class II towns (50,000 to 99,999 population), 18 Class III towns (20,000 to 49,999 population), 11 Class IV towns (10,000 to 19,999 population) and 9 small towns with less than 10,000 population.

The urban population in the region has grown faster than state urban population during the decades of 1961-71 and 1971-81. The decade population growth rates for the two periods in the region were 41.1 and 56.6 per cent and the corresponding growth rates for the state were 35.3 and 50.6 per cent. None the less the urban population growth in the region during 1981-91 has slowed down (27.6 per cent) compared to the state average (29.6 per cent). The high urban population growth in the region

TABLE 4.9: Occupational Pattern of Female Workers

(Percentage to Female Population)

Districts	Cultivators				Agricultural labourers				Other occupations			
	1961	1981	1981 (Main workers)	1991	1961	1981	1981 (Main workers)	1991	1961	1981	1981 (Main workers)	1991
Bellary	18.79	10.34	8.96	10.71	12.77	23.39	21.05	25.30	5.86	3.48	3.15	2.82
Bidar	13.72	5.56	3.86	6.32	18.33	23.39	17.55	21.55	4.57	1.96	1.54	1.67
Gulbarga	15.51	8.78	5.82	6.74	14.87	28.59	20.81	25.86	6.78	4.20	3.54	2.47
Raichur	18.61	6.84	4.95	6.63	11.02	25.19	21.24	26.29	5.19	2.32	1.98	1.93
Region	16.74	7.98	5.88	7.49	13.96	25.65	20.44	25.16	5.77	3.12	2.66	2.25
State	22.05	9.72	6.32	8.32	9.17	16.52	12.26	15.27	5.57	4.43	3.70	4.12

during the first two decades might have also been contributed by the push factor as evident from the earlier observation of out-migration of rural population due to economic compulsions.

Out of the 36 towns in the region with population exceeding 10,000 (in 1991) only 13 towns exhibited considerable growth (30 per cent and more) in population during 1981-91—the period marked by in-migration to rural areas. They are Siriguppa and Hadagalli in Bellary district; Bidar and Bhalki in Bidar district; Gulbarga, Sedam, Shahapur and Wadi in Gulbarga district and Raichur, Gangavati, Hatti, Manvi and Sindhnur in Raichur district. Apart from the district head-quarters, the three towns in Gulbarga district and Hatti in Raichur district have grown faster due to industrialisation. The other towns—one each in Bidar and Bellary district and three in Raichur district—might have grown mainly from the rural demand for urban services; and these towns are serving as growth centers. Thus the region has a few growth centers and there is need to develop growth centers distributed spatially in the region for the over all development of the region.

Conclusion

The Hyderabad-Karnataka region has low population density and is predominantly rural in character. The villages of the region are comparatively big excepting in the district of Raichur. The population has shown differential decennial growth rates in the districts of the region from 1961. There was net out-migration from Bidar and Gulbarga districts during 1961-71 though the region as a whole has a net in-migration. These two districts showed higher net out-migration during 1971-81, causing the region as a whole to lose population due to migration. However, in the decade 1981-91, all the four districts showed net in-migration. The migratory pattern over time shows that on balance the region was not a net loser of population but, in fact, it was a net gainer, particularly after 1981.

The urban population in the region has grown faster in the first two decades but it has slowed down in the latest decade. The faster growth in the earlier decades might also have been contributed by the push factor. The rural demand for urban services was weak and the weak demand might not have helped many towns to develop into growth centers.

The region has high proportion of agricultural labourers. Lack of year-long employment for them in the periods of drought appears to be a major factor for their temporary migration. The temporary migration brought more females into work force and most of them were agricultural labourers. The population in the region does not migrate on a permanent

TABLE 4.10: Proportion of urban population and its decennial growth rate

	Proportion of urban population				Decennial population growth		
Districts	1961	1971	1981	1991	1961-71	1971-81	1981-91
Bellary	22.57	27.15	33.05	29.86	47.56	61.48	14.68
Bidar	12.25	14.46	17.82	19.57	46.68	48.93	38.49
Gulbarga	16.18	17.78	22.86	23.62	36.59	53.82	28.18
Raichur	14.49	15.36	19.27	20.79	36.46	58.06	39.68
Region	16.52	18.63	23.45	23.64	41.14	56.63	27.60
State	22.33	24.31	28.89	30.92	35.23	50.65	29.62

basis and migration is not a solution to reduce the population pressure in the region.

The high female work participation rates and the tendency of return migration of population even with reduction in instability in agriculture production suggests that the region has the necessary human resource which only requires to be deployed in gainful economic activity. The region has to plan for employment generation to arrest the temporary out-migration of population. This calls for a strategy which provides gainful employment to the people in rural areas. This can be attempted through planned development of dry land agriculture in addition to the development of irrigation wherever feasible. Further, there is a need to introduce employment guarantee programme in this region on a regular basis with proper monitoring. This would need a clear understanding of unemployment levels of rural workers both during agricultural season as well as off season in the different talukas of the region. Such estimates on unemployment are not available even at the district level, which warrants a study in that direction.

The region has viability for locating employment generation projects in villages as there are good number of big villages and availability of persons to work on the projects.

There is a need to develop all the taluk-headquarters as growth centers in order to support the likely growth of agricultural production in the region due to expansion of irrigation and the encouraging results of dry land agriculture technology.

REFERENCES

1. P. J. Bhattacharjee, 1993: 'Estimates of Vital Rates for the Districts of Karnataka 1951-91', Population Centre, Bangalore.

2. M. Vivekananda and V. S. Satyapriya, 1994: 'Time Series Analysis of Agricultural Production in Karnataka - 1955-56 to 1990-91', ISEC, Bangalore.

5

INFRASTRUCTURE FOR REGIONAL DEVELOPMENT

M. Johnson Samuel

Introduction

The term infrastructure is an umbrella term for many activities referred to as 'social overhead capital' in development economics literature (World Bank, 1994 p. 2). An adequate and efficient infrastructure lowers production costs and raises productivity. It facilitates rapid industrialisation of a region by modernizing and diversifying production. A properly designed, well-managed and rightly located infrastructure can ensure environmental sustainability. The construction and maintenance of infrastructure especially roads, railway lines and similar civil works programme can contribute to poverty reduction by providing direct employment. Infrastructure represents, if not the engine, the wheels of economic activity (World Bank, 1994 p. 14). It can determine one region's prosperity and another's backwardness.

A study of regional disparities in the newly formed Mysore State noted that the Kannada speaking region of the erstwhile Hyderabad state lagged behind other regions of the state in infrastructural development (Government of Mysore). The pace and pattern of development of the state since then, has not reduced substantially the regional imbalances in infrastructure inherited from the past (I.S.E.C. 1989). This is a matter of grave concern to planners and administrators. If a backward region continues to be neglected, dissatisfaction and resentment are bound to increase.

Scope and Objectives of the Study

The paper draws up inventories for a number of economic infrastructural stocks and estimates the needed expansion to bring the region on par with the rest of the state. To the extent the data are available, the paper examines their usage patterns in an effort to assess the efficiency of infrastructural services. The term "economic infrastructure" includes transport networks, communication links, power generation and distribution facilities and credit institutions.

Data and Methodology

Most of the data used in the paper are drawn from periodically published government statistical reports. Some other data are compiled from administrative files of the concerned government departments. Not all the data pertain to the same year. The year of the data is indicated in the relevant table. While the latest data relate to the year 1993-94, the earliest data go back to March 1989. In any case, they are the most recent data available to researchers.

For each type of facility, a measure of coverage has been worked out. It is derived by dividing the total number of a given physical facility by the total population who are likely to benefit from the facility. A measure of accessibility is also worked out by dividing the total number of a given physical facility by the total area they are intended to serve. This is a rough and ready index which can often hide what can be a significant variation in physical accessibility of the facility to users. For example, in the case of post office, physical proximity such as share of population within a radius of one kilometre or by varying distance zones from the facility would be a good measure of accessibility, but such data are difficult to come by. Where data permit, some indicators of efficiency of the infrastructures have also been worked out.

Transport Network

An efficient and extensive transport network can reduce the time and cost of flow of goods and services and, therefore, is a sine-qua-non for economic development. Roads: Roads link villages to urban markets and help farmers to sell their crops and buy agricultural inputs. Road transportation is flexible and swift enough for carrying perishable agricultural commodities and they are economical over short distance movement. Roads feed the railways with passenger and goods traffic. By facilitating daily commutation of students and workers from their home in the village to urban centres, roads foster the social and cultural development of the villages.

Hyderabad-Karnataka region is served by 20,320 kms of roads of which National and State High Ways account for 13 per cent (2,601 kms). The road coverage of the region is less than in other parts of the state. The length of roads including National and State Highways for every 1,000 sq. km. works out to 446 kms in the region and 699 kms for the state as a whole. To reach the state standards with regard to road coverage 11,518 kms of road will have to be added to the existing road length in the region.

The region has only 18 registered motor vehicles per thousand population as against the state average of more than 38 vehicles. The fleet strength in the region needs to be doubled. (Table 5.1)

Road linkage within the region leaves much to be desired. According to government records, almost every revenue village in the region is connected by a road of sorts. Hidden behind the statistics are a large number of spatially dispersed hamlets, harijan *bastees* and tribal thandas which are tagged on to a nearby larger village for administrative convenience and counted as one single revenue village. The residents of these smaller human habitats do not enjoy direct access to a road. They often use a foot-path or badly rilled cart-track over long stretches to reach the nearest road. There is no precise estimate of their number. Even if one were to go by the 'revenue village' concept, only 52 per cent of the villages are connected by all-weather motorable roads and another 26 per cent by fair weather motorable roads. Nearly 22 per cent of the villages are connected by non-motorable roads only. Road linking of smaller villages with larger central places particularly hobli head-quarters, weekly shandis, marketing and manufacturing towns must receive greater attention in transport planning.

Black soil occurs over vast tracts of the region. During monsoon, the black soil becomes soggy and swells disrupting road alignment and structure. This pushes up the cost of maintenance of roads in the region. The roads in the region require liberal grants for their maintenance. Inadequate maintenance will shorten the useful life of the road, reduce the service quality and increase the costs to users. Besides, only a small proportion of the road capacity would be available at a given time.

Railways

Railways can transport bulk commodities over long distance relatively at cheaper cost. They link the region with national market for commodities and skilled labour. The region is served by 452 kms of broad gauge railway line and 271 kms of metre gauge line. The number of railway stations (2

TABLE 5.1: Levels of Transport Development, Hyderabad-Karnataka Region

Indicators	Bellary	Bidar	Gulbarga	Raichur	Hyderabad Karnataka Region	Karnataka State as a whole
Registered Motor Vehicles per 1000 Population 91-92	24.62	14.22	16.55	17.27	18.30	38.33
All roads per 1000 sq.km (Length in km.) 91-92	494.38	527.53	412.47	418.56	445.86	698.60
National and State High Ways per 1000 sq.km (Length in km) 91-92	56.74	64.42	49.12	63.63	57.06	69.26
Per cent villages connected by all weather motorable roads, as on 31.3.94	67.5	59.4	42.7	51.0	52.0	N.A
Per cent villages connected by fair weather motorable roads, as on 31.3.94	18.5	21.4	22.9	34.5	26.2	N.A
Per cent villages connected by non-motorable roads only, as on 31.3.94	14.1	19.2	33.9	14.0	21.5	N.A
Per cent villages not connected by any road, as on 31.3.94	0	0	0.5	0.5	0.3	N.A
Railway Stations per 1000 sq.km 91-92	3.64	1.65	1.41	1.07	1.82	2.05
All gauges of railway lines per 1000 sq.km (Length in km) 91-92	33.48	14.50	12.75	7.56	15.86	16.10
Broad gauge railway lines per 1000 sq.km (Length in km) 91-92	11.63	14.50	12.75	3.63	9.91	4.34

Note: 1991 Census Population is used as the base for computing ratios.

Sources: 1. Government of Karnataka, Directorate of Economics and Statistics (1994) *Karnataka at a Glance 1992-93*.

2. Personal communication from the Superintending Engineers, P.W.D., Gulbarga and Bellary Circles.

per 1000 sq. km) and the length of railway line (16 kms per 1000 sq. km) per unit of area are roughly the same in the region as well as in the state. But there is wide disparity within the region. Large parts of Raichur district and Gulbarga district, west of Shorapur are devoid of railway network.

The Southern Railways and the South Central Railways operate train services in this region. The railway network consists of Bombay-Bangalore broad gauge passing through Gulbarga and Raichur, Guntakal-Hubli metre gauge passing through Bellary, and Bidar-Hyderabad broad gauge serving Bidar district. Hospet is an important nodal centre where Bellary-Gadag metre gauge and Bangalore-Guntakal broad gauge converge. The eighty-three railway stations in the region serve as transit points between roads and railways. Gauge differences hamper the running of through trains. The flow of traffic, particularly goods, can be increased if Hubli-Guntakal metre gauge is converted to broad gauge line. There is also a persistent demand from the local opinion makers to strengthen the cohesion of the region by laying a railway line between Bidar and Gulbarga and another line between Hospet and Harihar. Co-ordination between road and railway services must also be ensured. With weak internal road linkages but with strong external railway linkages with metropolitan cities like Bombay, Madras, Hyderabad and Bangalore, the region has certain characteristic features of being a peripheral region tied to the fortunes of metropolitan cities located far away from it.

A disconcerting fact is that no city or town in the region is on the air map of India. It is said that this has driven away many outside entrepreneurs who would have otherwise invested in the region and helped its industrialisation. Gulbarga city seems to be a good candidate for locating the airport.

Communication

Cheap and extensive network of communication is essential for disseminating information and transacting business quickly. There are 1,883 post offices, 559 telegraph offices, 325 telephone exchanges and 36,200 telephones in the region. If one were to go merely by the number of post offices and telephone exchanges per unit of population, the region is on par with or even better than the rest of the state. The number of telegraph offices and telephones per unit of population is, however, lower than the state averages. When these physical facilities are related to area rather than population, the low level of communication development in the region becomes very obvious. The region has 41 post offices, 12 telegraph offices, 7 telephone exchanges and 794 telephones for every 1,000 square kilometre of area. But the state of Karnataka has as many as 51 post offices, 19 telegraph offices, 9 telephone exchanges and 2,265 telephones for the same unit area (Tale 5.2).

TABLE 5.2: Levels of Communication Development, Hyderabad-Karnataka Region

Indicators	Bellary	Bidar	Gulbarga	Raichur	Hyderabad Karnataka Region	Karnataka State as a whole
Post Offices per lakh population 1992- 93	24.03	24.37	24.04	21.84	23.46	21.78
Telephone exchanges per lakh population 1992-93	4.38	3.99	4.58	3.2	4.04	4.01
Telephones per lakh population 1992-93	575.89	399.66	419.59	411.78	451.10	969.26
Telegraph Offices per lakh population	6.7	7.7	6.7	7.0	7.0	8.2
Post Offices per 1000 sq.km. 1992-93	46.02	55.98	38.15	35.95	41.31	50.89
Telephone exchanges per 1000 sq.km. 1992-93	8.39	9.17	7.27	5.27	7.13	9.38
Telephones per 1000 sq.km 1992-93	1,102.68	917.76	665.68	677.74	794.31	2264.96
Telegraph Offices per 1000 sq.km	12.8	17.8	10.7	11.5	12.3	19.1

Note: 1991 Census Population is used as base for computing ratios

Sources: (1) Government of Karnataka, Directorate of Economics and Statistics (1994) *Karnataka at a Glance* 1992-93.

(2) Figures relating to telegraph offices were gleaned from different sources as noted below:

(a) Government of Karnataka, District at a Glance, Bellary 1991-92.

(b) State Bank of India, Annual Credit Plan, Bidar District, 1993-94.

(c) Government of Karnataka, District at a Glance, Gulbarga, 1990-91.

(d) Government of Karnataka, District at a Glance, Raichur, 1991-92.

(e) Government of Karnataka, Economic Survey 1991-92, Karnataka State as a whole 1989-90.

To approximate the level of Karnataka state, 436 post offices, 311 telegraph offices, and 102 telephone exchanges will have to be added to the existing stock. The number of telephones in the region must be trebled. These expansions are needed in order to extend the reach of services to the people in remote areas.

Electric Power

Power is important not merely for the expansion of industrial sector but also for ensuring stability of output in the agricultural sector through supplementary well and lift irrigation. By promoting indoor economic activities and by lengthening productive time beyond sunset, electricity can contribute to the prosperity of a region.

There are at present three power generating units in the Hyderabad-Karnataka region. The major generating unit is Raichur Thermal Power Section with an installed capacity of 420 million kWh. Besides, there are hydro electric power stations at Munirabad in Raichur district and across river Thungabhadra in Bellary district. The installed capacity of all the three plants put together is 462 million kWh, constituting only 18 per cent of the total installed capacity in the state. The state itself is deficient in power generation and obliged to buy power from neighbouring states (Table 5.3)

There is scope for improving the plant load factor capacity utilisation which can, to some extent, ease the scarcity situation. The proposed

TABLE 5.3: Power Generation - March 1989, Hyderabad-Karnataka Region

Name of the Generating Unit	Installed Capacity in Million kWh
Bellary District-Tunga Bhadra Dam - 20% of the Hydel Power - Share of Karnataka	15
Raichur District Munirabad Hydro Electric Station	27
Raichur District-Raichur Thermal Power Station	420
Total Installed Capacity Hyderabad-Karnataka Region	462
Total Installed Capacity in Karnataka State	2,530
Per cent Contribution of Hyderabad-Karnataka Region to the State's Power Resources	18.3

Source : Government of Karnataka, Directorate of Economics and Statistics, *Statistical Abstract of Karnataka 1988-89.*

thermal plants at Hospet and Raichur, and the diesel based project at Bidar, when materialised, may perhaps put the region in a comfortable position with regard to electricity (Government of Karnataka, 1992: 11).

The process of rural electrification in the region is apparently impressive. If the statistics based on the official terminology of 'Revenue Village' are accepted on their face value, almost all villages are electrified. But the sobering fact remains that electric power is yet to reach a large number of hamlets, harijan *bastees* and tribal thandas and there is no precise estimate of population living in such smaller habitats.

There are 84,900 energised electric pump-sets, 67,468 kms of distribution lines (LT and HT lines combined) and 861,632 power connections in the region. The coverage works out to 2.5 pump-sets per 100 ha. of gross cropped area, 1,480 kms of distribution lines per 1,000 sq. km and 107 power connections per 1,000 population. The coverage rates for the state as a whole are 5 pump-sets, 2,120 kms of distribution lines and 160 power connections for the relevant base units. The per capita consumption of power in the region is 112 kWh, which is considerably lower than the state average of 313 kWh. To reach the standard of the Karnataka state, it will be necessary to energise 98,000 more pump-sets, to lay 29,150 kms of additional distribution lines and to provide 422 thousand new connections in the region. The present level of electricity consumption in the region is 898 million kWh units and this may have to be raised by another 1,613 million kWh units.

The regional disparities in the generation and distribution of power, make the uneven growth of several sectors of the regional economy a stark reality. For example, the domestic sector consumes four times more power than the agricultural sector in the region. In contrast, at state level, agriculture consumes three times more power than the domestic sector. On an average, as much as 512 kWh of electricity is used for raising crops over one hectare of land in the state. But, in Hyderabad-Karnataka region hardly 12 kWh of electricity is used for raising one hectare of crop. Bidar district compares favourably with the state regarding availability of energised pump-sets per hectare of gross cropped area. But Bidar's agriculture consumes very low level of electricity. There appears to be large idle capacity in irrigation pump-sets in Bidar as well as in the other three districts of the region. The malady needs further investigation for initiating corrective measures.

There is inter-district disparity in the consumption of electricity in industries. Out of the four districts in the region, Bellary consumes 130 kWh of power per capita and Gulbarga 110 kWh of power per capita in their industries. The per capita industrial consumption of power in the

TABLE 5.4 :Levels of Development in Electricity Use, Hyderabad-Karnataka Region

Indicators	Bellary	Bidar	Gulbarga	Raichur	Hyderabad Karnataka Region	Karnataka State as a whole
Per cent Villages & towns electrified March 1989	96.50	98.17	98.33	97.80	97.84	97.09
Energised electric pumpsets per 100 ha. of gross cropped area March 1989	2.84	5.44	1.40	2.18	2.45	5.28
Consumption of Power for agriculture per Ha. of gross cropped area, KWH 1993-94	22	23	5	9	12	512
Distribution Line (LT & HT combined) per 1000 sq.km.(Length in KM) 1993-94	1,714	2,347	1,236	1,261	1,480	2,120
Electric connections per 1000 population 1993-94	124	116	94	104	107	160
Per capita consumption of power all uses KWH, 1993-94	177	43	140	65	112	313
Per capita domestic consumption of power KWH 1993-94	29	17	22	20	22	48
Per capita consumption of power in agriculture KWH 1993-94	8	8	2	4	5	137
Per capita consumption of power in industries KWH 1993-94	130	16	110	35	79	90
Per capita consumption of power in other sectors (street light-ing,public water supply, sewerage pumping, commercial lighting etc.) KWH 1993-94	10	1	5	5	6	39

Note: The bases used for computing ratios are 1981 census villages and towns, 1991 census population and 1989-90 three year moving averages for gross cropped area.

Sources:(1) Government of Karnataka, Directorate of Economics and Statistics *Statistical Abstract of Karnataka 1988-89.*

(2) 'Distribution and Consumption of Power' Files in the Karnataka Electricity Board Office, Cauvery Bhavan,Bangalore.

other two districts, namely, Raichur and Bidar are abysmally low being 35 kWh and 16 kWh respectively. The latter two districts appear to be less industrialised and special schemes are necessary to attract industries to these two districts.

The per capita consumption of power in street lighting, drinking water supply, sewerage pumping etc., in the region is also very low being 6 kHw. The state consumes six times more power in the same sector for one person. This would suggest that the region is disadvantaged by poorly developed civic amenities. In sum, the region has got to make up a lot of leeway with regard to power generation, distribution and consumption.

Credit Institutions

Credit institutions mobilise the savings of the community and make them available for investment in agriculture, industries, transport, trade etc.
Commercial Banks:

They provide short term finance to meet working capital requirements of industries, trade or any other productive enterprise. Their role in agricultural credit is also on the increase. There are 602 commercial branch banks in the region (Table 5.5).The total deposits mobilised by them amounts to Rs.802 crores and credit disbursed amounts to Rs.722 crores. The region has 8 commercial branch banks for every one lakh population as against 10 for the entire state. Overall in the state, a branch bank serves an area of about 43 square kilometres. In Hyderabad-Karnataka region, a branch bank caters to an area of about 76 square kilometres. The jurisdiction of a branch bank is very unwieldy in the region. The region needs another 446 banks to raise the status of this crucial infrastructure to the standard obtaining in the state.

There is lack of banking habit among the people. There are only 349 deposit accounts and 94 credit accounts for every thousand population in the region. The corresponding state prevalence rates are 588 and 128 respectively. On an average, a person in the region has a bank deposit of Rs.1,000 and a credit liability of Rs.899. This is less than half of the state figures of Rs. 2,501 and 1,921 respectively. This calls for vigorous efforts to take banking services to the door steps of the village community.

The banks in the region transact lower volume of business than their counterparts elsewhere in the state. On an average, a bank in the region mobilises Rs.133 lakh as deposit and deploys Rs.120 lakh as credit. A bank in other parts of the state transacts almost two times more business.

Another disturbing feature of the region is that the people have lower credit absorptive capacity and their ability to save is also limited. The

TABLE 5.5 : Scheduled Commercial Banks March 1992, Hyderabad Karnataka Region

Indicators	Bellary	Bidar	Gulbarga	Raichur	Hyderabad Karnataka Region	Karnataka State as a whole
Scheduled commercial banks per lakh population	9.29	7.35	6.66	7.06	7.50	9.86
Deposit accounts per 1000 population	467	251	263	400	349	588
Credit accounts per 1000 population	118	76	84	95	94	128
Average Area served by a Bank Sq.Km.	56	59	95	86	76	43
Deposit Mobilisation on an average by a Bank Rs.in lakh	122	108	159	133	133	254
Credit disbursement on an average by a Bank Rs.in lakh	137	77	106	139	120	195
Per capita deposits Rs.	1,132	798	1,053	941	1,000	2,501
Per capita credit Rs.	1,277	570	707	984	899	1,921
Average amount of deposit Rs	2,423	3,183	4,004	2,351	2,867	4,250
Average amount of outstanding credit Rs.	10863	7,511	8,413	10372	9,594	15,040
Credit deposit ratio	113	71	67	105	90	77
Sectoral Pattern of Outstanding Credit:						
(a) Per capita credit for agriculture Rs.	460	254	247	556	387	413
(b) Per capita credit village industries & artisans Rs.	13	7	8	7	9	10
(c) Per capita credit small scale industries Rs.	131	54	99	49	85	244
(d) Per capita credit medium and large industries Rs.	332	75	67	68	131	572
(e) Per capita credit trade Rs.	121	73	116	132	115	196
(f) Per capita credit transport Rs.	23	21	12	10	15	40
(g) Per capita credit professional services and personal loans Rs.	162	105	124	121	129	292

Note: 1991 Census Population is used as base for computing ratios

Source: Reserve Bank of India, Bombay, *Banking Statistics*, Vol. 21, March 1992.

average size of a bank deposit is Rs.2,867 and a bank loan Rs.9,594 in the region. They do not compare well in relation to the state level figures of Rs. 4,250 and Rs. 15,040 respectively. The credit deposit ratios stand at 90 for the region and at 78 for the state as a whole. As a matter of fact, the credit-deposit ratio is above 100 in Bellary and Raichur districts. It is evident that banks in the region have lent more than what they have mobilised locally. This would mean that the banks operating in the region are obliged to bring funds from elsewhere to meet the credit needs of the region.

The per capita credit disbursement in Hyderabad-Karnataka region is Rs. 387 for agriculture, Rs. 225 for industries, Rs.115 for trade, Rs. 15 for transport and Rs. 129 for professional services. The corresponding figures for the state are Rs. 413, Rs. 826, Rs. 196, Rs. 40 and Rs. 292 respectively. In general it is seen that industries have been neglected in credit deployment. Bellary and Raichur districts have received more than their share of credit for agriculture. Within the region, trade has absorbed more credit at the expense of more productive sectors like industries. Credit disbursement within the region seems to be lop-sided and flows into sectors which do not produce tangible goods.

Credit Co-operative Societies

Co-operative movement in Karnataka has had a long history (Government of Karnataka, 1970). The credit requirements of agriculture is mainly met by agricultural credit co-operative societies and their number in the region is 772. They have mobilised deposits in the order of Rs. 65 lakh and disbursed credit to the tune of Rs. 1,316 lakh. Non-agricultural credit co-operative societies provide credit for housing and production and marketing of non-agricultural commodities like hand-loom cloth. Deposits mobilised by them total to Rs. 174 lakh and credit disbursement to Rs. 468 lakh. There are 136 non-agricultural credit co-operative societies in the region.

The number of agricultural credit societies for every one lakh population works out to 10 for the region and also for the state. It looks as though certain norms like one society for every ten thousand population are observed for creating agricultural credit societies. With regard to non-agricultural credit societies, there is no such straight-jacketting into population norm. The number of non-agricultural societies in the region is two for one lakh population as against four for the state as a whole.

An agricultural credit society in the region serves an average area of about 59 square kilometres, whereas a typical society in the state serves only about 44 square kilometres. The non-agricultural credit societies in the region on an average cater to an area (335 square kilometres) three

TABLE 5.6: Credit Co-operative Societies 31.3.1992, Hyderabad-Karnataka Region

Indicators	Bellary	Bidar	Gulbarga	Raichur	Hyderabad Karnataka Region	Karnataka State as a whole
Primary Agricultural Credit Co-operative Societies						
Number per lakh population	9	14	9	9	10	10
Average area served by a society Sq.km.	60	32	70	68	59	44
Membership per 1000 population	110	83	62	91	85	101
Deposit Mobilised on an average by a society Rs.	25,726	269	4,358	6,122	8,460	158,000
Loans disbursed on an average by a society Rs.	384,585	278912	31,095	66,229	170411	277,072
Per capita loan given Rs.	33	38	3	6	16	27
Percentage of overdues to outstanding	72	42	94	92	73	65
Primary Non-Agricultural Credit Co-operative Societies						
Number per lakh population	2	1	2	1	2	4
Average area served by a society Sq.km.	241	419	280	584	335	116
Membership per 1000 population	6	3	7	3	5	21
Deposit mobilised on an average by a society Rs.	3,08,927	25,000	59,224	40,208	1,27,875	4,81,780
Loan disbursed on an average by a society Rs.	6,90,537	4,82,769	1,72,414	2,17,583	3,44,191	7,89,208
Per capita loan given Rs.	15	5	4	2	6	29
Percentage of over dues to outstanding	2	1	58	37	12	9

Source : Registrar of Co-operative Societies, Bangalore, 1992 *Co-operative Movement at a Glance in Karnataka.*

times larger than the area (116 square kilometres) served by a similar society located elsewhere in the state. The region needs another 258 agricultural credit societies and 256 non-agricultural credit societies to come up to the level that the state has already achieved.

Another disturbing feature is that a large mass of people in the region are outside the orbit of credit system. Out of every thousand persons only 85 persons are members in agricultural co-operatives and 5 persons are members in non-agricultural co-operatives. The corresponding figures for the state are 101 and 21, respectively.

An average agricultural co-operative in the region mobilises Rs.8 thousand as deposit and disburses Rs.1.70 lakh by way of loans. This is much lower than the state level averages of Rs.1.58 lakh and Rs.2.77 lakh, respectively. Similarly a non-agricultural co-operative in the region, on an average, collects Rs.1.28 lakh as deposits and disburses Rs.3.44 lakh as loans. The corresponding state level averages are Rs.4.82 lakh and 7.89 lakh, respectively. The paradox is that even though there are fewer co-operatives in the region, they suffer from low levels of turnover.

The per capita loan given by agricultural co-operatives works out to Rs.16 and by non-agricultural co-operatives to Rs.6. This is much lower than the state level figures of Rs.27 and Rs.29, respectively. The region's share in the credit provided by co-operative sector is indeed small. But for the higher levels of agricultural loans disbursed in Bellary and Bidar districts, the position would have been still more appalling.

The over-dues as a percentage of outstandings are as high as 73 among agricultural co-operatives and 12 among non-agricultural co-operatives in the region. The state level overdues to outstandings are 65 percentage for agricultural and 9 percentage for non-agricultural co-operatives. Bidar, however, records higher levels of loan repayment. The overdues and wilful default plague the co-operatives of Gulbarga and Raichur districts retarding the flow of credit to potential investors.

The region's credit system is characterised by inadequacy of institutions, general apathy of the people towards co-operative movement, tardy deposit mobilisation, low levels of credit absorptive capacity, smaller volume of business transactions, and unsatisfactory recovery of overdues. The full benefits of co-operative credit institutions cannot be realised in the region as long as these deficiencies persist.

Policy Issues

Whichever way we look at, the region trails far behind the rest of the state in infrastructural development. While the existing infrastructural units are woefully inadequate to meet the needs of the regional economy, they are also very much under-utilised. Lack of adequate infrastructural services deprives the region of dynamism along industrial and agricultural fronts. This results in low standard of living for the people, which, in turn, keeps the infrastructure in a perpetual state of under-development. This is a vicious circle which must be broken through state intervention, by way of creating infrastructure wherever it is inadequate. If historical experience is any guide, in a free market society, profit motives and the pull of agglomeration economics are so strong that private sector would accentuate rather than reduce regional disparities.

The data by revenue village do not lend themselves for pursuing a vigorous programme of rural electrification or rural roads. There is need to generate data on the availability of infrastructures in smaller habitats like hamlets, harijan bastees, lambani thandas by their population size.

It must be recognised that every region is unique in its own way. Hyderabad Karnataka region has low population density and human habitats are diffused over a wider geographical area. The planners seem to rely on the procrustean bed of population size for distributing resources for the creation of infrastructure. The size of area to be served by a unit of infrastructure is seldom taken into consideration. The spatial distribution of infrastructure appears to be uneven and random, forcing people to trudge long distances and spend considerable time and money to avail themselves of the infrastructural services. It may not be possible to locate a unit of infrastructure in each and every village. But aggregate travel time and cost for potential users can be minimised if infrastructure is located at central villages situated at more or less uniform distance from one another. Special campaigns would be necessary in villages without infrastructure, to make their inhabitants aware of whatever infrastructure services are available in the central village nearest to them. Maintenance grants for roads need liberalisation, considering the soil condition of the region.

The poor performance of certain infrastructure provides strong reasons for doing things differently in more effective and less wasteful ways. Idle capacity in infrastructure can be minimised if the services are taken to the door steps of the villagers who happen to live in villages which cannot support on their own, a permanent unit of the infrastructure. In this context, the strategy of delivering services through mobile post offices, periodic credit camps etc., must be tried.

Our study has shown that there is lop-sided development of infrastructure within the region itself. The causes for intra-regional spatial inequalities could be deep-seated and may refuse to budge if sectarian interest groups are allowed to influence location decisions. The Hyderabad-Karnataka Area Development Board should be given the freedom to decide objectively where and what level of infrastructure should be created. Development of infrastructure requires some attention to be given to identification and selection of service points and manageable service areas. The delivery system for the services must be integrated horizontally and vertically so that services of different kind and order are located at convenient points. This calls for the preparation of a master plan for the region. In sum, systematic and co-ordinated efforts are called for to lift the region from the quagmire of poverty and backwardness.

REFERENCES

Government of Mysore, *Mysore After Integration—A Survey of Development of Different Regions :* Government Press, Bangalore, 1969.

Government of Karnataka, Bureau of Economics and Statistics (1970) *Economic Development of Mysore 1956-69,* Bangalore.

Government of Karnataka, Planning Department (1992) *Economic Survey 1991-92,* Government Press, Bangalore.

Institute for Social and Economic Change, Bangalore (1989) - papers presented in a seminar on *Karnataka's Eighth Five Year Plan Perspective* 16-17 November (mimeographed).

World Bank (1994) - *World Development Report 1994-Infrastructure for Development,* Oxford University Press, New York.

6

IRRIGATION DEVELOPMENT
Problems and Prospects

M. Venkata Reddy

1. Introduction

It is needless to over emphasise the role of irrigation in the economic development of any region. For, it augments agricultural production by facilitating higher intensity of cropping and higher levels of productivity. The fact that the scope of the genito chemical technology of the Green Revolution is almost limited to irrigated lands reinforces the crucial importance of irrigation (Hiremath *et.al.*, 1988). Irrigation not only is being used as a production augmentating input but also as one of the strategies to ensure balanced regional development. In a democratic polity like India where balanced regional development is considered as one of the constitutional obligations, it becomes necessary to evolve appropriate strategies to exploit water resources available in a region taking into account the local needs. An attempt is, therefore, made in this paper to analyse the problems and prospects of irrigation development in the Hyderabad-Karnataka region and to suggest appropriate measures for optimising the utilisation of water resources.

Karnataka is one of the backward states in terms of irrigation potential. While the state accounts for 5.81 per cent of the total area and 5.31 per cent of the total population of the country, the ultimate potential of irrigation (major, medium and minor, including ground water) is 5.5 million hectares accounting for only 4.8 per cent of the total potential in the country. According to the figures available upto 1991-92, only 21.6 per cent* of the net sown area is irrigated in the State as against the

* Bureau of Economics and Statistics, Karnataka at a Glance 1992-93, Government of Karnataka, Banglore.

national average of about 33 per cent. This is indicative of the relative backwardness of the state as a whole when compared with the national average. Unfortunately, Karnataka is unable to harness fully even the available river water because of the unfavourable terrain which does not facilitate construction of storage reservoirs. This is particularly true in the case of west-flowing rivers, whose contribution to the total yield in the state is more than 50 per cent. Therefore, the state has to be content with the utilisation of only 1724 TMC out of the 3440 TMC of the annual average yield from all the rivers. That apart, in Karnataka irrigation potential is also beset with sharp imbalances between the regions. Table 1 which gives the details of net area irrigated as a per cent of net area sown in the state adumbrates this point. Though in recent years there has been some narrowing down of disparities the inter-district imbalances in irrigation development, as revealed by the data presented in Table 6.1, seem to have persisted in the state. Further, it is interesting to note that in 10 out of 19 districts, the percentage of net irrigated area to net sown area was found to be less than the state average in all the three periods under reference. There was some change in the relative positions taken by the districts. The change is quite perceptible in some districts like Raichur and Bellary where the area irrigated had increased from 1.2 per cent in 1957-58 to 25.4 per cent in 1991-92 and from 3.5 to 27.7 per cent, respectively. The reason for such phenomenal increase seems to be the efforts of the State to encourage canal irrigation which increased the net area irrigated by canals to the level of 76.2 per cent in Raichur and 63 per cent in Bellary districts. The increase in net area irrigated in Gulbarga was also significant, though it is much less than the state average. On the other hand, in some districts like Bidar, where there is no much scope for canal irrigation, the change in net area irrigated is not significant.

2. Irrigation in H. K. Region: An Overview

The HK region accounts for almost one-fourth (23.6 per cent) of the total geographical area of the State and 28.3 per cent of the net sown area. While the proportion of net sown area to the total geographical area of the State (as per 1991-92 figures) is of the order of 56.2 per cent, it is 67.5 per cent in the case of the HK region. Furthermore, the region is endowed with fertile deep black cotton soils. Moderate irrigation in these soils promotes higher productivity while heavy irrigation is hazardous in the long run. Optimum and judicious use of irrigation potential in the region is, therefore, critical for ensuring sustainable agricultural production. Because of scanty and erratic rainfall* fertile soils of the region remained less productive. It may look somewhat paradoxical to think about more irrigation facilities in a low rainfall region. Ironically this region, which is drought-prone, is blessed with one of the major river systems, namely, Krishna river basin. However, for historical reasons this important river system has not been adequately tapped for irrigation purposes.

TABLE 6.1 : District-wise Net Area Irrigated as Per Cent of Net Area Sown in Karnataka

Sl. No.	District	Net area irrigated as per cent of net sown area		
		1957-58	1983-84	1991-92
1.	Bangalore	10.9	19.0	19.2
2.	Belgaum	5.9	20.6	28.9
3.	Bijapur	1.8	10.8	20.8
4.	Chickmagalur	32.7	11.2	10.0
5.	Chitradurga	7.3	18.5	20.2
6.	Dakshina Kannada	24.7	39.3	43.0
7.	Dharwad	5.0	8.7	14.7
8.	Hassan	15.7	14.6	17.1
9.	Kodagu	6.7	3.0	2.4
10.	Kolar	17.0	23.8	27.3
11.	Mandya	26.0	38.2	37.6
12.	Mysore	1.2	12.4	25.2
13.	Shimoga	41.5	41.8	44.6
14.	Tumkur	9.6	13.2	13.6
15.	Uttara Kannada	20.5	19.4	29.9
16.	Bellary	3.5	20.7	27.7
17.	Bidar	2.7	7.7	11.7
18.	Gulbarga	1.4	2.5	14.1
19.	Raichur	1.2	12.4	25.4
	State:	7.5	15.0	21.6

Source: Government of Karnataka, *Bureau of Economics and Statistics,* Govt. of Karnataka, Bangalore. Computed from the data obtained for different years.

The river Krishna and its tributaries form the life line of the H-K. region because, the entire culturable area of the three districts, namely, Bellary, Gulbarga and Raichur falls under Krishna basin.* In the case of Bidar, a small proportion (17.9 per cent) of the culturable area comes under Krishna basin and the remaining area (82.1 per cent) falls under Godavari basin. In view of the fact that about 28 per cent of the annual

* Normal rainfall in the region ranges from 599 mm in Raichur district to 847 mm in Bidar. Gulbarga and Bellary fall in between with 777 mm and 639 mm respectively.

yield in the state comes from the Krishna basin and that the HK region forms a major part of the basin, the need for harnessing available water gains importance. Attempts were, therefore, made in 1960s and 70s to utilise the available water by initiating a number of major and medium projects in the basin. The ultimate utilisation in Krishna basin in the state is likely to be 1156 TMC, the details of which are presented in Table 6.2.

TABLE 6.2 : Water Available in the Krishna Basin

1.	As per the Krishna Tribunal's allocation presently in force	734 TMC
2.	By way of Godavari Diversion to Krishna as per the Godavari Tribunals award	23 TMC
3.	When the surplus waters of the Krishna River are allocated under the scheme 'B' formulated by the Krishna Tribunal's award*	183 TMC
4.	If the scheme known as Peninusular Rivers Development materialises	216 TMC
	Total	1156 TMC

* This scheme can come into force on the formation of an authority to be called Krishna Valley Authority by consent of the party-states by an Act of the parliament.

Source: *Irrigation in Karnataka* - 1993-94, Government of Karnataka, Irrigation Department, Bangalore, 1993.

As observed from the above table, 1156 TMC of water in the Krishna basin envisaged under different schemes, would be available for utilisation. That would, however, ultimately depend upon the successful implementation of the various projects, the possibility of which under the given politco-administrative dynamics relating to sharing of river waters appears to be a distant dream. Nevertheless, the utilisation of 734 TMC of water allocated to the state needs to be taken up on a priority basis in order to extend irrigation facilities in the HK region. Keeping this objective in view, the state has, no doubt, initiated the construction of a number of major and medium irrigation projects in the region, to the discussion of which we may now turn our attention.

3. Irrigation Potential and Utilisation under Major and Medium Projects in Hyderabad-Karnataka Region

Most of the major and medium irrigation projects in the HK region were started in 1970s. Thungabhadra was the first large storage reservoir in the Krishna basin, the major beneficiaries of which are Bellary and

TABLE 6.3 : Major and Medium Irrigation Projects in Hyderabad- Karnataka Region

Sl. No.	Name of the Project	Year of Starting	Ultimate Potential	Potential as on Dec. 1992	Taluks to be benefitted
Gulbarga District					
1.	Soudagar	1973	1417	1417 (100.0)	Yadgir
2.	Lower Mullamari	1975	9713	-	Chincholi
3.	Amarja	1975	8903	-	Aland
4.	Bennythora	1976	20236	-	Chitapur, Sedam
5.	Upper Krishna Stage I	1969	288551	135318	Jevargi, Shahpur Shorapur
		Total	328820	136735 (41.6)	
Bidar District					
6.	Upper Mullamari	1976	3279	3279 (100.0)	Basavakalyan, Humnabad
7.	Karanja	1972	44972	4250 (9.5)	Bhalki, Bidar
8.	Chulukinala	1976	4047	-	Basavakalyan, Bhalki
		Total	52298	7529 (14.4)	
Raichur District					
9.	Maskinala	1976	2833	-	Lingasugur
10.	Hirehalla	1977	8013	-	Koppal
11.	Thungabhadra	1945	244381	243900	Deodurg, Gangavathy, Koppal, Manvi, Raichur, Sindhanur
		Total	255227	243900 (95.6)	
Bellary District					
12.	Thungabhadra	1945	118414	104384 (88.2)	Bellary, Hospet, Sandur, Siruguppa
13.	Bhadra	1959	3724	3724 (100.0)	Harapanahalli
		Total	122138	1081.08 (88.5)	
		Grand Total	758483	496272 (65.4)	

Note : Figures in brackets indicate percentage of potential created to the ultimate potential.

Source : Major and Medium Irrigation in Karnataka.

Raichur districts. The details of all the on-going projects are presented in Table 6.3. It can be seen from that Table that there are 12 on-going major and medium irrigation projects in the region with an ultimate potential of about 7.58 lakh hectares. About 65 per cent of this potential is already being utilised. When all these on-going projects are completed, 25 out of the 32 taluks of the four districts will get irrigation facilities.

A careful look at the data presented in the table tends to raise certain questions. In spite of a great need to augment irrigation facilities in the region, many of the projects have remained incomplete even after two decades. While in some projects potential is realised partially, in some others not even a single acre potential is created even after two decades of their starting. Furthermore, the projects which are located in the districts where there is greater need to increase irrigation potential, have remained incomplete. For instance, the percentage of irrigated area in Gulbarga district at present is only 14 per cent. If all the projects are completed, the percentage could be doubled. Same is the case with Bidar district. But it is unfortunate that the projects in these two districts remained incomplete. For instance, the Lower Mullamari, Amarja and Bennithora projects in Gulbarga district started in 1975 and 1976 have not been completed. So far, not even a single hectare of potential is created, though the ultimate potential under these three projects is estimated to be about 39 thousand hectares, benefiting four taluks in the district. Same is the case with Bidar district where Karanja and Chulkinala projects have been lingering for years. In spite of the fact that Bidar has limited scope for increasing canal irrigation, the only major irrigation project in the state, namely, Karanja did not seem to have got the attention it deserved. It has the potential of about 45 thousand hectares; but so far, only about four thousand hectares of potential is being exploited under the project. Therefore, it calls for a policy change to prioritise the completion of on-going projects in these two districts so that optimum utilisation of available water resources may be ensured.

The utilisation of irrigation potential in Bellary and Raichur districts has almost reached a saturation point, though two medium projects, namely, Maskinala and Hirehalla in Raichur district remain incomplete. The problems in these two districts are different and are related to optimum and efficient utilisation of the potential already created. Large areas in these districts under Thungabhadra command area have gone out of cultivation because of water logging, salinity and alkalinity. If this is allowed to recur, the production potential of the region will get adversely affected in spite of availability of more irrigation facilities. Therefore, there is a need to have a fresh look at the irrigation methods, strategies and programmes in this region besides concentrating on completion of the on-going projects.

4. Minor Irrigation Schemes in Hyderabad-Karnataka Region

Table 6.4 gives the status of minor irrigation (surface) in Hyderabad-Karnataka Region. It can be observed from the data presented in the table that the contribution of minor irrigation to the irrigation potential in the Hyderabad-Karnataka region is not very significant. Lift irrigation schemes appear to be more prominent in the region as they account for about 40 per cent of the potential in the State. Within the region, lift irrigation is prominent in Bellary and Gulbarga districts accounting for about 39 per cent and 30 per cent respectively of the total potential. But it is not clear from the available data whether the potential created is actually realised or not because, lift irrigation schemes are beset with

TABLE 6.4 : Potential created under Minor Irrigation as on 1-4-1992 (Area in Hect.)

Sl. No.	Districts	MINOR IRRIGATION SCHEMES									
		Tanks		Anicut/Pick-ups		Others		LI Scheme		Total	
		Nos.	Area	Nos.	Area	Nos.	Area	Nos.	Area	Nos.	Area
1.	Bidar	93	17805	44	823	2	25	11	3419	150	22072
2.	Bellary	268	16125	28	558	2	87	53	14999	351	31769
3.	Gulbarga	514	25200	177	5359	22	800	36	11502	749	42861
4.	Raichur	671	20974	42	1068	8	300	25	8394	746	30736
5.	H.K. Region	1546 (4.2)	80104 (11.9)	291 (11.7)	7808 (11.4)	34 (2.8)	1212 (1.9)	125 (28.8)	38314 (40.8)	1996 (4.9)	12743 (14.2)
6.	State	36639	673253	2484	68714	1211	63784	434	93880	40768	8996

Source: Minor Irrigation in Karnataka 1993. Chief Engineer, Minor Irrigation, Bangalore.

Note: Figures in brackets are the percentage share of the Hyderabad-Karnataka Region in the total potential of the state.

several technical and operational problems. A fresh look at the lift irrigation schemes in the region would be very much in order in view of their high potential.

It is interesting to observe that the average potential per tank in HK region is much higher at 52 hectares when compared with about 18 hectares per tank in the state as a whole. Within the region, tanks in Bidar district seem to have higher capacities, their average potential being 191 hectares per tank. From the modern and scientific management point of view, tanks in the HK region merit special attention taking the viability factor into account. Furthermore, the scope for increasing tank irrigation in the region appears to be much less, because of low and scanty rainfall on the one hand and the unfavourable topography (Plateau) in most parts of the region on the other. Therefore, it becomes relevant to modernise tank irrigation in terms of conveyance and distribution net work, followed by an institutional approach to sustain tank capacities to store water.

5. Ground Water Potential

Ground water potential in Karnataka state as a whole is estimated to be about 10 lakh hectares. It is well known that the availability of ground water, like surface water, depends upon the intensity of rainfall. The HK region being a low rainfall area is subjected to frequent droughts. Therefore, ground water potential tends to be low there. However, since canal irrigation is going to be a dominant feature in the region, the possibilities of ground water recharge are likely to be more. This may hopefully help augment ground water potential in the region. The present status of ground water exploitation in the HK region is discussed in what follows.

Ground water is being exploited in the region by resorting to both traditional dug wells and modern tube wells (shallow and deep) the details of which are presented in Table 6.5.

It is evident from the table that more than one-third of the dugwells in the HK region are located in Gulbarga district, accounting for about 30 per cent of the gross potential, followed by Bidar and Raichur with 23 per cent each and Bellary with 22.7 per cent. Shallow tube wells are predominant mainly in Bellary (53.4 per cent) and Raichur (12.9 per cent) districts. This could, perhaps, be due to the prevalence of the widespread canal irrigation in these districts which must have improved the ground water table over years. Deep tubewells are also more in Bellary (51.7 per cent) followed by Bidar (26.3 per cent). Augmentation of ground water potential appears to be one of the positive externalities of canal irrigation. This is borne out from the fact that the potential per well is high in the districts where canal irrigation is stabilised. For instance, gross potential per dugwell works out to 3.1 hectares in Bellary, while it is 1.9 hectares in other districts. This could possibly be due to higher intensity of canal irrigation in Bellary district. One could visualise the same situation in other districts also, especially in Gulbarga, when canal irrigation under upper Krishna project gets extended and stabilised. This is one of the aspects which needs to be carefully examined. Higher potential realised under shallow and deep tube wells further explains the association between canal irrigation and ground water potential. Because, the potential per well is more than four hectares in Bellary and Raichur districts where canal irrigation under Tungabhadra project was introduced

TABLE 6.5 : Ground Water Irrigation in HK region (1986-87)

Districts	Dugwells Potential			Shellow Tube Wells Potential			Deep Tube Wells Potential			Total Potential		
	No.	CCA	Gross	No.	CCA	Gross	No.	CCA	Gross	No.	CCA	Gross
Bellary	9733	20361	30488	1182	3072	5310	317	826	1522	11232	24259	37320
	(14.8)	(17.4)	(22.7)	(53.4)	(54.2)	(59.2)	(51.7)	(58.9)	(63.7)	(16.4)	(19.6)	(25.7)
Bidar	16326	31061	31061	204	495	495	161	268	318	16691	31824	31874
	(24.8)	(26.5)	(23.12)	(9.3)	(8.7)	(5.5)	(26.3)	(19.1)	(13.3)	(24.3)	(25.6)	(21.9)
Gulbarga	23059	39002	40809	253	348	461	42	95	100	23354	39445	41370
	(35.00)	(33.4)	(30.5)	(11.4)	(6.2)	(5.1)	(6.9)	(6.8)	(4.2)	(34)	(31.8)	(28.5)
Raichur	16721	26583	31654	574	1755	2697	93	214	450	17388	28552	34801
	(25.4)	(22.7)	(23.6)	(25.9)	(30.4)	(30.2)	(15.1)	(15.2)	(18.8)	(25.3)	(23)	(23.9)
HK region	65839	117007	134012	2213	5670	8963	613	1403	2390	68665	124080	145365
	(100.00)	(100.00)	(100.00)	(100.00)	(100.00)	(100.00)	(100.00)	(100.00)	(100.00)	(100.00)	(100.00)	(100.00)

Note: Figures in brackets are percentages; CCA : Canal Command Area.

Source: Government of Karnataka: *Minor Irrigation Census 1986-87.*

long ago. In the other two districts, the potential per well is much less. There is greater scope to increase ground water potential in the HK region when Krishna waters get fully utilised.

Another strategy that needs to be adopted in the canal command areas is to encourage and provide for conjunctive use of canal and ground water (Reddy, 1990). This provision in the design of all the irrigation projects in the region not only helps increasing irrigation facilities but also avoids or minimises adverse effects like water logging. One has to draw lessons from the experiences of Tungabhadra project and incorporate corrective measures in all the on-going new projects in the HK region.

Among the four districts of the HK region, well irrigation (both dug and tube wells) is more popular in Bidar district. As per the latest available figures (1991-92) more than 90 per cent of the net area irrigated in Bidar district is by wells; there is no scope to increase canal irrigation here. Therefore, wells continue to be the main source of irrigation in the district. In the other three districts, at least in Gulbarga, there is scope to increase canal irrigation and also to ensure its sustainable use. Encouraging more and more watershed programmes in Bidar might help ground water recharge and promote well irrigation.

6. A Resume

The above discussion reveals that the scenario of irrigation development in the HK region looks encouraging. Canals and wells are the two important sources of irrigation; tank irrigation is not prominent. More than one-third of the potential created under major and medium irrigation projects lies in the HK region. Even so, the need for harnessing waters from the Krishna basin is more. Unless adequate funds are made available in the next 10 years, it may not be possible to utilise the 734 TMC of water by 2000 AD that is allocated to the Karnataka state by the Krishna Tribunal. For the completion of the on-going projects and for starting new projects in the Krishna basin an outlay of Rs.3,300 crore is required with an annual outlay of Rs.330 crore for the next 10 years.* Paucity of funds appears to be one of the main reasons for not completing projects on time which has led to cost over runs. Therefore, there is an urgent need to priorities the schemes taking local needs into account and complete them with available funds, instead of starting new projects and making scarce funds less productive.

More efforts are also needed to encourage farmers to utilise Krishna water for irrigation by promoting lift-irrigation all along the river course.

* Government of Karnataka, Irrigation Department, *Report of the Working Group on Major and Medium Irrigation Programme for the Eighth Five Year Plan*, Bangalore, 1989.

This has proved very efficient and cost effective in other districts of the Krishna basin. Since canal irrigation is going to be expanded when all the on-going projects are completed in the region, ground water potential is bound to increase. Therefore, proper planning is needed to encourage conjunctive use of canal and ground water. This will not only avoid adverse effects like water logging, salinity and alkalinity but also increase productivity of land.

In the existing major and medium irrigation projects drainage is totally neglected. With the result, thousands of hectares of fertile soils have gone out of cultivation. Thungabhadra project is the worst affected one in this aspect. Since black cotton soils are ubiquitous in the region, drainage should be treated as an integral part of the project design. Otherwise, like in Thungabhadra, fertile soils of the region tend to become unfit for cultivation. Apart from providing drainage in the command areas, there is a greater need to protect and maintain the natural drainage system in irrigation projects. One could even think of acquiring all the natural drains in irrigation projects by the government and take-up the responsibility of their maintenance. This would certainly help minimise the intensity of adverse effects in the long-run.

The importance of some of the institutional factors like farmers' cooperatives should be recognised right from the design stage of an irrigation system. In view of the contemporary policies of government, like economic liberalisation, the need for farmers' participation and the consequent privatisation in a phased manner becomes more relevant. The ways and means of involving the water users in irrigation management needs to be carefully articulated while designing the irrigation projects. For instance, *Warabandi* is one of the best strategies to ensure efficient irrigation system. Unless farmers' cooperation is ensured, it would be difficult to implement such programmes successfully.

REFERENCES

Government of Karnataka, Bureau of Economics and Statistics *Karnataka at a Glance 1992-93*, Bangalore, 1993.

Government of Karnataka, Irrigation Department :

(a) *Irrigation in Karnataka 1993-94.*

(b) *Irrigation Projects in Karnataka (Major and Medium) 1985.*

(c) *Report of the Working Group on Major and Medium Irrigation Programme for the Eighth Five-Year Plan.*

(d) *Minor Irrigation Census, 1986-97.*

Hiremath K C and Ramanathan Chetti R (1988), "Irrigation Development in Karnataka - Investment and Utilisation" - *Bhagirath*, Vol.XXXV, October-December.

Venkata Reddy, M (1990) - *Dynamics of Irrigation Water Management*, Ashish Publishing House, New Delhi.

7

POLITICO-ADMINISTRATIVE INSTITUTIONS IN THE H-K REGION

N. Sivanna and C. Charles Nelson

Introduction

The development of a backward region has become imperative not only in the advancement of that region in terms of infrastructure, strengthening of economic, social and political institutions, but also in the improvement of the living conditions of the people. Intended efforts in this direction have aimed at bringing in necessary socio-economic transformation. However, while pursuing such a path of transformation, many constraints will have to be faced. They can be of varied nature such as physical, institutional, political and administrative. In order to release these constraints necessary corrective measures have to be brought in by initiating specific policy measures. To comply with this requirement, there is a need for massive investment of resources, and effective guidance and direction.

Seen in the above perspective, the main initiator as also the motivator, to carry out such desired changes, is the government itself which comprises of both political leaders and bureaucracy. The effective coordination and proper understanding between these two principal functionaries would certainly bring in the necessary changes in the economy. The dynamics of governmental process can be understood through two approaches : political and administrative. The political approach specially emphasises on the political process; that is, formulation of policies and programmes which should be based on the felt needs of the people, area or region. It is to be noted that the decisions taken to initiate developmental activities, to create necessary institutions for executing such activities, and to devolve required powers, functions and resources to institutions, are politically initiated and determined. The administrative approach to political process is very much exemplified by 'efficiency' criterion. The success or failure of development programmes depends to a great extent on their effective implementation, which is the prime responsibility of the field level bureaucracy.

With the above as a backdrop, the present paper attempts to study the politico-administrative dynamics in the development of the Hyderabad-Karnataka region. As part of this attempt, efforts are made here to study and analyse the organisational and functional aspects of institutions that are involved in the development process, more importantly, the Hyderabad Karnataka Area Development Board (HKADB) which has recently been established to promote the development of the region.

The objectives of this paper are:(1) to study the organisational and functional aspects of the institutions such as HKADB in order to assess their strengths and weaknesses; (2) to examine the performance of both political and administrative leadership in the articulation of people's felt needs; and (3) to assess the nature of development process, specially to identify constraints, if there are any, and to suggest possible corrective measures. In addition, the paper has tried to analyse the local dynamics keeping in view the environmental dimension of the process.

The data base of the paper consists of the qualitative information gathered through interviews with eminent persons drawn from political, administrative, knowledgeable local leaders, beneficiaries of various development programmes and general public. This is supplemented by secondary data collected from the offices of HKADB and local development departments and panchayats.

Hyderabad-Karnataka Area Development Board

The HKADB was established by an Act (Karnataka Act No. 35 of 1991) which is officially called The Hyderabad-Karnataka Area Development Board Act, 1991. As enunciated in the preamble of the Act, the Board is entrusted with the responsibilities of preparing annual plans containing programmes and projects for the development of the Hyderabad-Karnataka area, supervise the implementation of projects and programmes, and monitor and evaluate the implementation of its plans. This means, the Board is expected to carry out key functions like plan formulation and plan implementation of various development programmes.

The Board has an impressive list of members comprising members of Parliament, State Legislature, Adhyakshas of Zilla Panchayats belonging to four districts of the region, up to ten persons nominated by the State Government of which one each from SC/ST, and the Secretary of the Board (appointed by the Government not below the rank of Divisional Commissioner). The Chairman of the Board is appointed by the Government from amongst the Board members. His term of office is for a period of three years. The Board can hold its sitting once in every three months. The important functions of the Board are : to monitor development projects through its Implementation Committee comprising almost all top officers and Heads of Departments (including the Gulbarga University Vice-Chancellor); prepare annual plan, give approval to plans prepared by the development departments and zilla panchayats; supervise and review the progress of expenditure, performance of various development departments; coordinate the functioning of all development departments and zilla panchayats; implement the schemes; and more importantly, to reappropriate funds from one development department to another. All these functions have facilitated the Board to be a 'nodal development agency' catering to the needs and demands of the region.

To carry out all these responsibilities, the Board has been entrusted with both financial and man-power resources. The assigned development works so far are: construction of roads and bridges; major, medium, minor irrigation schemes; education; rural development and panchayati raj; health; cooperation; youth services; electrification; social welfare; commerce and industries. The financial assistance to carry out these activities ranges between Rs. 50 crore and Rs. 60 crore per annum and it comes from the State Government as grant-in-aid.

Functioning of the Board

The Act has entrusted heavy responsibilities to the Board to organise and execute plans for developing the region to the level of the state average. Although the Board holds a key position in the development of the region, at the same time it suffers from many drawbacks. For instance, the Board as an organisation is found to be inadequate compared to its responsibilities. The organisation chart reveals that it has one Secretary (at present the Divisional Commissioner as Secretary in- charge), one Deputy Secretary of IAS Cadre, one Under Secretary of KAS Cadre, one Deputy Director of Class II Cadre, one Assistant Executive Engineer, one Controller of Finance, one Assistant Controller of Finance and one Accounts Superintendent. Out of the 38 posts sanctioned, 28 posts are of Non-Gazetted officers, to be filled through deputation. Owing to insufficient and untrained staff, the Board is unable to fully shoulder its responsibilities. To quote some of the Board officers "Though we are expected to supervise, monitor and evaluate the schemes (according to the Act), we are unable to do the same due to lack of sufficient technical and extension staff. Hence, we depend mainly on the progress reports furnished by the concerned development departments". This kind of organisational and management deficiency is seen as a hindrance for the full attainment of developmental goals set for the Board.

The importance accorded to the Board in matters of development mainly originates from its superior position compared to zilla panchayats and development departments. For instance, as mentioned earlier, the Board has the powers to approve the plans prepared by zilla panchayats and departments, to review the works and to coordinate the functioning of these institutions and departments. The Board may not be in a position, at present, to carry out all these responsibilities but in course of time it would be possible to do so provided the Board is strengthened with sufficient technical and extension staff. However, the Implementation Committee is able, to a certain extent, to review the works executed by departments and institutions. Through this body, the Board is able to exercise its control over other departments and institutions.

One of the significant and much discussed aspects of the Board is about the allocation of funds; it follows a two-way pattern, that is, it has two components—MLA works and non-MLA works. Under the MLA works, each MLA is given Rs.50 lakh to undertake developmental activities in his\ her constituency. It is the MLA's prerogative to suggest what types of works should be carried out and how much money should be allotted for such works. This practice has been going on in this region since the inception of the Board. Interviews with the officials and the general public, especially in rural areas, indicated that there is a strong opposition to this practice since in many a instance, works carried out under this scheme were in and around MLA's village and villages of his close associates. This growing disenchantment is also due to encroachment of MLAs in the works slated under non-MLAs category. It was suggested by the officials and people that this scheme should be withdrawn and the funds could be used better by giving them to Panchayats.

One serious drawback of the above practice is that the power of allocation of funds rests with the district headquarters and with the State leadership. There is a strong urge from the members of village panchayats that it would be better on the part of the authorities if they took Panchayats (taluk and village level) into confidence for executing works which are at present done by the Board. Then only will there be real and meaningful devolution of powers and resources. As such, there is no serious effort by the Board to identify felt needs of the region and the people. As it is, whenever there is a proposal from the MLA or from the development department, the same is accepted and executed without cross-checking such proposals for their rationale.

The meetings of the Board are not taken seriously both by the officials and non-officials. For instance, the General Body and Implementation Committee meetings have hardly been called regularly, and even when called, they were poorly attended. According to the Act, the Board should meet at least once in three months and the Implementation Committee once in a month. So far, only three General Body and two Implementation Committee meetings have been held. In one of the Implementation Committee Meetings held on February 26, 1994 the Secretary took serious note of the absence of officers like Chief Executive officers of Zilla Panchayats, Deputy Commissioners and other district level officers. All this clearly indicates the luke-warm attitude of the officials and the non-officials towards the Board.

There are many reasons for such attitude towards the Board. Our interviews with some selected officials and non-officials brought out the following points. Some MLAs opined that it was very difficult for all of them to attend the meetings owing to pressing work at their respective constituencies. Instead, they felt that it would be enough if they sent requests and proposals through writing to Chairman and Secretary of the Board. Some of the Zilla Panchayat officials held that it would become unwieldy and burdensome to correspond with all the members and at times it would become very difficult to observe the protocols. A lot of money on these formalities is spent which is really unnecessary and instead it can be used for a better purpose.

The foregoing indicates that both organisationally and managerially, the Board appears to be weak which in turn may be affecting the effective execution of development works. Organisationally, we feel that the Board should be strengthened not only at the headquarters but also at the field level. It is necessary to establish its field level offices so that both supervision, monitoring and evaluation are taken care of. There is need to have a 'Governing Council' instead of a General Body as an executive and policy-making body. To make it representative of the entire region one-third of the MLAs of each district, through 'rotation system', may represent on this body and the Chairman should be elected (and not appointed) from amongst the members of the council. These changes would certainly strengthen the Board both organisationally and functionally.

Interface with the People

It is clear from the above discussion that the Hyderabad-Karnataka area has been given special attention by the Government especially by establishing a separate institution to look after the development of the region. This is in addition to the existing institutions like Panchayati Raj institutions. A question that arises in this context is: in spite of institutional support and necessary financial assistance, why is the region not responding to the efforts initiated by the government? We posed this question to many important political leaders of the region, senior officials, panchayat leaders, beneficiaries of various programmes and the general public. The views they shared with us are quite revealing - a reference to which may be quite in order.

The discussions with the villagers revealed that there was no proper assessment and identification of needs of the people while formulating the programmes; programmes are formulated and implemented at the behest of the MLAs and other influential leaders. In such cases, party considerations weighed while identifying the location of an amenity or a beneficiary. They also expressed the view that they were not familiar with the new schemes that had been implemented by the institutions and departments. Some persons belonging to a village reported that though they voluntarily came forward to contribute in cash and kind to lay a road, the government authorities did not show any interest and concern. They pointed out that there was total indifference among officials (district and block) and non-officials towards implementing developmental activities.

A much related issue is that the political leadership, especially at the panchayats level, is still in the grip of dominant castes; other communities have hardly made any dent into the power structure. Recent elections to panchayats also reflect the same trend. For instance, the information on socio-economic background of the members of two village panchayats in Gulbarga district (Taj Sultanpur and Kalangarga) indicates that majority of them are from Lingayat community (dominant community in the region). This dominance continues to play a crucial role in the rural power structure despite the fact that Panchayats have members drawn from SC\ST and other backward class communities. A larger question that arises in this regard is, why this perpetuation of caste dominance? This indeed is a difficult question to answer. Because more than the intended institutional reform measures, there is a need for a thorough and in-depth understanding of rural power structure. Unless there is a serious and sincere attempt to understand the socio-economic base of rural power structure, the reforms so perceived will have no substantive effect.

Furthermore, the reforms so perceived, to change the rural power base and other social inequalities like land reforms and anti-poverty programmes, have been sluggish due to improper implementation. These hurdles could be removed only when the rural people, especially the poor, are mobilised and organised. In this stupendous task both political and administrative leadership has a crucial role to perform.

Pivotal Planning Role

With the presence of several institutions, there prevails a total confusion between the institutions as far as linkages and coordination is concerned. The multiplicity of controls and supervisions have kept the middle level bureaucracy in dark. For instance, the Zilla Panchayat officials, who are incidentally in charge of implementing both panchayats and HKADB works, have been finding it difficult to carry out their assigned tasks. The ultimate question is, to whom are they responsible? From whom should they receive instructions, orders and directions? Which works, whether panchayat's or HKADB's works, should be given priority? To whom should they report when there are field level problems? There are many such problem areas which the middle and lower level functionaries have been confronting with while carrying out their tasks. This is due to the absence of a clear cut demarcation of functions and duties between the Board and other institutions. There is, therefore, a need to reallocate functions and responsibilities of these organisations in the light of institutional and related administrative changes.

The above situation leads to one of the significant aspects of development administration, that is, the problem of coordination. For the success of a programme/scheme, it is a necessary condition that a proper and effective administrative organisation is evolved by creating appropriate organisational design and culture. The imperative of coordination in the politico-administrative system, especially at the sub-state level, is quite understandable considering the operation of multiple organisational and institutional structures. An important reason why stupendous problems of coordination exist is that in an important way there persists even now pre-development administrative structures and cultures. Also, owing to the existing administrative arrangement, which provides more for disintegration than for integration, for single line of command than team work, coordination of developmental activities seems to be more crucial.

What we feel with regard to the administrative set up in this region is that the HKADB should become the principal body for the management of all development programmes which can be handled at that level. With this arrangement the Board should be able to exercise its control and supervision to bring in coordination and integration for the genuine implementation of development programmes. For this purpose, the Board should open its branches in all the four districts. However, mere creation of new structures or incorporating some changes will not be enough because such changes may not be functional enough for achieving coordination in the development programmes. There is need to introduce 'a culture of management' which is more problem—oriented and less concerned with status and power. In doing this, emphasis should be placed on the reorientation of the attitudes and values of local government functionaries, particularly those steeped in the bureaucratic tradition. In order to create a right atmosphere, there is a need for the removal of hierarchical hurdles, free flow of communication (bottom-up) both horizontally and vertically.

If the HKADB is treated as a nodal institution for the development of the region, the Board has to adopt new strategies to bring in desired development. The Board, instead of adhering to the present method of 'departmental approach', which is often steeped in 'red tapism' and 'formalism', should develop 'project management approach'. Of course, such a shift calls for reorientation of bureaucracy to the required skills and techniques of this approach. But it is worth trying.

Notwithstanding all these, what is most important is that there is a need for a cordial relationship between non- officials and officials in order to bring in effective and desired changes in the region. A positive relationship between these two will certainly have a direct bearing on bridging the gap between the role expectation and role performance of institutions and development departments involved in the process of development. This point is more poignantly brought out by Shri Veerendra Patil, former Chief Minister of Karnataka when he observed as follows in our interview with him: "As long as there is an absence of a proper understanding and coordination between political leadership and administrative leadership in pursuing a task like the development of Hyderabad-Karnataka region, whatever efforts the government may make, in terms of providing financial assistance and creating necessary institutions, there would not be any long-standing effect on the development of the region". In order to make both political and administrative leadership work together at the sub-state level, he further observed that the state level leadership should play a promotive role or a role like a 'big-brother' by giving encouragement and assistance at various critical levels to usher in an all-round development of the region.

Awareness Among the People

The field level observations and discussions with the villagers unfold issues like lack of awareness about the programmes, poor mobilisation of the socially and economically disadvantaged groups, not-so-effective. participation of women, and, more importantly, absence of community participation in the development process. The local-level authorities should accord top priority to these issues before they formulate and implement the development programmes. There is an immediate need to organise 'awareness camps' in all the four districts of the region to educate the general public with regard to the crucial aspects of region's development. This would certainly motivate the people to participate in the activities initiated by the government. To further strengthen this, it is imperative to constitute 'people's committees' at the project-site level to monitor and evaluate programmes and schemes. This would work as a ' feed back' to line agencies. The poor should be mobilised and motivated to participate, through their contributions, in the development process since they are the ultimate beneficiaries of the programmes and schemes.

To make this process a fruitful exercise, the district level institutions and departments should utilise the skills and expertise of the private sector especially to maintain the services like electricity, water supply, repair works, sanitation, parks, transport, etc. Given the opportunities, the private sector would certainly be able to play a supportive and useful role to government initiated development programmes and schemes.

Conclusion

To sum up, the HKADB is given a unique position to carry the mantle of developing the Hyderabad-Karnataka region. The Board is endowed with both statutorily sanctioned powers and responsibilities and necessary financial resources. This itself reflects the strength of the Board and opportunities it has to initiate and execute various development programmes in order to promote the region's development on par with the development of other regions in the State. To carry out this important task, both non-officials and officials have a crucial role to play especially in the application of resources and in exploiting the opportunities that are available to the Board. The constraints, seen in organisational and functional terms, are, however, natural in a newly created institution like HKADB. These constraints that could be rectified by the Board itself by strengthening its technical and extension staff. The Board has enough strength and capacity to provide both political and administrative leadership to promote the region's all-round development.

8

INTRA-REGIONAL DISPARITIES IN HYDERABAD-KARNATAKA REGION
An Analysis

Hemlata Rao and M. Devendra Babu

I. The Background

At the time of States-reorganisation, the then Mysore State inherited a very backward region, which was earlier a part of Hyderabad State. This region, originally comprising of Gulbarga, Bidar and Raichur, was lagging behind both in terms of social and economic development. As quoted in a report of the government, the average road mileage for every 100 sq. miles of area was just 8.6 miles in the Kannada speaking areas of Hyderabad, while the average road mileage in Mysore State excluding village roads was 36.7 miles per 100 sq. miles. In terms of health facilities, the region had a fourth of the facilities available in other parts of Karnataka. Even in the sphere of education, facilities were half of the facilities in the rest of the state. After the merger of these areas in the old Mysore State, Government of Mysore became responsible for the administration and welfare of 19 districts.

The Government was also charged with the special responsibility for bringing the new integrated areas to the level of development of old Mysore without affecting the pace of development in the old Mysore State.

Development efforts began in Hyderabad-Karnataka region in 1960's. By 1968-69, the region was provided with roads, both surfaced and unsurfaced, irrigation wells and industrial estates. As a result, a number of small-scale industries got established. While in 1956-57 there were 3462 primary schools, by 1968-69, another 1686 were added. The number of high schools increased from 171 to 323. During this period 40

Government high schools, and eight private colleges were established. However, these efforts did not really succeed in pulling up the lagged Hyderabad-Karnataka region. Hence in 1980, the Government of Karnataka constituted a committee for identifying the strategy for an all round development of this region, including the district of Bellary. Thus, now four districts with 32 Taluks constitute the Hyderabad-Karnataka region. Special emphasis is laid on the overall development of these four districts.

II. Regional Planning

Hyderabad-Karnataka, while it suffers from some historical factors, is also at some disadvantage in terms of natural factors like low rainfall, poor soil, low underground water potential and so on. This region needs a proper regional plan with differential strategies of development. In fact, there exists sharp intra-regional diversity and disparities. While the sub-region comprising of taluks like Hospet, Bellary, Gangavathi is endowed with rich water resources, there are talukas like Jevargi, Sedam where water resources are inadequate.

Two important tasks before a regional planner are : (a) to improve the average level of development of the region as a whole and (b) more important, to take care of the intra-regional disparities. Efficient operation of the economic organisation requires balanced development of all the sub-regions, in the sense that resources are not left relataively underutilised in any region. In perfect competition, the optimal regional allocation/ utilisation of resources maximises national output. In fact, it represents pareto-optimum, a situation where it is impossible to increase output in one region without decreasing some output in another region. In order to reach this stage, initiating development of all the sub-regions is very important. Special efforts towards development of backward sub-regions are required for the rapid growth of the macro-region.

Backward sub-regions are of two types. One type consists of those which are resource poor and do not possess adequate development potential. The other type consists of those which have rich natural resources like water, forest, minerals, good soil and so on but owing to historical and political factors could not exploit the resources for development purposes and, therefore, remained backward. These differences in the nature of the sub-region are important while formulating a regional plan, which is to be based on the assessed levels of development and typology of backwardness. A study which concentrates on the average performance of the region e.g., Hyderabad-Karnataka as a whole, may place the region as the most backward in the state. However, a disaggregated analysis may show that some of the sub-regions like Hospet and Bellary are developed or more developed than some of the developed taluks in other parts of Karnataka. Further, the region as a whole may record a reasonably good rate of growth, but it may still comprise of taluks which are stagnating. Hence, a study of sub-regional disparities within the macro-region like Hyderabad-Karnataka, assumes special importance. This necessitates going below a district unit while formulating regional development plans. Such a unit, while planning for sub-regions, could be a taluk which satisfies the following eight norms of planning unit:

(i) Planning unit should be geographically a contiguous unit;
(ii) People of the region should have social and cultural cohesion;
(iii) Region should be a separate unit for data collection and analysis;
(iv) The region should have an economic existence which can be assessed from statistical records;
(v) It should be under one administrative agency;
(vi) It should have fairly homogeneous topography;
(vii) It should have one or more growth points; and
(viii) And there should be common appreciation of local problems and common aspirations and approaches to their solution so that it should permit and encourage competition but not rivalry or apathy between one and the other unit of planning.

From the above eight points, 'Taluka' appears to be a good unit of regional planning. Hyderabad-Karnataka has 32 taluks as given below.

Districts	Taluks
Bellary	8
Bidar	5
Gulbarga	10
Raichur	9
Total	32

An inter-taluk analysis brings forth sharp contrasts, diversities and disparities among these 32 talukas. These are analysed in thc following sections.

III. Regional Diversity and Delineation of Homogeneous Regions within Hyderabad-Karnataka

Diversity indicates variations in terms of structural factors like demographic aspects, natural resources, rainfall, minerals, soil type etc. For the present study we could not get information on all the relevant structural variables. Hence, we had to be contended with a few structural variables (Table 8.1):

1. Population per village,
2. Population density,
3. Rainfall,
4. Percentage of forest area,
5. Percentage of uncultivable land,
6. Percentage of working population, and
7. Percentage of net sown area.

A more meaningful delineation of homogeneous groups of taluks requires more information on other structural variables. However, based on the available indicators, the 32 taluks were distributed into different groups according to their structural homogeneity. In order to delineate homogeneous groups we used a full-fledged factor analysis method of the following type:

$Zj = aj1p1 + aj2\,p2 + - - - - + ajn\,pn$ - - -(1).
Zj = standardised variable
$aj1$ = factor loadings on component one.
pj = per 'J'th principal component.

The regions which emerged homogeneous on factor I reflecting such structural variables as percentage of forest, percentage of uncultivable land, percentage of net sown area and average size of the village are put under the following groups:

Group I : Hospet, Sandur, Kudligi, Harapanahalli, H.B. Halli, Humnabad , Koppal, Yadgir, and Gangavathi (9 talukas).
Group II : Chincholi, Hadagalli, Basavakalyan, Bidar, Bellary, Gulbarga, Chitapur, Lingsugur, Shorapur, Sirguppa, Shahpur, Kushtagi, Bhalki, Sedum and Deodurga (15 talukas).
Group III : Aurad, Sindhanur, Aland, Manvi and Raichur (5 talukas).
Group IV : Jevargi, Afzalpur, and Yelburga (3 talukas).

The factor II represented percentage of workers. On this variable, three groups were formed:—

TABLE 8.1 Structral Indicators

	District/ Taluk	Total Population (00) (1991)	Area in Sq. Kms	Population per village	Population per Sq. KM Area	% of Workers to total Population	Normal Rainfall (1901-70) in M.M	% of Forest in total Geographical area	% of Uncultivable land	% of Net Sown Area
	Bellary District									
1.	Bellary	4952	1689	4952.00	293.19	30.74	525.4	1.70	9.55	84.19
2.	Hadagalli	1468	948	2823.08	154.85	34.06	615.5	5.00	12.81	77.02
3.	H. B. Halli	1347	974	2590.38	138.30	32.29	554.5	4.59	25.75	30.95
4.	Harapanahalli	2334	1438	3154.05	162.31	33.42	656.7	15.54	12.23	66.45
5.	Hospet	3128	934	4344.44	334.90	48.24	658.0	26.74	15.99	42.86
6.	Kudligi	2190	1602	2737.50	136.70	35.43	628.2	21.09	12.08	54.98
7.	Sandur	1562	1258	2055.26	124.17	34.70	806.8	25.56	26.36	36.77
8.	Sirguppa	1886	1042	2272.29	181.00	39.55	663.8	2.08	9.05	71.15
	Bidar District									
1.	Aurad	2100	1224	1418.92	171.57	41.00	840.1	1.90	4.83	65.54
2.	Basavakalayna	2463	1206	2218.92	204.23	43.04	674.1	5.98	9.16	68.91
3.	Bhalki	2229	1117	1842.15	199.55	40.20	939.2	2.37	5.15	70.81
4.	Bidar	3315	926	2455.56	357.99	34.96	940.7	5.05	4.79	55.19
5.	Humnabad	2450	985	2987.80	248.73	39.55	841.8	8.46	14.29	57.25
	Gulbarga District									
1.	Afzalpur	1509	1305	1734.48	115.63	43.80	707.4	0.06	5.29	86.37
2.	Aland	2608	1735	2037.50	150.32	45.97	834.0	1.65	3.60	81.96
3.	Chincholi	1892	1569	1444.27	120.59	48.57	880.2	12.59	10.11	61.47
4.	Chitapur	3095	1765	2622.88	175.35	40.19	794.2	3.49	7.27	72.77
5..	Gulbarga	5239	1730	3880.74	302.83	32.51	766.4	2.38	6.86	72.38
6.	Jevargi	1887	1822	1292.47	103.57	48.33	696.5	0.17	3.56	77.36
7.	Sedam	1632	1025	1600.00	159.22	47.55	920.6	1.81	9.57	74.66
8.	Shahapur	2402	1694	1679.72	141.79	45.00	723.4	3.13	7.42	81.74
9.	Shorapur	2817	1820	1609.71	154.78	46.22	709.7	2.64	11.02	62.15
10.	Yadgir	2741	1709	2108.46	160.39	48.34	732.8	13.96	9.63	50.41
	Raichur District									
1.	Deodurga	1768	1508	1021.97	117.24	33.77	632	3.51	6.61	77.50
2.	Gangavathi	3201	1328	2148.32	241.04	35.05	523	10.94	9.33	65.38
3.	Koppal	2514	1375	1835.04	182.84	34.92	600	7.88	19.88	59.80
4.	Kustagi	1895	1366	1162.58	138.73	29.82	571	3.03	7.36	73.63
5.	Lingsugur	2613	1948	1412.43	134.14	31.88	564	4.68	6.71	52.34
6.	Manvi	2690	1791	1650.31	150.20	35.69	640	1.29	2.30	64.52
7.	Raichur	3586	1541	2359.21	232.71	29.25	688	0.26	1.43	68.28
8.	Sindhnur	2843	1598	2016.31	177.91	38.37	582	0.67	7.09	65.77
9.	Yelburga	1960	1490	1420.29	131.54	37.55	593	0.05	4.05	79.15

Source: District Statistical Office, District At a Glance of Bellary, Bidar, Gulbarga (1992-93), and Raichur (1991-92), Government of Karnataka.

Group I : Sandur.

Group II : All the remaining taluks except those included in groups I and III.

Group III : Bellary, Afzalpur, Yelburga and Raichur. As the first factor explained the highest variation for delineation of homogeneous taluks, we retained the scores on factor-I. The talukas which are homogeneous are shown in Table 8.2.

Group I consisted of areas with good forest areas (within Hyderabad-Karnataka region) with large percentage of uncultivable land.

Group II consisted of talukas with high percentage of net sown area and good rainfall.

Group III consisted of negligible forest area with negligible percentage of uncultivable waste. Even percentage of net sown area was average. Population density and average size of village were also medium and rainfall was average.

Group IV consisted of talukas with low density of population, low average size of village, with high net sown area, and average rainfall.

The above delineation of regions based on structural factors, helps the policy makers to frame a regional plan suitable to the natural factors..

Once regions are identified and grouped according to their homogeneity in terms of natural factors, the next task before a regional planner is to assess the levels of development realised by different sub-regions within the homogeneous groups. This is done by an analysis of intra-regional disparities.

IV. Intra-Regional Disparities in the levels of Development

In order to assess the relative levels of development of the 32 talukas in Hyderabad-Karnataka Region, we selected 36 indicators of development which are displayed in Table 8.3. We have used coefficient of variation to observe the level of disparity with regard to selected indicators. As may be seen from Table 8.4, the coefficients for the first range of indicators are very low and are between 0 and 25 per cent, indicating negligible level of disparities. Inter-taluk disparities are more pronounced in the case of adoption of new technology, irrigation, motor vehicles, factory sector, telephones, hospital beds, railway length and employment percentage. The last four ranges show the areas where disparities are considerable and need to be brought down considerably by way of a proper regional planning.

While the coefficient of variation just reflects the relative extent of

TABLE 8.2 : Delineation of Homogeneous Regions

	Taluk	Index
Group I		
1.	Hospet	3.900595
2.	Sandur	3.681512
3.	Kudligi	3.349011
4.	Harapanahalli	3.270538
5.	H. B. Halli	3.243048
6.	Humnabad	3.196801
7.	Koppal	3.088807
8.	Yadgir	3.068209
9.	Gangavathi	3.040093
Group II		
1.	Chincholi	2.799735
2.	Hadagalli	2.797617
3.	Basavakalayna	2.740847
4.	Bidar	2.686908
5.	Bellary	2.619493
6.	Gulbarga	2.579265
7.	Chitapur	2.470878
8.	Lingsugur	2.450762
9.	Shorapur	2.377744
10.	Siraguppa	2.344909
11.	Shahapur	2.217412
12.	Kustagi	2.177678
13.	Bhalki	2.138711
14.	Sedam	2.126035
15.	Deodurga	2.084046
Group III		
1.	Aurad	1.957194
2.	Sindhnur	1.858892
3.	Aland	1.808119
4.	Manvi	1.625988
5.	Raichur	1.109088
Group IV		
1.	Jevargi	0.807296
2.	Afzalpur	0.658084
3.	Yelburga	0.555554

TABLE 8.3: Sectoral Development Indicators

(a) *Agriculture* (b) *Industry*

District/ Taluk	% of Net Sown Area	% of Gross Cropped Area	Cropping Intensity	No. of I P Sets per hectare of N S A	% of Net Irrigated area in N S A	% of HYV area in Net Sown Area	Fertiliser per ha of G S A in KGs.	Veterinery Centres per lakh Livestock	No. of Factories per 100 Sq. Kms	No. of Factories per lakh population	No. of Employees Per Factory	% of Employees to total population
Bellary District												
1. Bellary	84.19	94.69	112.47	2.07	51.30	50.76	97.64	6.57	6.99	23.83	63.72	1.52
2. Hadagalli	77.02	88.35	114.71	6.47	14.95	44.98	33.34	12.03	1.27	8.17	18.67	0.15
3. H. B. Halli	30.95	39.49	127.56	13.79	69.70	77.25	106.28	9.76	1.75	12.62	19.12	0.24
4. Harapanahalli	66.45	74.10	111.52	4.61	12.04	58.20	61.33	6.53	0.35	2.14	19.60	0.04
5. Hospet	42.86	53.61	125.09	7.53	53.79	57.75	201.36	5.08	3.85	11.51	188.50	2.17
6. Kudligi	54.98	64.53	117.36	6.78	13.15	38.09	50.48	5.95	0.87	6.39	63.29	0.40
7. Sandur	36.77	38.98	106.01	5.74	10.87	64.11	130.04	6.50	0.16	1.28	13.50	0.02
8. Sirguppa	71.15	87.77	123.37	2.52	37.97	55.80	141.62	6.51	2.02	11.13	42.00	0.47
Bidar District												
1. Aurad	65.54	75.16	114.68	3.75	4.40	19.98	24.56	10.30	0.08	0.48	10.00	0.00
2. Basavakalayna	68.91	76.95	111.67	8.66	9.48	20.23	29.67	9.35	0.33	1.62	102.50	0.17
3. Bhalki	70.81	91.24	128.86	5.28	7.38	10.87	22.17	15.28	0.36	1.79	11.25	0.02
4. Bidar	55.19	61.28	111.05	16.20	20.95	12.36	64.63	9.02	6.16	17.19	34.56	0.59
5. Humnabad	57.25	65.61	114.61	16.85	22.74	23.27	56.62	15.03	1.42	5.71	86.21	0.50

TABLE 8.3 CONTD.

Gulbarga District												
1. Afzalpur	86.37	88.38	102.33	4.93	8.16	50.71	25.15	14.14	0.54	4.64	4.86	0.02
2. Aland	81.96	93.48	114.05	4.90	7.00	22.08	19.12	9.20	0.40	2.68	5.00	0.01
3. Chincholi	61.47	79.91	130.01	2.13	3.73	14.75	23.28	13.03	0.83	6.87	4.23	0.03
4. Chitapur	72.77	73.67	101.24	0.82	0.78	35.36	23.85	11.50	2.95	16.80	6.77	0.11
5. Gulbarga	72.38	79.53	109.88	4.23	4.63	5.38	23.96	8.34	7.92	26.15	5.44	0.14
6. Jewargi	77.36	78.13	100.99	0.83	0.99	5.73	16.15	12.39	0.66	6.36	7.58	0.05
7. Sedam	74.66	82.27	110.21	1.11	0.75	12.43	23.73	10.37	2.54	15.93	5.92	0.09
8. Shahapur	81.74	89.79	109.84	0.67	17.86	18.40	23.74	5.27	0.94	6.66	5.56	0.04
9. Shorapur	62.15	89.20	143.51	1.20	71.44	42.12	24.78	5.00	1.48	9.58	4.96	0.05
10. Yadgir	50.41	57.24	113.55	1.01	6.12	14.65	35.74	7.99	1.23	7.66	4.00	0.03
Raichur District												
1. Deodurga	77.50	78.79	101.67	1.95	2.39	12.77	26.52	4.91	1.53	13.01	26.09	0.34
2. Gangavathi	65.38	86.33	132.04	3.64	64.25	59.03	206.06	6.74	4.74	19.68	31.75	0.62
3. Koppal	59.80	74.39	124.39	7.55	27.14	32.22	102.43	7.11	3.20	17.50	70.45	1.23
4. Kustagi	73.63	80.57	109.42	3.88	7.40	24.84	37.66	7.70	0.37	2.64	20.00	0.05
5. Lingsugur	52.34	57.25	109.38	3.72	4.23	31.60	36.83	6.57	1.44	10.72	25.00	0.27
6. Manvi	64.52	80.53	124.80	2.00	42.10	36.20	140.20	8.48	1.23	8.18	22.73	0.19
7. Raichur	68.28	81.27	119.03	3.62	17.80	38.37	134.29	7.15	8.18	35.14	68.25	2.40
8. Sindhnur	65.77	92.37	140.44	1.69	64.26	92.78	173.86	5.88	1.56	8.79	32.00	0.28
9. Yelburga	79.15	81.86	103.43	4.59	7.69	17.34	29.42	9.37	1.61	12.24	20.83	0.26

(Contd.)

TABLE 8.3 CONTD.

District/ Taluk	(c) Finance			(d) Transport				(e) Communication		
	Commercial Banks per lakh pop	No. of Comm. Banks per 100 Sq. Kms	Members per Co-op. Society	% of Coop. Members to population	No. of Vehicles per lakh per pop	Railway Length 100 Sq. Kms	Road Length per 100 Sq. Kms	Post Offices per lakh population	Telphone Exchanges per lakh population	Telephones per lakh population
Bellary District										
1. Bellary	6.87	2.01	6.11	19.39	5129.44	5.62	73.71	19.59	5.45	1126.82
2. Hadagalli	3.41	0.53	2.28	21.80	582.43	0.00	47.47	27.93	4.77	229.56
3. H. B. Halli	3.71	0.51	1.22	40.09	888.64	3.08	36.45	25.24	5.20	296.21
4. Harapanahalli	1.71	0.28	1.63	23.14	642.25	0.00	41.66	26.99	4.28	212.94
5. Hospet	7.03	2.36	2.19	23.02	3591.43	10.17	57.07	17.58	2.88	890.35
6. Kudligi	3.65	0.50	1.41	21.00	514.16	1.25	40.45	34.70	4.57	208.22
7. Sandur	5.12	0.64	1.33	17.29	1825.22	7.23	41.41	23.05	5.12	266.97
8. Sirguppa	3.71	0.67	2.40	24.92	1301.17	0.00	56.43	28.10	5.30	231.71
Bidar District										
1. Aurad	3.81	0.65	3.30	20.48	402.86	1.96	52.21	20.48	3.33	149.52
2. Basavakalayna	3.65	0.75	2.87	15.83	1132.36	0.00	40.38	13.80	4.06	289.89
3. Bhalki	5.38	1.07	3.41	17.50	823.24	3.04	61.95	14.36	5.38	208.61
4. Bidar	4.83	1.73	2.61	25.04	3003.02	2.27	57.67	8.75	2.71	759.28
5. Humnabad	4.08	1.02	3.20	20.00	968.16	0.00	47.01	15.51	4.90	430.20

(Contd.)

Gulbarga District											
1.	Afzalpur	9.94	1.15	0.25	15.31	802.52	2.38	36.48	29.82	9.94	239.89
2.	Aland	5.75	0.86	0.42	12.12	648.01	0.00	29.05	27.99	4.60	182.13
3.	Chincholi	5.81	0.70	0.41	8.03	347.78	0.00	34.29	29.60	5.29	128.44
4.	Chitapur	5.82	1.02	0.46	6.53	943.13	3.74	30.82	22.94	5.17	438.45
5.	Gulbarga	8.59	2.60	0.39	17.87	5296.43	2.20	30.17	15.46	2.86	1085.89
6.	Jewargi	6.36	0.66	0.23	12.19	487.02	0.00	27.28	28.62	4.24	135.14
7.	Sedam	6.13	0.98	0.24	13.05	825.98	3.12	29.37	28.80	5.51	234.07
8.	Shahapur	5.00	0.71	0.47	8.37	882.18	0.00	24.50	21.65	5.83	285.18
9.	Shorapur	6.03	0.93	0.69	7.95	641.46	0.00	21.26	23.07	3.90	217.96
10.	Yadgir	5.11	0.82	0.46	9.01	801.53	3.39	31.01	28.09	2.92	286.39
Raichur District											
1.	Deodurga	1.70	0.20	5.00	5.66	746.04	0.00	31.43	26.02	1.70	60.52
2.	Gangavathi	4.06	0.98	5.88	7.50	1943.14	0.00	42.70	18.74	1.87	531.40
3.	Koppal	3.98	0.73	13.07	5.57	1086.12	4.00	45.02	20.68	4.77	362.77
4.	Kustagi	2.64	0.37	5.83	6.33	426.91	0.00	46.85	27.97	2.11	115.04
5.	Lingsugur	2.68	0.36	5.93	5.74	809.41	0.00	33.88	21.43	1.91	135.48
6.	Manvi	2.23	0.34	4.17	8.55	1097.77	0.00	26.47	20.07	1.86	145.72
7.	Raichur	5.58	1.30	4.73	12.55	3496.37	3.31	34.91	20.64	3.63	779.42
8.	Sindhnur	2.81	0.50	6.91	7.74	2101.30	0.00	24.66	20.40	3.52	300.74
9.	Yelburga	2.55	0.34	9.73	5.61	321.94	0.00	37.72	23.47	3.06	85.71

(Contd.)

TABLE 8.3 CONTD.

District/ Taluk	*(f) Education*								*(g) Health*		
	Literacy Rate (1991)			No. of Schools Per 100 Sq. Kms.	High Schools Per lakh pop	No. of High Schools per 100 Sq. Kms	P U Colleges per 100 Sq. Kms	P U Colleges per lakh popu-lation	Health Units per lakh popu-lation	No. of Beds per lakh popu-lation	No. of Health Units per 100 Sq. Kms
	Male	Female	Total								
Bellary District											
1. Bellary	52.19	30.7	41.68	13.85	6.46	1.89	0.41	1.41	2.63	241.92	0.77
2. Hadagalli	49.09	26.38	37.85	13.92	10.90	1.69	0.32	2.04	3.41	28.61	0.53
3. H. B. Halli	49.29	25.62	36.95	12.32	11.88	1.64	0.21	1.48	4.45	11.88	0.62
4. Harapanahalli	44.83	24.03	34.65	17.18	14.14	2.29	0.28	1.71	3.00	11.14	0.49
5. Hospet	51.1	31.08	41.27	19.27	7.99	2.68	0.54	1.60	1.92	47.63	0.64
6. Kudligi	47.83	24.75	36.49	15.61	12.79	1.75	0.25	1.83	3.20	39.27	0.44
7. Sandur	43.92	21.62	33.03	10.57	7.68	0.95	0.16	1.28	3.84	42.25	0.48
8. Sirguppa	35.82	14.99	25.46	12.96	5.30	0.96	0.19	1.06	3.18	12.73	0.58
Bidar District											
1. Aurad	53.00	25.43	39.5	16.75	16.19	2.78	0.16	0.95	3.81	43.81	0.65
2. Basavakalayna	57.71	27.77	42.95	16.33	12.59	2.57	0.25	1.22	3.65	43.85	0.75
3. Bhalki	61.92	30.26	46.47	16.74	13.91	2.78	0.36	1.79	3.59	32.30	0.72
4. Bidar	62.91	37.92	50.95	25.81	13.57	4.86	0.97	2.71	2.11	99.25	0.76
5. Humnabad	57.1	28.07	42.87	15.23	13.06	3.25	0.81	3.27	3.27	45.71	0.91

(Contd.)

TABLE 8.3 CONTD.

Gulbarga District												
1.	Afzalpur	52.29	22.09	37.62	10.34	11.93	1.38	0.15	1.33	3.98	38.44	0.46
2.	Aland	55.01	22.45	39.12	13.08	8.82	1.33	0.58	3.83	4.22	42.94	0.63
3.	Chincholi	48.27	18.28	33.41	12.05	8.46	1.02	0.13	1.06	4.76	40.17	0.57
4.	Chitapur	52.3	24.7	38.72	13.88	10.99	1.93	0.23	1.29	3.23	45.23	0.57
5.	Gulbarga	70.12	43.41	57.33	21.45	14.51	4.39	0.87	2.86	1.53	141.63	0.46
6.	Jewargi	48.42	17.09	32.85	9.82	10.07	1.04	0.16	1.59	4.24	38.16	0.44
7.	Sedam	47.73	21.13	34.5	15.61	9.19	1.46	0.29	1.84	3.06	58.82	0.49
8.	Shahapur	41.04	17.04	29.14	12.69	4.58	0.65	0.18	1.25	3.33	29.14	0.47
9.	Shorapur	46.39	18.84	32.74	14.34	5.32	0.82	0.27	1.77	3.19	31.95	0.49
10.	Yadgir	35.96	15.62	25.88	14.80	6.93	1.11	0.29	1.82	4.38	46.70	0.70
Raichur District												
1.	Deodurga	24.46	8.69	16.68	12.27	1.70	0.20	0.20	1.70	3.39	14.71	0.40
2.	Gangavathi	38.59	18.48	28.63	16.87	4.06	0.98	0.38	1.56	2.81	8.75	0.68
3.	Koppal	46.19	21.61	34.04	11.85	6.36	1.16	0.36	1.99	3.18	24.26	0.58
4.	Kustagi	41.5	14.31	28.01	14.20	5.80	0.81	0.29	2.11	3.17	9.50	0.44
5.	Lingsugur	39.65	16.29	28.09	12.42	5.36	0.72	0.26	1.91	3.06	16.07	0.41
6.	Manvi	32.59	14.33	23.5	11.45	2.23	0.34	0.22	1.49	2.97	8.92	0.45
7.	Raichur	45.47	25.69	35.81	16.22	6.41	1.49	0.52	2.23	1.95	94.26	0.45
8.	Sindhnur	37.43	17.2	27.38	12.58	3.52	0.63	0.13	0.70	2.81	7.03	0.50
9.	Yelburga	44.9	17.22	31.19	10.54	8.67	1.14	0.27	2.04	3.57	7.14	0.47

Source: Same as in Table 8.1.

TABLE 8.4: Coefficient of Variation 1992-93

Indicators	C. V. %	Coefficient of Variation Range (Percent)						
		0—10	10—25	25—40	40—60	60—80	80—100	100 & above
% of Medium and Large Holdings (Area)	8.970367	8.970367	-	-	-	-	-	-
Cropping inensity	9.353612	9.353612	-	-	-	-	-	-
% of Workers to total population	15.58935	-	15.58935	-	-	-	-	-
Normal Rainfall(1907- 70) in M.M	17.04773	-	17.04773	-	-	-	-	-
% of Medium and Large Holdings (No.)	17.06636	-	17.06636	-	-	-	-	-
% of Gross Sown Area	18.90391	-	18.90391	-	-	-	-	-
Male Literates (%)	19.41703	-	19.41703	-	-	-	-	-
% of Net Sown Area	19.93358	-	19.93358	-	-	-	-	-
Area in Square Kilometer	21.61259	-	21.61259	-	-	-	-	-
Health Unit per lakh population	22.38896	-	22.38896	-	-	-	-	-
No. of Schools per 100 sq. kms	22.86994	-	22.86994	-	-	-	-	-
Total Literates (%)	22.87837	-	22.87837	-	-	-	-	-
Post Offices per lakh pop	24.68513	-	24.68513	-	-	-	-	-
Road Length per 100 sq. km	30.47572	-	-	30.47572	-	-	-	-
Female Literates (%)	31.51908	-	-	31.51908	-	-	-	-
% of Small and Marginal Holdings (Area)	31.62954	-	-	31.62954	-	-	-	-
Veterinery Centre per lakh live stock	33.57728	-	-	33.57728	-	-	-	-
Total pop(00)1991	34.95318	-	-	34.95318	-	-	-	-
Population per Sq. km Area	35.41871	-	-	35.41871	-	-	-	-
P U Colleges per lakh population	36.76486	-	-	36.76486	-	-	-	-
Tel.Exc per lakh pop	39.06155	-	-	39.06155	-	-	-	-
Population per village	40.03753	-	-		40.03753	-	-	-

TABLE 8.4 Contd.

Commercial Banks per lakh population	40.16463	-	-	-	40.16463	-	-	
High schools per lakh pop	43.71008	-	-	-	43.71008	-	-	-
% of Coop. Members to population	54.12724	-	-	-	54.12724	-	-	
% of Uncultivated land	56.18395	-	-	-	56.18395	-	-	
% of Uncultivable land	61.99001	-	-	-	-	61.99001	-	-
% of HYV area in Net Sown Area	62.55821	-	-	-	-	62.55821	-	-
P.U Colleges per 100 sq. kms	62.89397	-	-	-	-	62.89397	-	-
% of Fallow Land	64.19812	-	-	-	-	64.19812	-	-
No. of Comm. Banks per 100 sq. kms	64.27564	-	-	-	-	64.27564	-	
No. of High Schools per 100 sq. kms	65.07490	-	-	-	-	65.07490	-	-
% of Small and Marginal Holdings (No.)	65.48792	-	-	-	-	65.48792	-	-
No. of Factories per lakh pop	74.85767	-	-	-	-	74.85767	-	-
Telephones per lakh pop	80.12839	-	-	-	-	80.12839	-	-
Fertiliser per ha. of GSA in Kgs.	84.29507	-	-	-	-	-	84.29507	-
No. of IP Sets per ha. of NSA	84.56685	-	-	-	-	-	84.56685	-
No. of Vechiles per lakh pop	92.86338	-	-	-	-	-	92.86338	-
Members per Co-op. Society	96.14353	-	-	-	-	-	96.14353	-
% of Net Irri. Area in Net Sown Area	103.0072	-	-	-	-	-	-	103.0072
No. of Factories per 100 Sq.kms	103.6766	-	-	-	-	-	-	103.6766
No. of Beds per lakh population	104.1826	-	-	-	-	-	-	104.1826
% of Forest in total Geographical Area	113.6362	-	-	-	-	-	-	113.6362
No. of Employees per Factory	116.8982	-	-	-	-	-	-	116.8982
Railway Length per 100 sq. kms	136.8801	-	-	-	-	-	-	136.8801
% of Employees to total population	151.8529	-	-	-	-	-	-	151.8529

disparities with regard to individual indicators, it does not tell us anything about the position of individual talukas with regard to various sectoral and aggregate levels of development. In order to capture this dimension vertical form of factor analysis method is used in the study thus:

A. Methodology

SID = $a11^* z1 + a21^* z2 + - - - - + an1^* zn.$

here:

SID = Index of development of sectors.

aji = Factor loading of 'j'th variable on factor I

$j = 1,2$ —— n.

$Zj = xj\text{-}xj / sxj$

x = average of xj variable

sxj = standard deviation of 'j'th variable.

In order to derive a Composite Index of Development, first we computed sectoral indices (SID) for the following sectors:

1. Agriculture = A
2. Industry = I
3. Finance = F
4. Transport = T
5. Communication = C
6. Education = E
7. Health = H.

The selected 36 indicators were divided into 7 sectors. Then 7 sectoral indices were used to derive the final composite index:

CD = .231 A1 + .476 I1 + .597 F1 + .844 T1

.914 c! + .769 E1 + .862 H1 ————(3)

The subscript '1' indicates Factor-I.

CD = Composite Index of Development

The first principal component explained more than 50% of total variance and hence we took that as the composite index of development.

B. Results of Analysis

1. Agricultural Development Based on the sectoral indices, the taluks were grouped according to their levels of development in terms of sectoral development. In Table 8.5, we have shown the talukas according to their levels of development. It is evident from the table that the entire Bellary evident from the table that the entire Bellary district is highly developed. Even talukas like Harapanahalli, Kudligi and Hadagalli come under the developed region. Thus, the entire northern part of Hyderabad-Karnataka, comprising of Yelburga, Kustagi, Lingsugur and Deodurga of Raichur district, the entire Gulbarga district except Shorapur, the entire Bidar district except Bidar and Humnabad emerged as backward sub-regions. The three talukas of Gulbarga District - Jevargi, Chitapur and Chincholi— emerged as the most backward taluks in terms of agricultural development.

2. Industrial Sector

In terms of industrial development, the talukas are put under the following five groups:

Group I Highly developed: consisted of six talukas.
Group II Developed: consisted of 11 talukas.
Group III Average level: consisted of 4 talukas.
Group IV Backward: consisted of 7 talukas.
Group V Highly backward: consisted of 4 talukas.

These talukas with their respective scores and ranks are displayed in Table 8.5. In terms of industrial development also the position of Bellary district is better except Harapanahally and Sandur, and all other talukas are above average. In Raichur district, except Kustagi, other talukas are average, and Raichur taluk is developed. The entire Gulbarga and Bidar districts are industrially still lagging far behind the other two districts.

3. Finance Sector

In terms of banking and cooperative finance, intra-regional disparities are not very pronounced. In fact, the 32 talukas fall under three categories only:

Group I : Developed.
Group II : Average
Group III: Backward

The most backward talukas are Deodurg, Yelburga, Lingsugur, Kustagi and Manvi. Thus, on the whole Raichur district is lagging behind in terms of Finance sector. Whereas the positions of Gulbarga and Bidar districts are better. Taluks with their scores and ranks are shown in Table 8.5.

4. Transport Sector

In terms of transport sector development, it is heartening to observe that all the talukas have scored high values and in fact they can be put under two groups, namely,

Group I: Highly developed
Group II: Developed.

While the taluks of Bellary, Hospet, Sandur, Bidar, Raichur, Gulbarga, Koppal and Bhalki come under the first group and rest of the talukas come under the second group (refer Table 8.5).

5. Communication

In terms of communication, the entire region is backward with negative scores (refer Table 8.5).

6. Educational Development

In terms of educational development, the taluks can be put under the following categories:

Group I : Extremely developed - Gulbarga, Bidar.
Group II : Highly developed - consisting of 10 talukas.
Group III: Developed - consisting of 14 talukas.
Group IV : Average - consisting of 6 talukas, out of which Manvi and Deodurga occupied the last two ranks (refer Table 8.5).

7. Health Development

In terms of health sector, the entire region is deficient as the talukas have scored very low values. The talukas can be put under two groups. The first group consists of developed taluks like Bellary, Gulbarga, Bidar, Raichur, Hospet, Humnabad, Sedam, Basavkalyan, Chitapur and Yadgir, while the remaining talukas come under the second group i.e., backward talukas (see Table 8.5).

The above analysis shows the levels of development of various talukas at disaggregate level. In order to capture an over view, we have constructed a composite index of development. The last column of Table 8.5 gives the Factor scores on composite index. Based on this exercise, the talukas are grouped under the following five groups:

Group I : highly developed
Group II : developed

TABLE 8.5 : Taluk-wise Sectoral and Composite Index

Taluk	Agricultural Development Index	Taluk	Industrial Development Index	Taluk	Finance Development Index	Taluk	Transport Development Index
Group-I		Group-I		Group-I		Group-I	
1. Hospet	5.93	1. Raichur	3.71	1. Gulbarga	2.13	1. Bellary	6.08
2. H. B. Hall	5.88	2. Bellary	3.28	2. Afzalpur	1.98	2. Hospet	6.06
3. Sindhnur	5.81	3. Hospet	3.20	3. Sedam	1.69	3. Sandur	5.57
4. Gangavathi	5.80			4. Jevargi	1.56	4. Bidar	5.45
5. Siraguppa	5.35	Group-II		5. Hospet	1.56	5. Raichur	5.43
6. Bellary	5.22	1. Koppal	2.79	6. Aland	1.44	6. Gulbarga	5.35
7. Manvi	5.15	2. Bidar	2.55	7. Chitapur	1.36	7. Koppal	5.21
8. Koppal	5.08	3. Gangavathi	2.50	8. Chincholi	1.29	8. Bhalki	5.15
9. Sandur	5.06			9. Yadgir	1.29		
		Group-III		10. Shorapur	1.26	Group-II	
Group-II		1. Sirguppa	1.89	11. Bidar	1.26	1. Chitapur	4.97
1. Raichur	4.94	2. Humnabad	1.72	12. Shahapur	1.20	2. H. B. Hall	4.95
2. Shorapur	4.81	3. Gulbarga	1.72	13. Bellary	1.16	3. Yadgir	4.88
3. Harapanahalli	4.68	4. Deodurga	1.57	14. Sandur	1.02	4. Gangavathi	4.87
4. Humnabad	4.61	5. Sindhnur	1.41	15. H. B. Hall		5. Siraguppa	4.85
5. Kudligi	4.60	6. Yalburga	1.39			6. Sedam	4.84
6. Bidar	4.52	7. H. B. Hall	1.39	Group-II		7. Afzalpur	4.82
7. Hadagalli	4.34	8. Kudligi	1.39	1. Bhalki	0.97	8. Humnabad	4.67
		9. Lingsugur	1.36	2. Raichur	0.89	9. Aurad	4.67
Group-III		10. Chitapur	1.11	3. Humnabad	0.88	10. Basavakalyana	4.66
1. Basavakalyana	3.94	11. Manvi	1.02	4. Sirguppa	0.81	11. Sindhnur	4.66
2. Afzalpur	3.92			5. Kudligi	0.81	12. Hadagalli	4.50
3. Kustagi	3.91	Group-IV		6. Basavakalyana	0.70	13. Harapanahalli	4.48
4. Lingsugur	3.84	1. Sedam	0.92	7. Aurad	0.68	14. Kudligi	4.47
5. Shahapur	3.77	2. Hadagalli	0.89	8. Hadagalli	0.67	15. Lingsugur	4.47
6. Yelburga	3.67	3. Basavakalyana	0.23	9. Gangavathi	0.48	16. Manvi	4.47
7. Aland	3.58	4. Shorapur	0.18	10. Harapanahalli	0.26	17. Deodurga	4.41
8. Yadgir	3.46			11. Koppal	0.06	18. Kustagi	4.39
9. Aurad	3.42	Group-V		12. Sindhnur	0.03	19. Shahapur	4.36
10. Bhalki	3.34	1. Jevargi	-0.19			20. Aland	4.33
11. Chincholi	3.11	2. Shahapur	-0.22	Group-III		21. Jevargi	4.20
12. Deodurga	3.07	3. Yadgir	-0.23	1. Manvi	-0.05	22. Yelburga	4.20
13. Gulbarga	3.01	4. Chincholi	-0.44	2. Kustagi	-0.11	23. Shorapur	4.19
		5. Kustagi	-0.47	3. Lingsugur	-0.13	24. Chincholi	4.19
Group-IV		6. Harapanahalli	-0.67	4. Yelburga	-0.33		
1. Chitapur	2.62	7. Afzalpur	-0.83	5. Deodurga	-0.50		
2. Sedam	2.32						
3. Jevargi	1.90	Group-VI					
		1. Bhalki	-1.18				
		2. Aland	-1.36				
		3. Sandur	-1.65				
		4. Aurad	-2.92				

TABLE 8.5 CONTD.

Taluk	Communication Development Index	Taluk	Education Development Index	Taluk	Health Development Index	Taluk	Composite Development Index
Group-I		Group-I		Group-I		Group-I	
1. Deodurga	-0.18	1. Gulbarga	7.74	1. Bellary	1.77	1. Hospet	16.23
2. Yalburga	-0.31	2. Bidar	7.45	2. Gulbarga	1.57	2. Bidar	15.99
3. Chincholi	-0.33			3. Bidar	1.48	3. Bellary	15.91
4. Kustagi	-0.37	Group-II		4. Raichur	1.35	4. Gulbarga	15.89
5. Jewargi	-0.38	1. Humnabad	6.88	5. Hospet	1.19	5. Raichur	14.91
6. Kudligi	-0.45	2. Hospet	6.62	6. Humnabad	1.10		
7. Aland	-0.49	3. Bhalki	6.55	7. Sedam	1.08	Group-II	
8. Afzalpur	-0.51	4. Basavakalyana	6.28	8. Basavakalyana	1.04	1. Humnabad	13.53
9. Lingsugur	-0.55	5. Aurad	6.26	9. Chitapur	1.01	2. Koppal	12.69
10. Sedam	-0.55	6. Harapanahalli	6.22	10. Yadgir	1.00	3. Gangavqathi	12.42
11. Aurad	-0.56	7. Aland	6.19			4. Chitapur	12.37
12. Harapanahalli	-0.56	8. Raichur	6.09	Group-II		5. H B Hall	12.24
13. Sirguppa	-0.56	9. Kudligi	6.03	1. Aurad	0.99		
14. Hadagalli	-0.57	10. Bellary	6.01	2. Aland	0.95	Group-III	
15. Manvi	-0.60			3. Bhalki	0.92	1. Basavakalyan	11.96
16. Shorapur	-0.64	Group-III		4. Sandur	0.89	2. Sedam	11.94
17. Yadgir	-0.68	1. Hadagalli	5.97	5. Kudligi	0.89	3. Kudligi	11.80
18. Sandur	-0.69	2. Chitapur	5.93	6. Chincholi	0.87	4. Bhalki	11.68
19. H. B. Hall	-0.70	3. Sedam	5.77	7. Shorapur	0.84	5. Siraguppa	11.46
20. Shahpur	-0.73	4. H. B. Halli	5.75	8. Afzalpur	0.84	6. Hadagalli	11.43
21. Bhalki	-0.79	5. Koppal	5.60	9. Jevargi	0.81	7. Afzalpur	11.23
22. Sindhnur	-0.81	6. Afzalpur	5.57	10. Hadagalli	0.80	8. Yadgir	11.18
23. Koppal	-0.85	7. Yelburga	5.38	11. Shahapur	0.78	9. Sandur	11.08
24. Chitapur	-0.88	8. Yadgir	5.35	12. Koppal	0.78	Group-IV	
25. Basavakalyana	-0.94	9. Gangavathi	5.32	13. Lingsugur	0.54	1. Shorapur	10.80
26. Humnabad	-1.03	10. Chincholi	5.27	14. Siraguppa	0.54	2. Aland	10.72
27. Gangavathi	-1.10	11. Shorapur	5.21	15. Deodurga	0.48	3. Sindhanur	10.40
28. Raichur	-1.15	12. Sandur	5.18	16. Gangavathi	0.47	4. Harapanahalli	10.39
29. Bellary	-1.28	13. Jevargi	5.12	17. Harapanahalli	0.45	5. Shahpur	10.25
30. Hospet	-1.28	14. Kustagi	5.11	18. H. B. Hall	0.45	6. Lingsugur	10.01
31. Gulbarga	-1.40			19. Kustagi	0.35	Group-V	
32. Bidar	-1.50	Group-IV		20. Manvi	0.35	1. Aurad	9.93
		1. Lingsugur	4.96	21. Sindhnur	0.30	2. Chincholi	9.92
		2. Sirguppa	4.89	22. Yelburga	0.23	3. Jevargi	9.81
		3. Shahpur	4.86			4. Yelburga	9.48
		4. Sindhnur	4.47			5. Manvi	9.42
		5. Manvi	4.10			6. Kustagi	8.90
		6. Deodurga	3.29			7. Deodurga	7.99

Group III: Average
Group IV : backward and
Group V : highly backward.

The talukas are shown according to their levels of development in Table 8.5. It may be seen from the table that the four district head quarters and Hospet talukas emerged as the highly developed taluks. Here again, the position of Bellary district appears to be the best as only one taluka, namely, Harapanahaily, emerged as an average taluk. The other three districts are more or less similar in the composition of differentially developed talukas. The talukas of Deodurga, Kustagi, Manvi, Yelburga, Jevargi, Chincholi and Aurad emerged as the highly backward ones.

V. Trends in Intra- Regional Backwardness

An intra-regional analysis of sectoral and composite index of development brings out inter-taluk disparities as observed in 1992-93. The Hyderabad-Karnataka Region has attracted the attention of the government since 1980 and huge investments were made to develop the area as a whole. In order to assess whether the development efforts of the government have yielded any positive results, it is important to make a study of the trends in development and disparities. For this purpose, in this paper an attempt is made to compare the relative factor scores on composite index of all the 32 taluks in 1979-80 and 1992-93. We have used the indicators used in the construction of a composite index by Rao in her earlier study for this purpose.

In Table 8.6, relative ranks obtained by various talukas in the two benchmark years are displayed along with the respective index values. An important point which is apparent from the table is that the index values which were negative for most of the taluks in 1979-80 have assumed positive values in 1992-93. This is a clear indication of the fact that development has taken place over the past 12 to 13 years. On an average, the Hyderabad-Karnataka region has developed in absolute sense, and this is a welcome feature.

Secondly, there have been changes even in the relative ranks obtained by various taluks. Though the rank coefficient is still high at 0.85, yet the relative changes in the ranks indicate to the balanced regional development that emerged in this region. In Gulbarga district, we observe marked changes. This may be seen from Table 8.6. Jevargi, which occupied 32nd place in 1979-80 moved to 28th place. Similarly, Shahpur moved from 31st place to 24th place, Shorapur from 30th place to 20th

TABLE 8.6: Relative Changes in the Ranks between 1980 and 1993

	Taluk	1979-80 Index	Rank	1992-93 Index	Rank
1.	Afzalpur	-16.619	28	11.233	17
2.	Aland	-15.264	25	10.718	21
3.	Aurad	-14.696	23	9.926	26
4.	Basavakalyana	-10.392	13	11.957	11
5.	Bellary	19.402	1	15.906	3
6.	Bhalki	-12.470	17	11.679	14
7.	Bidar	3.035	53	15.986	2
8.	Chitapur	-11.528	15	12.369	9
9.	Chincholi	-15.058	24	9.921	27
10	Deodurg	-17.270	29	7.993	32
11.	Gangavathi	-4.328	7	12.419	8
12.	Gulbarga	0.315	4	15.889	4
13.	Hadagalli	-9.378	11	11.434	16
14.	H.B. Hall	-0.831	5	12.239	10
15.	Harapanahalli	-11.676	16	10.393	23
16.	Hospet	5.679	2	16.231	1
17.	Humnabad	-4.247	6	13.533	6
18.	Jevargi	-19.648	32	9.806	28
19.	Koppal	-6.877	9	12.691	7
20.	Kudligi	-8.475	10	11.803	13
21.	Kustagi	-15.514	27	8.901	31
22.	Lingsugur	-13.498	21	10.010	25
23.	Manvi	-13.433	20	9.421	30
24.	Raichur	-5.888	8	14.909	5
25.	Sedam	-10.799	14	11.939	12
26.	Sandur	-12.953	18	11.076	19
27.	Shahpur	-18.382	31	10.249	24
28.	Shorapur	-17.792	30	10.803	20
29.	Sindhanur	-13.739	22	10.403	22
30.	Sirguppa	-10.231	12	11.457	15
31.	Yadgir	-15.411	26	11.183	18
32.	Yelburga	-13.378	19	9.484	29

Rank Correlation Coeffient 0.850439

place, Afzalpur from 28th to 17th place and Aland from 25th to 21st place. Similarly in Bidar district also Bhalki improved its position from 17th to 14th. While Gulbarga district has recorded a positive movement, Raichur and Bellary talukas have moved from high positions to lower one.

VI. Policy Implications

The above method of delineation of homogenous regions and grouping of talukas on the basis of sectoral and composite index of development has policy implications, especially while allocating funds to different talukas and for different sectors. In order to allocate aggregate funds, the HKAD Board can use the following formula:

1. Take the inverse of composite index of development i.e.,
1. $CDj = Ij$ = index of backwardness j=1,.......32 taluks
CD = Composite Index
2. Gj = (Ij/ X100 Gj = Share of jth taluk in total funds

Similarly, sectoral allocation can be worked out by taking sectoral index share in the total value. While allocating funds to various sectors one can opt for either of the two approaches:

I (a) Combine the inverse of the sectoral index of development values of a taluk and derive a total backward index value (This will be different from the composite index, because the latter is a combination of weighted sectoral indices).
(b) After deriving the total backwardness index, one can workout the percentage share of each sector in this total.
(c) After ascertaining the percentage share of each sector, planners have to examine the development potential of the sector, and only if such potential is available, funds should be allocated for the development of that sector. If development potential is totally lacking, preference should be given to a sector where more potential exists. Thus the objective, should be to improve the aggregate level of development so that a taluk can reach an optimum level of development.

II. The second approach is: (a) to allocate funds to various sectors at the district or regional level, (b) to workout the talukwise sectoral percentage share, and (c) to assess the sectoral potential of the taluk and allocate the funds.

In fact, a faster and balanced regional development is more certain in the former method than in the latter.

The advantages of a composit index method are:

1. the composite index gives full credit to population factor, as population is taken as an important denominator while deriving indicators;
2. it also gives credit to area, as this also forms the basis of some of the important indicators;
3. the index takes note of the availability of goods, services and infrastructure; and
4. all the important activities like agriculture, industry, transport, power, finance, education and health are fully covered by the index.

The allocation based on the index helps in achieving the development as well as equity objectives of the allocating agency.

To conclude, within the Hyderabad-Karnataka region, though intra-regional diversity and disparities exist, during the last 10 years or so these disparities have got narrowed down and all the taluks have moved forward. However, the pace of development can be accelerated and sub-regional disparities mitigated, if proper regional plans are formulated and implemented. This requires formulation of a careful and an objective plan for allocation of funds. This also requires differential strategies of development for different sub-regions. If such a plan approach is adopted, there is some hope that by the end of this century, Hyderabad-Karnataka will be able to remove its label of backwardness and emerge as one of the prosperous regions of Karnataka.

9

DEVELOPMENT STRATEGY OF HKADB
A Critical Review*

Abdul Aziz

1. Introduction

With a sustained planned effort over years, the Karnataka economy has achieved a slightly higher growth rate of 3.7% per annum compared with the national average of 3.6 per cent. That apart, some desirable changes also have occurred in the economy such as: (a) a faster growth of the non-agricultural sector, (b) more diversified activities of the economy, and (c) building up of a stronger institutional and infrastructural base. However, these changes have not been uniform all over the State and across regions. For example, the Hyderabad-Karnataka region—an important segment of the Karnataka economy - has continued to remain backward. This fact attracted the attention of the policy-makers following which attempts are being made to accelerate development in the region by establishing a special development board viz., the Hyderabad-Karnataka Area Development Board (HKADB). The Board has since been made responsible for promoting development of this region. In the present paper, an attempt is made to critically evaluate the approach followed by the Board to promote the development of this region. As part of this exercise, we shall first present the development status of the Hyderabad-Karnataka region vis-a-vis that of the State. This will be followed by a critical account being presented of the strategy of development followed by the Board. The paper will conclude with some suggestions.

* Research assistance given by Mr.C.Charles Nelson is gratefully acknowledged.

2. H-K Region Economy : Level of Development

The H-K region economy comprising of Bidar, Bellary, Gulbarga and Raichur districts has always lagged behind in terms of development. This is evident from the composite index of development constructed by the Planning Department, Government of Karnataka for some selected years as presented here in Table 9.1 and also from the indicators of development presented in Table 9.2.

TABLE 9.1 : Composite Index of Development for H-K Region, (State Average - 100).

District	Index of Development 1960-61	Rank	Index of Development 1971-72	Rank	Index of Development 1974-75	Rank	Index of Development 1979-80	Rank
Bellary	89.23	14	83.9	15	86.4	15	94.98	11
Bidar	64.28	17	86.9	14	82.8	16	82.11	17
Gulbarga	60.10	19	63.2	19	67.0	19	65.77	19
Raichur	63.04	18	80.5	17	79.7	17	80.72	18

Source : Planning Department, Sixth Five-Year Plan; 1980-85, and Draft Eighth Five Year Plan, 1990-95, Vol. I, Government of Karnataka, Bangalore, Table 11.

From Table 9.1 it is clear that over the years, there is a gradual improvement in the development level of the H-K region districts—each of which having moved closer to the state average in this regard (except Gulbarga which has not made much progress). Yet, these districts remain far behind other districts of the state. Thus, of the 19 districts of the State, the three districts of the H-K region viz., Bidar, Raichur and Gulbarga respectively get the last three ranks viz., 17th, 18th and 19th, both during 1960-61 and 1979-80 though in between Bidar had moved a little up. Bellary, which held the 14th rank during 1960-61 moved upto the 11th place during 1979-80 showing some improvement in its development position. Even then its rank of 11 cannot be considered to be comfortable as its position in the development index is still below the State average.

We do not have comparable composite development index to ascertain the latest position regarding levels of development. However, from the development indicators presented by the Directorate of Economics and Statistics the position that emerges is not very encouraging. The selected development indicators viz., per capita income, gross irrigated area, net area sown, road length, literacy, population served by health institutions, banks, and the ranks obtained in regard to these indicators are presented in Table 9.2. From this table, it is evident that, though some districts of the H-K region have now moved above the State average in respect of a few indicators such as gross area irrigated, the region as a whole does not seem to be presenting any encouraging picture. Particularly in regard to indicators like per capita income, persons working in industries, banks, road length and literacy the position of the H-K region is below the State average indicating that it continues to remain comparatively backward. The three districts of this region viz., Bidar, Gulbarga and Raichur continue to remain backward and lag behind the State average in respect of most of the development indicators.

3. The Institutional Set-up for Development

On the whole, therefore, H-K Region's position has remained at the bottom and, what is worse, this has been so even after several years of planned effort. The backward nature of the H-K region had, of course, attracted the attention of a Fact Finding Committee appointed in 1954 to assess the level of development of the different Kannada-speaking areas likely to be integrated with the old Mysore State. After the States' reorganisation in 1956 there have been demands for constitution of a special development board for the H-K region following which a "Committee to Report on the Development of Hyderabad-Karnataka Area" was set up in May 1980. The Committee, which submitted its report in October 1981, among others, recommended: (a) that a statutory Board to formulate plans and monitor the implementation of these plans be constituted, and (b) that an area development corporation to execute and promote commercially viable schemes be established. The approach of the Committee to the development problem of this region is very simple : that is, to identify critical key sectors and to develop these sectors to the level of State average in about 10 years.

The cabinet accepted the recommendations of the Committee and approached the Planning Commission in 1985 for financial assistance. As the Planning Commission did not support the proposal, the Government decided to set up the Hyderabad-Karnataka Development Area Board (HKADB) making a provision of Rs.2 crores in the budget for the year 1989-90. The State Government subsequently approached the Union Government for special assistance to the proposed HKADB. In response, a central study team visited the H-K region in May 1990 to report to the Planning Commission. The Government of Karnataka prepared and submitted a blue print of development of H-K area to the Study Team proposing an outlay of Rs.634.52 crores for the years 1990-95.

Pending the constitution of the HKADB, the Government of Karnataka appointed a High Power Committee (HPC) in May 1990 with the Chief Minister as its Chairman, five ministers as members and a senior IAS officer as Secretary to oversee the development of this region. It also

TABLE 9.2 : Selected Development Indicators of H-K Region, 1990-91, Expressed as Proportion of State Average

State Average = 100

District	Per capita Income (Rs. at constant prices)	Rank	Persons Working in Indus -trial enter- prises per 1000 population	Rank	No.of Non-agricultu-ral enter-prises per 1000 population	Rank	Persons served by a commercial bank	Rank	Persons served by a co.opv. bank	Rank	Road length per100 sq. km area	Rank
Bellary	94.53	8	113.64	5	75.00	8	104.76	9	111.04	12	74.19	16
Bidar	77.54	16	60.61	14	75.00	8	132.26	17	88.09	9	83.87	14
Gulbarga	85.84	12	47.73	16	66.67	9	147.44	19	146.23	19	61.29	19
Raichur	75.63	18	59.85	15	66.67	9	135.99	18	141.86	17	62.90	18
State Average	(2048)	-	(132)	-	(12)	-	(10550)	-	(2174)	-	(62)	-
	100.00		100.00		100.00		100.00		100.00		100.00	

TABLE 9.2 (CONTD.)

District	Telephones Per lakh of population	Rank	Literacy rate	Rank	Population served by a medical institution (in lakhs)	Rank	Beds per lakh of population	Rank	Percentage of Gross area irri-gated	Rank	Percentage of net area sown to cultivable area	Rank
Bellary	50.33	7	81.32	16	100.00	13	91.18	6	142.08	5	109.18	1
Bidar	38.55	16	80.50	18	121.05	16	51.96	15	51.13	18	96.10	14
Gulbarga	38.96	15	68.77	20	105.26	14	60.78	13	55.20	17	101.53	10
Raichur	31.07	19	64.19	19	136.84	19	34.31	17	113.57	7	96.71	13
	(747)	-	(56.04)	-	(0.19)	-	(102)	-	(22.1)	-	(82.56)	-
	100.00		100.00		100.00		100.00		100.00		100.00	

Source : Compiled from Directorate of Economics and Statistics, *District Socio-Economic Indicators, 1993,* Government of Karnataka, Bangalore, 1994.

Note : Figures in brackets are in absolute numbers.

appointed an Implementation Committee with Secretary of the HPC as the Chairman to implement the schemes and programmes suggested by the High Power Committee. A full-fledged Hyderabad-Karnataka Area Development Board was constituted by a Government notification dated December 31, 1992 to plan and to supervise the implementation of the development programmes of the H-K region, and to monitor and evaluate the implementation of its plan.

The HKADB is now chaired by an elected member of the legislature; its Secretary—the Chief Executive - is a senior IAS officer with MPs, MLAs and MLCs of the region and a nominated person being members, who in all, add up to 52 members. The headquarters of the Board is Gulbarga city and it functions from there supervising the implementation of development projects for all the four districts. There is also an implementation committee which should meet every month with the Board Secretary as its Chairman and CEOs and DCs of all the districts of the region and the development departmental heads of the State including the Vice-Chancellor of the Gulbarga university as members. The Board has powers to raise loans, get grants, subventions, donations and gifts from the central and State Governments. It makes annual allocations to Zilla Panchayats and the development departments of the region for implementing the schemes formulated within the framework of the annual plan prepared and approved by the Board, and coordinates the HKADB schemes implemented by the development departments and Zilla Panchayats.

4. Thrust and Priorities of Development

Given the approach and thrust, it is proposed here to examine the resource allocation pattern suggested by the Government of Karnataka in its blue print presented to the Central Study Team, and the pattern of actual expenditure incurred by the HKADB in its budget (Table 9.3). In all this, our effort has been to understand the actual thrust given as a result of the resource allocation pattern. Before we get into this exercise it is desirable to mention here a peculiar practice that is in vogue with regard to resource allocation. That is, out of the total grant-in-aid received by the Board the latter delineates two components : one is what is called the MLA-Scheme component and the other (the balance) is the Board-Scheme component. Under the former, each of the 39 MLAs of the region gets annually allocated Rs.50 lakh for implementing schemes which he/she designs in his/her constituency. That takes away 40 per cent of the grants leaving 60 per cent for the Board-Schemes. When we talk about priorities here, for want of data, we are taking the aggregate of both the components to ascertain the priorities.

TABLE 9.3 : Thrust and Priorities of Development : Sectoral Perspectives

Thrust Areas	Sectoral Allocation for HKD Programme (in %) Govt. Blue prints	HKAD Committee	ResourceAllocation for different years by the HPC and the Board **				
	(1990-95)*	1981	1990-91	1991-92	1992-93	1993-94	1990-94
1. Roads and Bridges	68.41	40.85	11.53	22.25	24.16	25.46	21.06
2. Major and Medium Irrigation	Nil	Nil	4.65	4.38	1.50	0.28	2.60
3. Minor Irrigation	2.60	11.43	3.13	4.25	3.76	1.81	3.24
4. Health and Family Planning	8.58	8.57	5.88	3.27	5.30	4.79	4.84
5. Education	10.28	6.29	12.82	13.96	15.27	8.98	12.83
6. Water Supply & Drainage	10.12	Nil	19.29	11.66	8.52	8.76	11.85
7. Electrification	Nil	Nil	11.37	6.63	2.89	Nil	5.04
8. Cooperation	Nil	Nil	18.66	Nil	0.41	Nil	4.52
9. Rural Development & Panchayat Raj	Nil	24.28	12.66	32.17	37.86	48.45	33.23
10. Urban Devpt.	Nil	2.86	Nil	Nil	Nil	Nil	Nil
11. Miscellaneous	Nil	5.72	0.02	1.43	0.34	1.47	0.79
Total Outlay (in lakhs of Rupees)	63452.00	35000	5009.54	4899.10	6057.50	5272.13	21238.27

* Compiled from Draft Eighth Five Year Plan Vol. I. *Op.Cit.*

** Actual expenditure compiled from HKD Board Annual Report of Economic Progress, 1994-95.

The State perspective for H-K Region development seen in terms of priorities at the hands of the HPC, the Board and the Government's Blueprint submitted to the Study Team as it emerges from Table-3 is as follows :

1. In all the cases, the thrust is on key areas such as water supply, roads and bridges, education, health services and irrigation.
2. The additional thrust area in the case of the Board is on electrification programmes for hamlets and tandas which hitherto went without electricity because they were not recognised as revenue villages. This is a welcome step considering the importance of electricity use in the development process.

3. In the case of the Board, the resource allocation pattern across various thrust areas is less uneven across different heads of account. But the resource allocation pattern suggested by the Blue print and the HKAD Committee is highly uneven allocating respectively as much as 68.4 per cent and 40.85 per cent for roads and bridges leaving the balance for the other thrust areas. It is not clear as to why the Blue print and the Committee put so much emphasis on roads and bridges to the neglect of the remaining thrust areas which are equally important. Besides, in the blue print major and medium irrigation, electrification, cooperation and rural development did not figure as thrust areas, and in the Committee, though rural development did appear, water supply did not figure—a fact which is surprising looking at the development potential of these thrust areas.

From the above analysis, two points emerge : one is that the development programmes suggested emphasise on selected thrust areas. Secondly, the priorities worked out, however, differ. The resource allocation pattern of the Board is less uneven and also has a wider reach to different thrust areas. A more detailed analysis of the resource allocation pattern both across districts and across thrust areas/sectors may now be taken up.

4.1 Across Districts

The expenditure pattern by districts shown in Table 9.4 for the four-year period from 1990-91 to 1993-94 presents some interesting picture :

(a) Of the total amount spent during the period (Rs.212.38 crore) 38.5 per cent was taken away by the Gulbarga district leaving the remaining 61.5 per cent to be shared by the other three districts. One may perhaps justify the higher quantum of resource allocation to Gulbarga both in terms of its relative large area and population, and by its relative backwardness. But by the same criteria, Raichur also deserves similar treatment. Therefore, in the resource allocation exercise the Board did not appear to have used appropriate criteria for guidance.

(b) Rural development and panchayat raj takes the first priority in all the districts followed by roads and bridges, and education. Except in Gulbarga, in other districts, minor irrigation and electrification have not been given their due importance. Education is somewhat neglected in Bidar. This is surprising considering the importance of irrigation, electrification and education as thrust areas !

(c) In Bidar, cooperation comes in prominently but it is not known what programmes were formulated and implemented under this head. In other districts cooperation does not figure at all as a head of expenditure. This is also surprising considering the importance of cooperation in local development.

TABLE 9.4 : Expenditure Pattern by Districts during 1990-91 to 1993-94 Under the HPC and H-K ADB (in %).

Thrust Areas	Gulbarga	Bidar	Bellary	Raichur
1. Roads and Bridges	23.74	18.11	15.89	24.02
2. Major and Medium Irrigation	0.76	7.08	3.02	1.74
3. Minor Irrigation	5.20	0.66	2.82	2.36
4. Education	14.96	7.41	12.27	14.22
5. Rural Development and Panchayat Raj	28.81	27.63	36.97	42.28
6. Water Supply & Drainage	15.91	3.45	18.25	5.47
7. Health and Family Planning	5.95	4.96	4.43	3.23
8. Cooperation	0.31	23.64	0.00	0.54
9. Youth Services	0.25	6.95	5.89	5.77
10. Electrification	3.27	0.11	0.46	0.36
11. Social Welfare	0.06	0.00	0.00	0.00
12. Salaries	0.78	0.00	0.00	0.00
Total in lakhs of Rs.	8174.42	3849.08	4540.44	4636.63

Source: HKADB, *Annual Report of Economic Progress, 1994-95.*

4.2 Across Sectors

The priority structure that emerges from the expenditure pattern of HPC and HKADB for the region as a whole in regard to sectors during 1990-91 and 1993-94 presents the following picture: Rural development (33.2%), roads and bridges (21%), education (12.8%), water supply and drainage (11.85%) get priorities in that order over irrigation, electrification, health and miscellaneous services. The question is, whether the priority structure that emerges from the expenditure pattern is consistent with the priorities suggested by the development index of this region. As a step towards answering this question we may first look at the development index of the region vis-a-vis the state average with reference to the base year which is the year just resource allocation began to be made i.e., 1990-

91. Then, on the basis of the degree of distance between the region's development index and state development index we may identify the priority structure that suggests itself from the development index data.

Let us turn to Table 9.2 which presents information on some selected development indicators of the H-K region and its districts as of 1990-91 and examine the position of the region and its districts with regard to the thrust areas *vis-a-vis* the state average. In terms of distance as also the ranks obtained, Bellary district shows better performance compared with the other districts of the region. The latter woefully take the last three ranks in regard to literacy and road length, very low ranks—slightly above the lowest - in regard to persons served by commercial and cooperative banks, population served by medical institution, beds per lakh of population, and persons working in industrial enterprises. Though Bellary and Raichur are better off in regard to percentage of gross area irrigated, Bidar and Gulbarga fare very badly in this regard. Therefore, it seems that in regard to thrust areas such as health, education, irrigation, roads and bridges, commercial and cooperative banks, industry and perhaps electrification (in respect of which data are not available) more attention was needed. In this background the high priority actually given by the Board for education, roads and bridges is welcome. But what surprises is the low priority given to health, irrigation, cooperation, industry and electrification despite the fact that in their case the region has shown a wide gap between itself and the state average. This means that some where along the line there was a slip and it is desirable to search for this slip and to plug it.

Secondly, rural development was never listed as a thrust area by any of the Committees referred to above, yet, surprisingly rural development has been given first priority in resource allocation. Strictly speaking, this area falls into the ambit of responsibility of the district governments like Zilla panchayats. But the Board, by allocating a third of its resources to the area of rural development (Table 9.3), has caused a diminution of resources available for developing the thrust areas.

5. Some Recommendations

Based on the analysis of resource allocation pattern and the practices followed by the HPC and the Board, the following comments and suggestions may be made for the consideration of concerned authorities:

(1) Granting that the H-K region is expected to reach the state average in terms of development, and considering the distance that is seen with regard to thrust areas between the region and the State, the effort required is of a large magnitude. In our opinion,

the annual Rs.50 to 60 crore grant-in-aid from the State Government is too inadequate for the task in two senses : one, the amount earmarked annually is disproportionally low considering the area (23.7%) and the population (17.1%) involved. Second, even this amount, which is fixed in quantum, has been losing its real value over the years due to price escalation. Considering these points, there is a case for augmenting the financial resources of the Board.

(2) While the State Government grant can certainly be a source for annual additional funds, considering that State resources grow on a year-to-year basis, the Board ought to exercise its option to raise loans. Though the Act provides for borrowing by this body, the latter has not so far exercised this option. Once the Board borrows, it will, of course, be expected to service the debt and repay the loan. To be able to do so, it should exercise great caution in regard to spending. Investment in productive projects—projects that yield returns and pay for themselves—and imposing user charges would be the appropriate courses of action to be considered.

(3) The Act provides that the Board should plan, monitor and implement projects for development of the region. But currently the Board is engaged in funding the projects proposed by the ZP and other agencies, and in merely monitoring the progress of these projects. Its current role obviously falls short of the statutory role assigned to it. The Board should, therefore, take up the larger responsibility of planning for the region and not depend on ZP and other agencies for this purpose. It has to seriously take up this task not merely because it is expected to do so under law but also because planning by the Board would facilitate planning in the framework of integrated area development. Such an exercise can be carried out with ease if one single apex agency planned for the region taking into account the views of the development departments and people's representatives. Under such a framework, it is not the claims of departments and people's representatives as the claims of different sub-regions, sub-sectors and sections of the society that matter. Also, technically speaking, the projects designed should be meshed by considering the forward and backward linkages which fact will give the needed thrust to the region's economy to move automatically forward once it gets the push. Such a complex exercise can be carried out only when a single apex body

like the Board undertakes plan formulation in consultation with the district, taluk and village governments.

(4) If the above proposition is accepted, then the Board should not merely be engaged in disbursing funds and monitoring project progress ; it will also be expected to actively engage itself in planning and monitoring the projects leaving implementation to the development departments. The Planning cell of the Board should identify projects in thrust/key areas for development by its own studies and by inviting sub-regional plans from Village Panchayats, Taluk Panchayats and Zilla Panchayats. The village panchayats should prepare annual plans based on their needs and pass them on to the Taluk Panchayats which while adding their own projects should prepare a sub-regional plan for the taluk and pass it on to the ZP. The latter, adding its projects, should prepare an integrated district plan and pass it on to the Board. The Board in turn should examine the appropriateness of the project in terms of its thrust and its feasibility, ensure that backward and forward linkages are established across projects and then allocate funds for those projects which pass the tests of relevance, feasibility, productivity and integrative principles.

(5) In the proposed scheme of things there would be then no place for merely funding the projects and even for allocating resources to the so-called "MLA Schemes". When planning for the region has to be done in the integrated area development framework, allocation of funds to MLAs (currently Rs.50 lakh to each one of them) does not carry any economic logic for two reasons : one under the new dispensation, all the available funds have to be pooled and allocated to projects identified by the people's organisations and Governments, and not by individual political leaders. Secondly, experience has it that there is a tendency for individuals to spend money over some selected sub-regions and selected projects rather than spread them all over equitably. Therefore, it stands to reason to allocate funds to village, taluk and zilla panchayats than to individual MLAs. The latter, however, can propose projects of their choice and route them through the local governments of their constituencies. But the entire exercise should conform to the dictates of taking the region closer to the state average in regard to the identified thrust areas.

(6) As the *raison de etre* of the Board rests on the requirement of raising the development level of the key areas of the H-K region to the State average and as the Board is given the responsibility

of achieving this goal, the Board will be expected to allocate resources only to the key areas identified as such. Keeping these thrust areas in view, the Board will also be expected to work out a priority structure for purpose of resource allocation. However, the priority structures evolved ought to faithfully reflect the distance that obtains not only between the H-K region and the State average in regard to the key areas but also between the subregions—districts and taluks—in the H-K region and the State average. Therefore, in this exercise of working out priorities, care should be taken to avoid the past mistakes of: (a) allocating resources to non-key areas like rural development, and (b) allocating more resources to one region and less to others unless the carefully evolved resource allocation criteria dictate such course of action.

(7) As for the evolution of resource allocation criteria, the following points may be considered : Since the Board is charged with the responsibility of raising the development level of the key areas of the H-K region to that of the State average, it should obviously stick to allocating resources only for these key areas. The key areas as identified by various authorities are : roads and bridges, irrigation, education, health and family welfare electrification, water supply and drainage. The Board should workout the distance between the present development level of the key areas and of the state average in percentage terms and arrive at the resources required to bridge this gap over a given period of time, say, 10 years. Having arrived at the cost of (or more realistically the funds made available to it for) implementing the annual plan, the Board should then allocate resources to the four districts of the H-K region on the basis of a formula which is a weighted average of the distance between the district composite index of development of key areas and of the state average—the weight being the cost of implementing specific projects. The factor of weightage is added here to take care of the possibility of variations in the composition of projects to be taken up in different districts and the consequent differences in cost of implementing these projects. As the composite index of development in regard to key areas is standardised to area and population, there is no need to give weightage to area and population of the districts while allocating resources to the latter.

10

AGRICULTURAL DEVELOPMENT
Some Issues

V.S. Satyapriya and M. Vivekananda

1. Introduction

An attempt is made in this paper to highlight certain major issues concerning the development of agriculture in the Hyderabad Karnataka Region. This, however, is being attempted in a very limited way and the scope of the paper is restricted only to an examination of the changes in the cropping pattern, the growth in area and productivity, and the plausible association between cropping pattern changes and productivity growth. Only the major cereal crops, pulses, oilseeds, cotton and sugarcane are analyzed. Multi-cropping is a characteristic of this region and in such a situation shifts in cropping pattern may be an indicator of the direction of change occurring in the agricultural sector. It is hoped that the present attempt would highlight the direction of change that is taking place in the cropping system of this region and its possible implications for policy options. Section 1 presents a brief introduction. In sections 2 and 3 the cropping pattern and growth rates of area and productivity of crops, respectively, are discussed. In section 4 the policy options are presented.

The Hyderabad-Karnataka region comprising the four districts of Bidar, Gulbarga, Bellary and Raichur share nearly one-third of the total cropped area in the state (Table 10.1). Over the last three and a half decades gross cropped area in the state increased by 15 per cent while it was 4 per cent for the Hyderabad-Karnataka region. In the region gross cropped area showed a decline till 1980-81 and increased only during 1980-81 to 1990-91. Even this increase was not substantial: the region accounted for about 6 per cent of the increase in the gross cropped area with 94 per cent occurring in the other parts of the state. Changes in the gross cropped area would occur either through increase in net sown area or shifts in the cropping pattern towards short duration crops, which are largely governed by the level and nature of irrigation facilities, or both. These do not seem to have taken place on a perceptible scale in the region in the past.

It should, however, be recognised that given the physio-agronomic factors, there may not be a significant change in the area sown more than once though changes could occur in the cropping pattern. For with the introduction of irrigation, new crop varieties or the relative profitability of crops would bring about a shift towards more remunerative or profitable crops without altering the total cropped area. It is in this context an attempt is made to understand the changes in the cropping pattern and the plausible factors that could have induced such a change.

TABLE 10.1: Distribution of Gross Cropped Area: Hyderabad Karnata Region

(Area in hectares)

Districts	1956-57		1970-71		1980-81		1989-90	
	Area	%Share	Area	% Share	Area	% Share	Area	% Share
Bellary	622709	5.96	613355	5.63	546064	4.96	699295	5.82
Bidar	381414	3.65	404636	3.72	406906	3.70	444323	3.70
Gulbarga	1269597	12.16	1254402	11.52	1282728	11.65	1272189	10.60
Raichur	1080624	10.35	1050061	9.64	1049497	9.54	1074718	8.95
Region	3354344	32.12	3322454	30.51	3285195	29.85	3490525	29.07
State	10440955	100.00	10889526	100.00	11005884	100.00	12005535	100.00

2. Cropping Pattern

Changes in the cropping pattern are seen through shifts in the relative share of crops in the total cropped area spanning the period from 1955-56 to 1990-91. Triennium averages centred at 1956-57, 1970-71, 1980-81 and 1989-90 are considered to note the changes in the cropping pattern (Table 10.2). Are these shifts in the cropping pattern associated with the productivity levels of crops, is an important question. We have tried to answer this question by examining the trends in the growth rates in area and productivity. Compound rates of growth in area and productivity are calculated using the time series data for the period 1955-56 to 1990-91 and for three sub periods, namely, pre-green revolution, green revolution and post-green revolution. The important crops of the region selected for the present purpose are rice, wheat, bajra and jowar among cereals, pulses, oilseeds, cotton and sugarcane among non-cereals.

TABLE 10.2: Distribution of Area and Production of Major Crops: Hyderabad Karnataka Region (As percentage of State Total)

	Area				Production			
Districts	1956-57	1970-71	1980-81	1989-90	1956-57	1970-71	1980-81	1989-90
1	2	3	4	5	6	7	8	9
Total Cereals								
Bellary	5.49	5.47	5.52	6.07	4.69	5.34	5.74	6.70
Bidar	2.93	2.73	3.20	2.95	2.43	1.77	2.72	1.76
Gulbarga	12.70	9.28	9.94	9.26	5.77	5.68	5.90	4.18
Raichur	8.55	7.89	8.79	9.92	4.97	6.96	6.91	8.30
Region	29.67	25.37	27.45	28.20	17.86	19.75	21.27	20.94
Crop: Rice								
Bellary	1.21	2.37	2.63	3.45	1.19	2.94	2.78	4.18
Bidar	1.61	1.00	1.00	1.42	1.29	0.81	0.83	0.61
Gulbarga	2.36	0.89	1.14	1.49	1.62	0.78	0.84	1.16
Raichur	1.30	4.48	6.28	8.60	1.09	6.79	7.24	9.70
Region	6.48	8.74	11.05	14.96	5.19	11.32	11.69	15.65
Crop : Wheat								
Bellary	NEG	NEG	NEG	NEG	NEG	NEG	NEG	NEG
Bidar	3.19	1.93	3.73	4.46	3.54	4.69	6.75	4.66
Gulbarga	10.57	9.30	9.83	13.71	8.04	11.80	9.53	14.62
Raichur	9.83	9.42	7.24	7.27	6.25	12.58	8.47	3.11
Region	23.59	20.65	20.80	25.44	17.83	29.07	24.75	22.39
Crop : Bajra								
Bellary	5.50	5.76	5.31	5.54	8.47	8.68	8.37	8.28
Bidar	2.72	2.64	3.93	3.54	2.35	3.52	3.96	2.20
Gulbarga	14.22	17.25	24.17	18.07	10.98	25.99	31.12	17.82
Raichur	9.55	7.91	14.37	21.41	10.96	11.81	20.80	23.30
Region	31.99	33.56	47.78	48.56	32.76	50.00	64.25	51.60
Crop: Jowar								
Bellary	6.51	7.29	6.61	7.64	8.48	9.94	9.00	11.76
Bidar	4.29	4.41	5.90	5.33	5.53	3.50	7.31	5.42
Gulbarga	21.32	16.19	16.87	16.57	14.44	12.92	14.32	10.77
Raichur	12.36	11.25	13.15	14.09	11.98	10.09	9.92	13.01
Region	44.48	39.14	42.53	43.63	40.43	36.45	40.55	40.96

(Contd.)

TABLE 10.2 CONTD.

1	2	3	4	5	6	7	8	9
Crop: Pulses								
Bellary	3.76	3.13	2.86	3.07	2.30	2.14	4.12	4.27
Bidar	8.82	10.32	8.20	10.17	10.71	10.49	8.95	13.16
Gulbarga	13.68	18.01	20.79	23.98	13.77	21.03	21.15	20.10
Raichur	8.70	8.96	7.47	6.89	6.46	7.24	6.41	7.28
Region	34.96	40.42	39.32	44.11	33.24	40.90	40.63	44.81
Crop: Oilseeds								
Bellary	8.68	6.48	5.10	7.34	11.95	8.83	6.59	8.77
Bidar	4.81	3.89	4.62	3.20	3.30	3.55	2.72	2.15
Gulbarga	18.45	20.22	16.73	13.42	12.33	16.27	13.47	9.72
Raichur	12.75	11.55	12.24	12.93	11.84	10.56	13.34	12.09
Region	44.69	42.14	38.69	36.89	39.42	39.21	36.12	32.73
Crop: Cotton								
Bellary	9.69	11.85	8.79	15.92	13.72	11.58	15.80	18.72
Bidar	—	—	—	—	—	—	—	—
Gulbarga	4.13	11.12	11.83	1.16	2.94	11.69	7.31	0.57
Raichur	26.67	24.70	24.01	13.12	19.43	32.16	24.88	11.88
Region	40.49	47.67	44.63	30.20	36.09	55.43	47.99	31.17
Crop: Sugarcane								
Bellary	8.80	9.40	6.06	3.23	12.00	9.35	6.85	2.68
Bidar	8.55	4.95	8.16	8.07	9.72	4.53	7.54	7.37
Gulbarga	1.12	1.06	1.77	2.08	0.55	1.12	1.89	1.73
Raichur	3.50	4.53	3.32	0.83	2.09	4.80	3.73	0.74
Region	21.97	19.94	19.31	14.21	24.36	19.80	20.01	12.52

Cereals

The region accounts for 28 per cent of the total area under cereals and 21 per cent of cereal production in the state (1989-90). Among the districts in the region Gulbarga which accounts for 9.26 per cent of the area under cereals contributes only 4.18 per cent to the state's cereal production. It is only in Bellary where the proportions of area (6.07 per cent) and production (6.77 per cent) are of the same order. These proportions are indicative of the lower productivity levels of cereals as a group in the region relative to the state. However, the gap in the productivity level has narrowed over time (Table 10.2).

Coming to major cereal crops, rice accounting for about 5 per cent of the gross cropped area of the region (1989-90), shared only 1.75 per cent of the gross cropped area during 1956-67. The absolute area under rice increased by more than three times. With an increase of this magnitude the region's share in the area under rice in the state increased to 14.96 per cent from 6.48 per cent and that of production from 5.19 per cent to 15.65 per cent. As for as rice crop is concerned, the changing relative shares of the region is clearly indicative of the fact that it has emerged from a low productivity to a higher productivity region. The major rice producer of the region, namely, Raichur contributed as much as 75 per cent of this increase. Apart from being a high value crop, the introduction of irrigation gave a boost to the cultivation of rice in the region.

The region accounts for 25.44 per cent of the area and 22.39 per cent of production of wheat in the state (1989-90). However, the share of wheat in the gross cropped area of the region declined from 2.14 per cent to 1.66 per cent. Raichur contributed largely to this fall in wheat area. Within the region, Gulbarga has the highest share of 13.71 per cent of area and 14.62 per cent of production of wheat in the state.

In the case of bajra, a predominantly unirrigated crop, the region shared 48.56 per cent of area and 51.6 per cent of production in the state though it occupies a little over 6 per cent of the gross cropped area of the region (1989-90). The region's share in the area under bajra in the state increased from 32 per cent to 49 per cent between 1956-57 and 1989-90. Much of the increase in area under bajra has come from Raichur.

Jowar is the major cereal crop of the region and accounts for 28 per cent of the region's gross cropped area as against 18 per cent in the state as a whole. Further, 44 per cent of the area under jowar in the state is in this region. Within the region, the two districts namely, Gulbarga and Raichur share 30.66 per cent of area and 23.78 per cent production of jowar in the state. The lower contribution to production relative to area is largely in Gulbarga, which accounts for 16.57 per cent of area and 10.77 per cent of production.

Thus, cereal production in the Hyderabad-Karnataka region, with 46 per cent of its gross cropped area under cereals, is characterised by the predominance of jowar, essentially raised under rainfed conditions and has a lower productivity level relative to the state average.

Pulses

Pulses are a major crop of the region with a little over 20 per cent of its gross cropped area under various pulses (1989-90). The region's share in the area under pulses in the state increased from 35 per cent to 44 per cent and that of production from 33 per cent to 45 per cent between 1956-67 and 1989-90. Much of this increase in the region's share is contributed by Gulbarga which alone accounts for 24 per cent of the area under pulses and 20 per cent of its production in the state.

Oilseeds

The share of Hyderabad-Karnataka in the area and production of oilseeds in the state recorded a sharp decline, from 45 per cent to 37 per cent in the case of area and from 39 per cent to 33 per cent in the case of production between 1956-57 and 1989-90. However, in absolute terms area under oilseeds recorded an increase of over 55 per cent and continues to occupy nearly one-fourth of the gross cropped area in the region. Gulbarga and Raichur are the two major oilseeds growing districts with 71 per cent of the area under oilseeds in the region.

Cotton

With only about 6 per cent of its gross cropped area under cotton, the region shares 30 per cent of area and 31 of production of cotton in the state (1989-90). However, the region's share in cotton area declined from 40 per cent and that of production from 36 per cent (1956-57). The two districts, Raichur and Bellary, account for almost the entire crop in the region. While area under cotton in Bellary district remained around the same level, in Raichur district area under cotton declined considerably in relative as well as absolute terms.

Sugarcane

Sugarcane occupies 1.05 per cent of the gross cropped area of the region against 2 per cent at the state level. Area under sugarcane in the state increased by 4.75 times while in this region it was little over three times. Sugarcane in this region accounts for 14 per cent of area and 12.5 per cent of production in the state with Bidar being the major sugarcane producer. Thus the region is dominated by rainfed crops like jowar, bajra, pulses and oilseeds (91 per cent of gross cropped area) and to a small extent rainfed cotton and wheat. The overall productivity levels appear to be lower than the state average excepting for rice, wheat and bajra. These three crops, however, account for only 13 per cent of the gross cropped area. The region which was characterised by low value and low productivity cereal crops during 1956-57 moved towards high value cereal and non cereal crops: Rice 1.75 per cent to 5 per cent ; Pulses 13.74 per cent to 21 per cent; Oilseeds 16.79 per cent to 25 per cent; Sugarcane 0.36 per cent to 1.05 per cent of the gross cropped area. These changes in cropping pattern favouring high value cereal and non cereal crops occurred mainly during the eighties. How far these shifts were associated with productivity levels is discussed in the following section.

3. Growth Rates: Cerelas

Compound growth rates of area and productivity of the selected crops are presented in Table 10.3. Growth rates in yield of total cereals ranged between 2 and 4 per cent in the districts of the region for the total period of 36 years. In the pre green revolution (Period I) and green revolution periods (Period II) the growth rates were higher than the state average in all the districts excepting Raichur in the II period. The post green revolution period (period III) witnessed either a stagnation or decline in yield growth in all the four districts and also at the state level. The productivity growth obtained in the first two periods was not reflected in area growth excepting in the district of Bidar. The negative growth in the productivity in the III period is also accompanied by a decline in area. The aggregate picture of total cereals, however, conceals the area response of individual crops to productivity.

In the case of rice the region witnessed growth in yield rates coupled with growth in area in the first period; in the second period there was neither a significant growth in yield nor in area. In the third period though growth in yield rates either stagnated or declined, there was significant increase in area. The area response in the post green revolution period appears to have come from extension of irrigation in the region rather than from productivity growth.

Wheat experienced significant growth both in productivity and area during the green revolution period. However, this trend did not continue as the productivity declined in the III period.

In the case of bajra, a minor millet crop of the region, there was an impressive growth in productivity in the I period and area in the II period and a stagnation in productivity and decline in area in the III period.

Jowar, a major cereal crop, though showed an impressive growth in productivity in the green revolution period it did not bring about a corresponding growth in area. There was stagnation in productivity and area in the III period. Thus, the cereal crops in general showed stagnation in productivity and decline in area in the post green revolution period with the exception of rice. Though productivity of rice declined area under rice showed an increase.

TABLE 10.3: Compound Growth Rates of Area and Yield of Major Crops: Hyderabad Karnataka Region

District	Area				Yield			
	Total Period	Period I	Peiord II·	Period III	Total Period	Period I	Period II	Period III
1	2	3	4	5	6	7	8	9
Crop: Total Cereals								
Bellary	0.11	1.10	-0.90	1.40	3.08	2.53	3.87	0.94
Bidar	0.50	3.97	1.30	-1.43	2.11	2.23	4.60	-2.60
Gulbarga	-1.29	-0.66	0.31	-1.48	2.00	6.28	3.29	-1.99
Raichur	0.33	0.39	-0.43	0.80	3.84	1.87	2.77	1.11
State	-0.25	0.65	-0.43	-0.20	2.33	0.71	3.45	0.21
Crop: Rice								
Bellary	3.34	8.00	0.18	3.10	1.79	-1.73	2.19	2.01
Bidar	-0.40	-1.44	-0.88	3.86	0.26	2.79	1.59	-7.63
Gulbarga	-1.39	-0.40	1.77	3.00	1.76	3.13	-0.66	-0.18
Raichur	6.53	10.16	1.92	2.80	3.04	2.48	1.18	0.51
State	0.51	2.09	-0.43	0.28	1.57	0.43	1.16	0.12
Crop: Wheat								
Bellary	—	—	—	—	—	—	—	—
Bidar	1.36	-4.75	8.17	-3.12	4.18	3.27	6.54	-6.13
Gulbarga	0.37	-3.69	3.34	-0.81	4.18	2.12	5.03	0.37
Raichur	-1.59	0.93	-2.50	-4.43	2.67	2.08	5.23	-10.82
State	-0.32	0.54	1.00	-4.62	3.40	1.23	3.98	-0.86
Crop: Bajra								
Bellary	0.08	0.97	1.25	-2.14	2.62	4.68	0.56	2.98
Bidar	1.22	0.15	6.48	-4.80	2.29	6.57	0.85	-1.35
Gulbarga	1.42	1.18	6.86	-7.10	3.30	7.21	0.92	0.03
Raichur	2.53	0.16	11.62	1.58	3.26	3.29	-0.91	0.85
State	0.01	0.22	2.70	-2.94	2.75	3.18	0.78	2.63
Crop: Jowar								
Bellary	-0.76	0.92	-2.37	3.39	2.91	0.80	4.06	-1.34
Bidar	0.12	-0.10	1.43	-0.41	2.50	1.56	7.06	-2.83
Gulbarga	-2.00	-2.05	-1.79	0.33	1.90	6.64	6.46	-3.82
Raichur	-0.40	0.09	-1.66	1.29	2.26	0.89	2.06	0.40
State	-0.92	0.39	-2.29	0.82	2.20	3.15	3.10	-1.92

(Contd.)

TABLE 10.3 CONTD.

1	2	3	4	5	6	7	8	9
Crop: Pulses								
Bellary	0.37	-3.94	-0.49	1.85	2.35	5.94	8.03	-0.67
Bidar	0.78	1.96	-1.19	3.67	1.86	1.67	4.54	-1.29
Gulbarga	2.60	1.29	3.07	2.42	1.39	0.57	3.29	-0.79
Raichur	0.09	0.53	-1.46	0.06	1.60	0.86	2.50	5.04
State	0.86	-2.40	0.84	0.73	1.01	1.25	1.31	-0.81
Crop: Oilseeds								
Bellary	0.83	-1.40	-5.14	10.73	0.82	1.01	0.83	-1.78
Bidar	0.92	-0.08	1.21	2.04	-0.46	2.44	-3.84	2.06
Gulbarga	1.25	0.31	-1.64	5.33	0.98	1.02	1.01	-0.60
Raichur	2.10	0.10	-0.64	8.88	1.07	2.09	-0.28	-2.29
State	1.77	0.25	0.82	7.52	0.50	0.60	-0.54	-0.12
Crop: Cotton								
Bellary	-0.96	1.58	-4.06	-0.07	4.43	-4.63	4.56	3.71
Bidar								
Gulbarga	-1.82	7.96	0.43	-29.96	1.94	1.92	-2.61	5.13
Raichur	-3.01	-0.92	-0.73	-13.08	4.61	0.94	1.64	3.69
State	-1.43	-0.18	-0.79	-6.42	3.74	-1.38	-0.01	8.14
Crop: Sugarcane								
Bellary	0.98	5.65	-0.51	-2.07	-0.22	0.22	1.18	-2.18
Bidar	5.24	1.64	11.27	5.19	-0.36	3.22	0.17	-0.32
Gulbarga	6.70	6.64	14.98	5.91	2.26	9.92	-0.19	-1.73
Raichur	-1.00	8.29	3.57	-10.43	1.13	5.78	0.27	-2.01
State	4.35	5.25	4.70	5.20	0.50	2.36	-1.58	0.06

Pulses

Pulses as a group have shown an impressive growth in productivity during the second period in all the four districts with area growth only in Gulbarga district. During the post green revolution period the significant growth in productivity in Raichur district is accompanied by a stagnation in area, while in the other three districts though productivity stagnated there was growth in area.

Oilseeds

Oilseeds in the entire region showed neither growth in productivity nor in area for the total period. However, there was significant growth in area during the Third period though productivity stagnated in the three districts of Bellary, Gulbarga and Raichur. In Bidar district there was a significant growth in productivity and area.

Cotton

The region has shown an impressive growth in productivity and a substantial decline in area under cotton for the total period. This has occurred mainly in the Third period. This can be attributed to a decline of area under rainfed cotton. The higher productivity could not make up the fall in production caused by the decline in area.

Sugarcane

Productivity growth in sugarcane was observed only in the First period whereas the area under sugarcane increased in all the periods.

The crop-wise analysis has brought out that area under rice and sugarcane increased over time irrespective of the productivity levels. Addition of irrigated area and the high value and relative profitability of these crops are responsible for their area growth. As jowar, bajra, pulses and oilseeds showed a positive growth in productivity in the initial periods there was absence of any discernable shifts in the area under these crops. In spite of a stagnation in productivity of cereals, pulses, oilseeds and sugarcane a substantial increase in area under oilseeds and pulses and a modest increase of area under rice and sugarcane occurred in the post green revolution period. The shifts in area towards these crops was at the expense of cotton and bajra. The shift towards rice and sugarcane was conditioned by the extent of irrigation; the shift towards oilseeds and pulses was conditioned by the substantial increase in their prices. The changes in the relative prices made these crops relatively more profitable.

4. Policy Options

The region is thus well endowed with natural advantages for a multiple cropping system with a vast area under cultivation. The four districts account for one-third of the total cropped area in the state. The productivity levels of the crops have improved over time relative to the state average. The region was no exception to the general stagnation in productivity levels that prevailed in the state during the eighties and after.

Also the region has experienced a marked shift in the cropping pattern in the eighties. These shifts were in favour of rice, a high value cereal crop and non cereal crops, namely, pulses, oilseeds and sugarcane. The shifts towards rice and sugarcane, both demanding intensive irrigation, have come through an increase in the irrigated area though there was stagnation in productivity levels of these crops. These crops have higher profitability compared to other field crops, the only limiting factor for the expansion of area under these crops being the availability of irrigation. Extension of irrigation in the region also resulted in an increase in area under irrigated cotton. Consequently, productivity of cotton increased and released area under rainfed cotton to other crops. The shifts towards pulses and oilseeds, whose productivity was also stagnating, was at the expense of cotton and bajra. In a situation of stagnating productivity these shifts were in response to the relative profitability arising from price changes in favour of these crops. These changes indicate that the farmers in the region do respond to the provision of irrigation and to market signals.

The responsiveness of the cropping system to the price stimuli in the post-green revolution period in a stagnating productivity situation is thus evident. If the aggregate value of agricultural production is any indication then the region has experienced a real growth in production despite stagnation in the productivity of crops.

The advantages of relative prices of commodities may not really prove that advantageous in the long run. The changes in the relative prices of commodities in the long run with stagnating productivity of crops may bring in a cobweb type cropping pattern which may not benefit all sections of farmers equally. As a short term policy option one may choose consolidating the changes that have taken place in the positive direction by strengthening the efforts in providing appropriate infrastructure.

There is a need to break the stagnation in productivity of irrigated and rainfed crops to achieve sustained agricultural development. The region has large untapped irrigation potential. The irrigated area is likely to increase from the existing 10 to 30 per cent of the cropped area with the full exploitation of the irrigation potential the region has. Agricultural development of the region can be achieved in the long run, through rice and cotton under irrigated conditions and through oilseeds and pulses which are raised under both rainfed and irrigated conditions. Presently 45 per cent of the gross cropped area in the region is under pulses and oilseeds which are mainly raised under rainfed conditions. The development prospects of the region, therefore, depend on the speed with which the available technology at the research stations is transferred to the field. This calls for concerted policy efforts.

The policy efforts are to be in the direction of identifying appropriate cost effective technology for dry land agriculture, transfer of the available technology to the field level and strengthening marketing infrastructure for agricultural inputs and output.

Even after the full exploitation of the available irrigation potential, 70 per cent of the cropped area is likely to be under rainfed conditions. The production growth in the region would depend upon higher and stable productivity levels of rainfed crops. This calls for concerted efforts in the direction of retaining soil moisture with appropriate cost effective technology to harness the run off water through the watershed development programmes.

Transfer of technology from the research stations to the farmers' fields calls for a strong extension service base manned by motivated and knowledgeable extension workers. This can be achieved by strengthening and making more effective the operation of the existing extension wing through reorientation and constant up-gradation of their knowledge. This would equip the extension workers with the right kind of information to be carried to the farmers.

To achieve a sustained higher level of production it requires strengthening and expansion of the existing marketing institutions at various levels for assured supply of agricultural inputs and markets for the output. Thus the region has the potential to develop into a prosperous agricultural region with a strong base of commercial crops provided the policy efforts are in the aforesaid direction.

11

INDUSTRIAL DEVELOPMENT
Status and Prospects

M. Prahladachar

1. Introduction

The two striking aspects in the industrial growth pattern of Karnataka viz., slow-down since 1980s and lack of regional diversification (despite various efforts towards promoting and dispersing industry during the last three decades) need to be pinpointed to appreciate the current status of industry in the Hyderabad-Karnataka region. Without going into a diagnostic analysis of macro-policies, strategies and programmes that caused and shaped the trends cited at the state level which undoubtedly did cast their long shadows on the growth and performance of industry at the regional level, suffice it to mention that Hyderabad-Karnataka region is yet to secure a place of recognition in the industrial map of the State. The distributional profile of small, medium and large scale industries across districts in the State reinforces this observation.

2. Profile of Industries

1. Small Scale Industries

As on 31st March 1994 Hyderabad-Karnataka districts together accounted for a share of about 12 per cent in the state total number of SSI units (Table 11.1). In terms of number of units, Bellary, Raichur, Gulbarga and Bidar occupied 7th, 12th, 13th and 16th rank respectively in the state. Likewise, the shares of these districts and their ranks in the state total of employment

TABLE 11.1 : Cumulative Number of SSI Units in Karnataka - 1993-94

Sl. No.	District	Unit	Rank	Investment in lakhs	Rank	Employment	Rank
1.	Bangalore (Rural)	5804 (3.86)	9	4727.23 (12.82)	12	30522 (3.04)	12
2.	Bangalore (Urban)	29228 (19.48)	1	45773.15 (27.38)	1	261639 (26.09)	1
3.	Belgaum	13082 (8.72)	2	11765.53 (7.03)	4	59231 (5.90)	5
4.	*Bellary*	5862 (3.90)	7	3600.07 (2.15)	15	28314 (2.82)	13
5.	*Bidar*	3337 (2.24)	16	5036.24 (3.01)	11	20462 (2.04)	15
6.	Bijapur	5556 (3.70)	10	3870.93 (2.31)	14	32658 (3.25)	10
7.	Chitradurga	5608 (3.73)	8	7506.74 (4.49)	7	31490 (3.14)	11
8.	Chickmagalur	2646 (1.76)	19	1859.61 (1.11)	19	12814 (1.27)	20
9.	Dakshina Kannada	10229 (6.86)	5	17186.97 (10.28)	2	68597 (6.84)	4
10.	Dharwad	12672 (8.44)	4	12499.39 (7.47)	3	115796 (11.55)	2
11.	*Gulbarga*	4854 (3.23)	13	4305.71 (2.57)	13	27212 (2.71)	14
12.	Hassan	3305 (2.20)	17	2621.34 (1.56)	18	16836 (1.67)	18
13.	Kolar	5642 (3.64)	11	6920.48 (4.14)	8	38860 (3.87)	7
14.	Kodagu	1629 (1.08)	20	1614.70 (0.96)	20	15656 (1.56)	19
15.	Mandya	3340 (2.22)	15	2823.70 (1.68)	16	18346 (1.83)	17
16.	Mysore	13057 (8.70)	3	8720.34 (5.21)	6	76325 (7.61)	3
17.	*Raichur*	4927 (3.28)	12	6662.76 (3.98)	10	37936 (3.78)	8
18.	Shimoga	4723 (3.14)	14	6807.20 (4.07)	9	34050 (3.39)	9
19.	Tumkur	9152 (7.10)	6	10170.47 (7.08)	5	55833 (5.56)	6
20.	Uttara Kannada	2778 (1.85)	18	2680.96 (16.03)	17	19936 (1.98)	16
	Total	150021		167153.62		1002513	

Note: Figures in parentheses are percentages to the state total.

Source: Department of Industries and Commerce, Government of Karnataka, Bangalore.

and investment in the SSI sector respectively were not too impressive.

2. Large and Medium Scale Industries

By the end of March 1994, there were about 746 large and medium scale industries in the state with an investment of Rs.629802.42 lakh providing employment to 2.80 lakh persons (Table 11.2). The relative status of Hyderabad-Karnataka districts with respect to selected parameters of industry was as follows:

District	Rank in the State Total			Share in State Total			Per unit Emp-loy-ment	Per unit Inves-tment (Rs. lakhs)
	Units	Employ-ment	Invest-ment	Units	Employ-ment	Invest-ment		
Bellary	8	9	9	2.8	3.0	3.1	401	920.65
Raichur	7	8	9	2.9	3.4	4.5	435	1280.13
Gulbarga	12	6	1	1.9	3.8	30.7	750	13821.64
Bidar	10	16	5	2.3	1.0	0.8	159	292.50

The main point that emerges from the foregoing distributional profile of industries is that Hyderabad-Karnataka districts are placed generally on the lower side of the industrial ladder with respect to one industry parameter or the other. However, Gulbarga in particular stands out as an odd instance in this entire scenario with very high level of investment, but not accompanied by a commensurate level of employment generation.

If the interpretation that the Hyderabad-Karnataka districts are lagging behind industrially is accepted, more so when compared especially with industrially advanced districts of the state viz., Bangalore, Mysore, Dakshina Kannada and Dharwad, it serves a useful purpose from the point of view policy and strategy to examine the constraints that are responsible for the same. A good deal of explanation for the region's industrial backwardness may be sought in terms of its access to industrial finance, its resource utilization pattern vis-a-vis resource endowment, the level and quality of infrastructure facilities and the government's policy regime in general. A discussion of these aspects in succession follows.

3. Industrial Finance

It is useful to recall the seminal arguments made by Schumpeter that financial intermediaries—the ones that mobilise savings, allocate capital, manage risk, ease transactions and monitor firms—are essential for economic development. In the background of this conceptual framework

TABLE 11.2 :Large and Medium Scale Industries in the State of Karnataka as on 31.3.1994

Sl. No.	District	Unit	Rank	Investment in lakhs	Rank	Employment	Rank
1.	Bangalore (Rural)	337	1	129158.15	2	124192	1
2.	Bangalore (Urban)	(45.17)		(20.50)		(44.32)	
3.	Belgaum	30	5	21885.32	8	16960	4
		(4.02)		(3.47)		(6.05)	
4.	*Bellary*	21	8	19333.58	9	8421	9
		(2.81)		(3.06)		(3.00)	
5.	*Bidar*	17	10	4972.45	15	2697	16
		(2.27)		(0.78)		(0.96)	
6.	Bijapur	10	15	4519.23	16	4697	14
		(1.34)		(0.71)		(1.67)	
7.	Chicimagalur	5	18	67743.24	3	2638	17
		(0.67)		(10.75)		(0.94)	
8.	Chitradurga	26	6	2346.49	17	3211	15
		(3.48)		(0.37)		(1.14)	
9.	Dharwad	68	3	16019.27	10	10380	7
		(9.11)		(2.54)		(3.70)	
10.	Dakshina Kannada	34	4	23893.69	7	7106	10
		(4.55)		(3.79)		(2.53)	
11.	*Gulbarga*	14	12	193502.90	1	10508	6
		(1.87)		(30.72)		(3.75)	
12.	Kodagu	2	19	174.00	19	375	19
		(0.26)		(0.02)		(0.13)	
13.	Kolar	13	13	14073.82	11	27630	2
		(1.74)		(2.23)		(9.86)	
14.	Hassan	5	17	1497.61	18	1027	18
		(0.87)		(0.23)		(0.36)	
15.	Mandya	9	16	6570.45	14	5015	13
		(1.20)		(1.04)		(1.78)	
16.	Mysore	88	2	34442.08	5	20020	3
		(11.79)		(5.46)		(7.14)	
17.	*Raichur*	22	7	28162.86	6	9576	8
		(2.94)		(4.47)		(3.41)	
18.	Shimoga	15	11	39330.63	4	14864	5
		(2.01)		(6.24)		(5.30)	
19.	Tumkur	19	9	10612.07	13	51990	12
		(2.54)		(1.68)		(1.85)	
20.	Karwar	11	14	11564.58	12	5689	11
		(1.47)		(1.83)		(2.03)	
	Total	746		629802.42		280205	

Note: Figures in parentheses are percentages to the state total.
Source: Department of Industries and Commerce, Government of Karnataka, Bangalore.

which has got reinforced by empirical evidence assembled from several countries, we examine the aspect of industrial finance vis-a-vis industrial growth in Hyderabad-Karnataka region.

Despite the fact of an integrated structure of financial institutions having come about for providing term finance and other assistance to industrial sector, and despite many industrial finance institutions such as IDBI, KSFC, KSIIDC assuming a significant role with a conspicuous growth in their sanctions, the state's share in the country's total of All Financial Institutions dropped from about 8.8 per cent in 1980-81 to 5.99 per cent in 1991-92. Also the state's share in the cumulative sanctions upto March 1992 by the leading individual industrial financial institutions ranged from as low as 3.4 to 8.4 per cent.

These aggregate trends at the state level did naturally exert a limiting influence on the level of financial assistance that a given district in any region including Hyderabad-Karnataka was able to receive for industrial development. Moreover, Hyderabad-Karnataka districts have not been able to secure a niche in the sphere of industrial finance as is obvious from their comparatively low shares in the sanctions made by leading industrial financial institutions, viz., KSFC and KSIIDC in the state (see Tables 11.3 and 11.4).

No doubt, the analysis of industrial finance based on aggregated secondary data gives little insights into the intricacies involved in the operational dimensions of problems relating to industrial finance. Micro level surveys pertaining to industrial financial institutions and industries across districts in Hyderabad-Karnataka region should help obtain useful insights.

4. Resource Endowment and Use

4.1. Agro-Resources

Excluding the irrigated areas of the region wherein paddy and sugarcane are the major crops, the region's crop-economy is characterized by the dominance of jowar, bajra, millets, pulses and oilseeds. As the prospects of agriculture are subject to a great degree to the vagaries of monsoon, the prospect of agro-industries based on these agro-resources may also be surmised to be varying in nature. Perhaps, this explains why although pulses and oilseeds are major crops in the region the prospects of starting agro-industries based on these products are dampened and/or the industrial units have restricted themselves to primary processing. As a result, not only the contribution of these districts with respect to value-addition is low

TABLE 11.3 : District-wise Sanctions and Disbursments for Small Scale Sector by KSFC Since Inception upto March 1992

1	Sanctions No.	%	Amount (Rs.lakhs)	%	Disbursements No.	%	Amount (Rs.lakhs)	%
I. Backward Districts								
01 Bidar	1167	2.61	3631.99	3.68	1125	2.88	3483.65	4.22
02 Mysore	3264	7.29	7356.13	7.45	2742	7.03	6239.80	7.56
03 Dharwad	3871	8.65	6677.47	6.76	3000	7.69	5625.58	6.82
04 Raichur	995	2.22	2444.19	2.47	910	2.33	1815.54	2.20
05 Belgaum	3734	8.34	5224.33	5.29	3564	9.14	4719.17	5.72
06 Bijapur	3637	8.13	2231.36	2.26	3142	8.06	1632.07	1.98
07 Dakshina Kannada	2396	5.35	5468.34	5.54	1949	5.00	4624.47	5.61
08 Tumkur	3223	7.20	5279.41	5.35	2923	7.49	4581.26	5.55
09 Gulbarga	1464	3.27	2198.04	2.23	1218	3.12	1947.65	2.36
10 Uttara Kannada	788	1.76	1157.69	1.17	721	1.85	924.64	1.12
11 Hassan	1114	2.49	1773.43	1.80	907	2.33	1340.11	1.62
Total: I	25653	57.32	43442.38	43.98	22201	56.93	36633.94	44.40
II. Other Districts								
01 Bangalore	8147	18.21	39046.50	39.53	7014	17.98	32135.67	38.95
02 Shimoga	4519	10.10	2767.23	2.80	3937	10.09	2465.99	2.99
03 Kolar	1058	2.36	3402.96	3.45	1020	2.62	2837.81	3.44
04 Chitradurga	1789	4.00	4075.23	4.13	1637	4.20	3351.65	4.06
05 Mandya	1096	2.45	2036.32	2.06	1065	2.73	1851.69	2.24
06 Chickma-galur	700	1.56	709.59	0.72	574	1.47	707.59	0.86
07 Bellary	1329	2.97	2851.44	2.89	1132	2.90	2209.14	2.68
08 Kodagu	460	1.03	437.08	0.44	420	1.08	306.8	0.37
Total: II	19098	42.68	55326.35	56.02	16799	43.07	45866.34	55.60
State Total:	44751	100.00	98768.73	100.00	39000	100.00	82500.28	100.00

Source: KSFC Annual Reports, Various issues.

but also they are reduced to depend on the areas outside the region for product-processing. It is also possible that many other constraints on the fronts of finance, technology, entrepreneurship etc., have their bearing on this scenario.

TABLE 11.4 : District-wise Analysis of Assistance by KSIIDC Since Inception Upto March 1992

District	Total No.	%	Amount Sanction (Rs.lakhs)	%	Amount Disbursed (Rs.lakhs)	%
Backward Districts						
Category A						
Bider	23	3.17	1548.79	3.28	1447.19	3.98
Category B						
Raichur	26	3.58	1352.47	2.86	693.47	1.91
Dharwad	37	5.10	2225.82	4.71	1957.15	5.39
Mysore	115	15.84	9390.46	19.89	7091.71	19.52
Category C						
Belgaum	19	2.62	1233.22	2.61	837.42	2.30
Bijapur	10	1.38	490.99	1.04	396.56	1.09
Gulburga	6	0.83	325.28	0.69	324.28	0.89
Hassan	8	1.10	388.1	0.82	363.85	1.00
Kolar	18	2.48	1105.34	2.34	799.28	2.20
N. Canara	11	1.52	906.75	1.92	715.75	1.97
S. Canara	37	5.10	2211.5	4.68	1796.49	4.94
Tumkur	19	2.62	1162.33	2.46	1036.33	2.85
Coorg	1	0.14	27	0.06	26.5	0.07
Sub Total	330	45.45	22366.05	47.38	17485.98	48.12
Other Districts						
B'Lore	354	48.76	20488.29	43.40	16147.8	44.44
Bellary	9	1.24	649.01	1.37	336.41	0.93
C'Durga	24	3.31	2029.62	4.30	1325.37	3.65
CMLR	3	0.41	111.22	0.24	102.97	0.28
Mandya	10	1.38	591.7	1.25	341.7	0.94
Shimoga	13	1.79	970.21	2.06	598.33	1.65
Sub Total	413	56.89	24840.05	52.62	18852.58	51.88
Total	726		47208.1		36338.56	

Source: Calculated from KSIIDC Reports.

4.2. Mineral Resources

Important mineral resources of the region are manganese and iron ore in Bellary and limestone in Gulbarga. Considerable effort has gone in tapping these resources for industrial production. Nevertheless, it is gathered that several industrial units engaged in mineral production activities are faced with a variety of problems both technical and non-technical, which need to be attended to in order to ensure a sound and optimal production possibilities of these resources. Problems faced by cement manufacturing units in the small scale sector in the region may be specially noted in this regard.

4.3. Other Resources

Among other local resources, a special reference may be made to leather. Though pastoral farming is widespread, it is reported that the leather industry has not been able to achieve significant growth. On the contrary, out of 75 leather industries in Gulbarga district, most of them have closed down. In the event of leather industry having failed to stabilise, it is natural that the region's raw material (sheep and goat skin) is being transported to neighbouring Andhra Pradesh.

5. Infrastructure

Needless to mention that infrastructure plays a key role of a catalystic nature in the industrial development of a region. Making use of data on individual infrastructure items (railway route length, broad-gauge length, road length, National Highways and surface metalled, number of goods vehicles, number of post offices, telephone exchanges, telephone lines and electricity consumption by the industry), an overall infrastructure development indices for the districts in Karnataka for the years 1976-77 and 1990-91 were computed by resorting to the technique of Principal Component Analysis for the purpose. The wide gulf in the infrastructure development between industrially developed districts like

Bangalore, Dakshina Kannada, Mysore, Dharwad and Belgaum, on the one hand, and the industrially backward districts of Hyderabad-Karnataka region on the other is too striking to be missed (Table 11.5). Also the wide disparity in the level of infrastructure development between these two sets of districts persisted over the period 1976 to 1991, despite the professed objectives of the Government to develop infrastructure facilities in the backward areas with a view to promoting industrial development therein.

In the course of discussions with the industry department officials, local entrepreneurs and others concerned during our visit to Hyderabad-Karnataka region (July 1994), it was time and again emphasised that water, power, transport and communication (in terms of both quantity and quality) were the major bottlenecks in attracting entrepreneurs to this

TABLE 11.5 : Infrastructure Development Index for districts in Karnataka

Districts	1976 Index	Rank	1991 Index	Rank
Bangalore	44812	1	33140	1
Belgaum	8143	3	6860	3
Bellary	3338	8	2616	12
Bidar	1000	19	1306	19
Bijapur	4686	6	3186	8
Chickmagalur	2292	17	2310	15
Chitradurga	3802	7	3384	6
Dharwad	7291	4	6045	5
Dakshina Kannada	9460	2	10226	2
Gulbarga	2533	11	2660	10
Hassan	2416	16	2502	14
Kodagu	1471	18	1748	18
Kolar	2509	13	2659	11
Mandya	2519	12	2081	16
Mysore	6391	5	6151	4
Raichur	2471	15	2058	17
Shimoga	3287	9	3202	7
Tumkur	2560	10	2531	13
Uttara Kannada	2480	14	2668	9

Source: M,Prahladachar, et al., Industrial Potential in Karnataka, ISEC, Mimeo, 1994, Chapter 5, p.193.

region. Various concessions and incentives offered to industrialists with a view to coaxing them to set-up industrial units in under-developed/ undeveloped parts of backward regions including Hyderabad-Karnataka turned out to be mere palliatives in the absence of substantive pre-requisites being fulfilled.

6. Government Policy

Some of the features in the tax regime of the state such as turn-over tax, entry tax on specified items (though limited in number but vital in character), higher level of sales tax rates compared to those prevailing in the neighbouring states, withdrawal of sales tax benefits, withdrawal of investment subsidy to medium and large scale industries, are found to be exerting negative influence on the industrial development of a backward region like Hyderabad-Karnataka. Withdrawal of sales tax benefits on processing units under the latest policy package announced by the state Government would in particular affect the growth of industry in Hyderabad-Karnataka region (e.g., dal mills, stone polishing units, etc.). In essence, these features in the tax regime of the state have inadvertantly given room for concealed exploitation of the state's facilities and resources, diversion of trade, etc. to the benefit of the neighbouring states.

While on the one hand, the state seemed to be serious in attracting entrepreneurs to relatively backward areas, on the other it inadvertently discouraged them by showing laxity and tardiness in implementing many of the concessions and incentives (such as investment subsidy, sales tax refund etc.) earmarked for the backward regions.

There is a plea from the industry associations/entrepreneurs that as the escalation in land prices is exerting a dampening effect on their readiness to set up industrial units, the government should preferably make the land available to them at "reasonable" prices, if not free of cost. It is also pointed out that the level of efforts of the KIADB in developing industrial areas are not commensurate, due to a variety of factors, with the level of needs felt by the region.

7. Future Outlook

The fact that so far the Hyderabad-Karnataka region has lagged behind in industrial development is no reason why it should continue to remain so. The geographical location of Raichur and Gulbarga are strategically meaningful—connected as they are by broad-gauge rail to important cities like Hyderabad, Bangalore and Bombay—thereby offering rich possibilities to capitalise agriculture and industry linkages for the region's development. We may also mention that resource endowments of the region—be it agro-horticulture products, minerals—are not adequately exploited for industrial manufacturing due to a variety of factors. Improvements in base and quality infrastructure coupled with institutional network for finance, technology, technical training etc. would ensure a vigorous industrial activity in the region.

In order to tap the industrial potential of the region, it is essential that the Hyderabad-Karnataka Development Board assumes a lead role in preparing a perspective industrial plan, based among others, on the region's resource-inventory through the assistance of professional/research organisations that can serve as a useful and vital reference frame for entrepreneurs. It is a welcome step that such a study is already undertaken for Gulbarga by NIDC and their report is ready for consultation. Likewise, it is commendable that DIC of Bellary has carried out a survey which has indicated ample scope for small scale agro-based and service-based industries. The efforts of the DICs in organising exhibitions periodically with a view to educating the prospective entrepreneurs also deserve to be noted with satisfaction.

Further, it is necessary to forge close links between entrepreneurs and research institutions on the one hand and financial institutions on the other. Such an interaction becomes all the more imperative and urgent when we look into the sorry state of affairs with regard to cement industry in the small scale sector in the region - the problems and poor performance of which are attributed mainly to incompatible technology.

In order to obtain quick and visible results in the industrial sector, it seems to be a good strategy to identify a few clusters within the region with relatively high industrial potential and give top priority in providing and ensuring pre-requisites necessary for industrial development. Curiously enough, such a course would not only pre-empt the hijacking of incentives and concessions, if any, meant for the backward regions by unscrupulous elements in setting up industries, but also would stop the practice of deliberately allowing them to degenerate into sick units with an eye on associated pecuniary benefits!

Under the new economic policy, the inter-state competition in attracting entrepreneurs for setting up industrial units is further sharpened and it is plausible to argue that a state which offers mere concessions and incentives without the backing of required infrastructural facilities and development has lesser chances to win the race compared to the one which offers such concessions and incentives along with infrastructural facilities and development.

In conclusion, the region's pace of industrial development may be accelerated if increased attention is paid to the industrialisation process as such rather than merely attracting or setting up a few industries. Industrialisation process encompasses a wide ranging factors involving changes in the structure, technology, institutional arrangements and so on. The process of industrialisation has a definite agglomeration and self-reinforcing quality. Once a favourable environment for growth of industry is ensured in a region, industrialisation tends to feed on itself. The industrial growth experience of Bidar, which was once declared as a 'no industry' district is a standing testimony to this phenomenon and should help instil a sense of optimism and hope that such a phenomenon could be replicated in other districts of the region as well.

12

EDUCATIONAL DEVELOPMENT
Constraints and Prospects

A. S. Seetharamu

Perspective

The potential for development of a region depends to a large extent on the quality of the people of that region. By quality of people, we mean, their knowledge of the physical and natural resources of the region, awareness of the constraints and problems in exploiting these resources, the skills they possess at varying levels of operations and management, their attitudes to life and society in general, their work habits, savings habits, their values of personal and social life, etc. The quality of people in the region is determined by the spread, quality and content of education, defined in its broadest sense wherein formal schooling is only one component. This paper is intended to examine the status, challenges and opportunities for educational development in Hyderabad-Karnataka region from the perspectives of socio-politico-economic as well as spiritual development of the region.

Hyderabad-Karnataka Region in Karnataka State

Hyderabad-Karnataka Region with its four districts viz., Bidar, Bellary, Gulbarga and Raichur occupics 23.8 per cent of the area of the State. However, only eight million out of the 45 million people of the State live in Hyderabad-Karnataka Region, which will account for 17.89 per cent of the State total. The density of population is quite low as compared to State average though the growth rate of population during 1981 to 1991 is quite high in relation to the State. Two largest districts of the State, Gulbarga and Raichur (ranked 2 and 3 in terms of area) are in Hyderabad-Karnataka region.

The Hyderabad-Karnataka region is backward as reflected from several indicators of development. The literacy rate of the region is 32.71 per cent while the State average is 47.02 per cent. The male-female differentials in literacy are in the ratio of 2:1 while that for the State is 3:2. There are inter-district disparities in the region with Bellary and Bidar being better off as compared to Raichur and Gulbarga. This is a case of disparities within a backward region. Further, there are inter-taluk disparities within each district. There are also differentials in literacy rates between scheduled castes, scheduled tribes and others. The Hyderabad-Karnataka region has the highest concentration of Muslims as compared to other regions. Problems of bi-lingualism also affect this region as all the four districts of the region share their borders with Andhra Pradesh while Gulbarga and Bidar districts, in addition, share their borders with Maharashtra.

Sex and caste differentials as well as intra-regional disparities referred to in regard to literacy rates in Hyderabad-Karnataka region are also observed in regard to enrolment of students at all levels of education viz., lower primary, higher primary, secondary, higher secondary/vocational stage, graduate and post-graduate levels of education. There are also imbalances in the spread of educational facilities. The imbalances not only refer in a quantitative way to the number of educational institutions but also refer in a qualitative way to the structure of the spread such as opportunities for medical, engineering, polytechnic, science, commerce, arts, law, education, pharmacy, dental and other courses in post-secondary education.

In sum, the problems and prospects for educational development in the Hyderabad-Karnataka Region can be identified in terms of the following issues:

A. Issues of educational growth and quantitative expansion in regard to (i) universalisation of primary education and (ii) achievement (as compared to the State) at higher levels of education.

B. Issues of (a) equity in regard to (i) sex differentials, (ii) caste differentials, (iii) minorities (language/religion) differentials, and (b) parity in terms of intra-Hyderabad Karnataka region districts and inter-taluk imbalances within the districts, and finally, (c) Hyderabad- Karnataka region in relation to the State.

C. Issues related to the pursuit of relevance and excellence in the field of post-secondary vocational, polytechnic and higher education.

The present paper examines the status and constraints of education in Hyderabad-Karnataka region from the foregoing perspective.

Educational Infrastructure

The National Policy on Education, 1986 is a watershed in the development of education in Hyderabad-Karnataka region as it is in other regions of the country. Intensive efforts were made to make education available to every child within a walking distance of 1 kilometer. By and large, this target was reached by 1988 as revealed by the All India Fifth Educational Survey, 1988. A school is only a basic minimum, essential facility for educational development. Normally, a school implied at least one teacher for four standards of primary education, known as a Single Teacher School. The single teacher school is associated with low enrolment and high drop-out rates. Hence, as per the National Policy, it was decided to provide a second teacher to all the single teacher schools in the region under a scheme which is well known as OPERATION BLACKBOARD. All the schools in the region have been provided with a minimum of two teachers. The official position is that there is not a single Single Teacher School in HK region. Still, it is observed that HK region is far behind other regions of the State in terms of educational infrastructure. A comparison of these facilities as a proportion of such facilities in the State would clarify the above observation.

A Clear Case of Injustice

From a historical perspective it would appear that considerable progress has taken place in HK region in regard to growth of educational infrastructure. However, in a relational perspective, as compared to the share of population in the region, the available facilities fall very much below expectations.

The population of Karnataka State in 1991 is 44.82 million. The four districts of HK region viz; Gulbarga (2.57 m), Raichur (2.31 m), Bellary (1.89 m) and Bidar (1.25m) together account for 8.02 million or 17.89 per cent of the State's share. Age-specific population data is not available. Hence the general figure is taken as a proxy for each age-slab. Though this is incorrect, still the proportion for each slab will not be lower than the State average for the corresponding slabs, as the growth rate of population in this region is higher than that in the State. It is assumed that the share of educational infrastructure at all levels of schooling should be at least equal to the share of the region to the State's population, (that is, 17.89 per cent). Any deviation which is lower than this figure, is a case of deprivation and such deviations beyond a critical minimum of 2 percentage points should be construed as a clear case of injustice. It may be noted that the 2 percentage points workout to 8.964 lakh of people.

As compared to the State's share of the population in HK region which is 17.89 per cent, the share of lower primary schools is 14.13 per cent and that of higher primary schools is 11.40 per cent (Table 12.1). The shortfalls are 3.76 per cent and 6.49 per cent respectively. The higher primary schools carry with them I to IV standards of the lower primary stage. Together they add upto 5260 primary schools with facility at least for I to IV standards. It constitutes 13.61 per cent of total primary schools in the State which means a shortfall of 4.58 per cent. Completion of four standards of primary education, which may be considered as the first phase of universalisation of 7 years of primary education, is a much too difficult proposition with this type of shortage of facilities.

TABLE 12.1: Education Infrastructure 1992-93:

Number of Schools/Institutions

Expected Percentage: 17.89

	Pre-Primary	LPS	HPS	High Schools	Composite Junior Colleges
H.K.Region	542	3304	1956	687	157
Karnataka	5325	23383	17157	4699	938
Percentage	10.18	14.13	11.40	14.62	16.94
Gap	7.71	3.76	6.49	3.27	0.95

The shortage of infrastructure facilities in regard to high schools is around 3.27 per cent. It is only in regard to composite junior colleges that the shortage is the lowest, the gap being less than 1 per cent. The gap is the highest in regard to provision of pre-primary schools. It is of the order of 7.71 per cent. There is a supplementary pre-primary education programme operated by the Department of Women and Children's Welfare. The schools are known as the Anganwadis. It is not clear, how the picture will emerge when the total pre-primary schools in the region are juxtaposed with that of the State.

Number of Teachers

A few variables such as teacher-pupil ratios, teacher-standard ratios may be important. In the absence of reliable data on these variables, a crude analysis of the availability of teachers in HK region as a proportion of State average is made here.

There has been notable recruitment of primary school teachers in the last few years under the Operation Black Board. In spite of such a teacher-recruitment drive the proportion of teachers in the region juxtaposed with the proportion of population is lower by 3.78 per cent for lower primary schools, 2.73 per cent for higher primary schools and as high as 7.51 per cent for high schools. It is somewhat tolerable only in regard to composite junior colleges (Table 12.2).

TABLE 12.2: No. of Teachers in HK Region, 1992-93

[Proportion of Population in the State= 17.89 per cent]

	LPS	HPS	High Schools	Composite Junior Colleges
HK Region	6198	14592	4173	2409
Karnataka	43921	96251	40199	14717
Percentage	14.11	15.16	10.38	16.37
Gap	3.78	2.73	7.51	1.52

A significantly large proportion of untrained teachers have been recruited in the last few years. Many of them had passed their school final 8 to 10 years before and now they are teaching all of a sudden higher primary standards.

Though teachers' vacancies have been filled up still there is a shortage of teachers from a normative perspective. A significant proportion of teachers (over 20 per cent) have taken transfers to neighbouring non-HK region districts rendering the HK region again with single teacher schools and 2 to 3 teachers with seven standards higher primary schools, especially in certain most backward talukas such as Deodurg, Kusthagi, Siruguppa, Afzalpur, Shahpur, Jewargi and Aurad. Hence, in the records of the Ministry of Education at Vidhana Soudha, Bangalore, the teachers' vacancies in HK region have been filled up. But in actual real-life, functional situations HK region has a shortage of teachers.

College and University Education

The HK region has one University located at Gulbarga with two P.G. Centres located at Bellary and Raichur. There are 29 PG departments at Gulbarga, six at Bellary and two at Raichur. One pleasing feature about the University is in regard to its policy of student-admissions or in-take policy. There is no unregulated, excessive admissions. Admissions are tailored to infrastructure facility. As such, the in-take is fixed at 865 students for the whole University, with a provision for 746 students at the

Gulbarga campus during 1994-95. The in-take capacity also provides for students from other universities, children of army personnel, freedom fighters, university employees, NCC/NSS cadets, SC/ST/ABCDE of BC apart from general merit categories. Certain off-beat courses are also offered, viz., Folklore studies, Micro-Biology, Electronics, Bio-chemistry, TV Technology, Mineral Exploration, Mineral Processing, Instrumentation Technology etc. The number of students preparing for research degrees such as M.Phil/Pre.Ph.D/Ph.D during 1991-92 was 170. There is also a centre for women's studies.

Colleges in Taluks

HK region is guilty of the same sin which it alleges against the State in regard to disproportionate developmental attention. Large-scale imbalances are observed especially in regard to provision of college/ higher education.

There are 90 colleges of general education and 48 professional

TABLE 12.3: Distribution of Colleges in HK Region (1994)

	Gulbarga	Raichur	Bellary	Bidar	Total
General Education					
Arts	11	5	3	6	25
Arts & Commerce	12	6	5	2	25
Commerce	2	2	-	-	4
Arts/Science/ Commerce	4	4	6	6	20
Commerce/Science	1	-	-	-	1
Science & Arts	4	1	1	4	10
Science	3	1	-	1	5
Totals	37	19	15	19	90
Professional Education					
Engineering	2	1	1	2	6
Medicine	1	-	1	-	2
Ayurvedic	-	-	2	1	3
Homeopathy	1	-	1	-	2
Dental	2	1	-	2	5
Pharmacy	4	2	2	3	11
Law	2	1	1	1	5
Education	5	2	3	2	12
Nursing	1	1	-	-	2
Totals	18	8	11	11	48

colleges, excluding colleges of agriculture, in HK region. The distribution of colleges in the four districts, course-wise is as follows: Nearly 40 per cent of the colleges in both general higher education and professional education categories are in Gulbarga district only. This imbalance is understandable.

However, the position in regard to distribution of colleges in the taluks presents a dismal picture. Leaving out the four taluks of district head-quarters, only six out of 28 taluks have professional colleges. There are nine out of 48 professional colleges in these six taluks only one of which is an engineering college and a position of no-medical college.

Poor Status of Science Education*

The status of science education is very poor. In fact, only 36 out of 90 colleges in the region provide for science education; 50 colleges provide for commerce and 80 out of the 90 colleges offer arts courses leading to the B.A. degree. There are 19 taluks in the region, out of a total of 32 which have only one degree college. Out of these 19 taluks, there are 16 taluks, which do not provide for facilities for science education. That is, 50 per cent of taluks in the region do not have facilities for science-based higher education.

The position in regard to status of science education in schools also is extremely poor as revealed by an intensive study of Raichur district by this author, when he prepared the DPEP report for the district [Commissioned by the Government of Karnataka, 1993]. Consequently there is no demand for science education at higher levels.

Vocational Education

47 vocational courses are offered in the region out of a total of over 500 courses offered across the State. Only 80 out of 2409 Junior colleges offer vocational courses, the lowest tally being in Bellary district. Thirteen vocational courses are offered through polytechnics. There is a great potential for the strengthening of vocational education at the +2 stage in the region.

---

* Note: A historical and comparative analysis of growth and development of education in advanced countries highlights the premier status that had been given to the widespread dissemination of scientific knowledge and science education. Even Jawaharlal Nehru strongly emphasised the significance of the popularisation of science education and creation of a scientific community for national development when he moved the Science Policy Resolution, adopted by Parliament in 1956.

Educational Performance in the Region

Educational performance in HK region can be best described through the proverb "As you sow, so you reap". The infrastructure facilities are poor and the performance is equally poor.

Enrolment in Schools

By and large, enrolment at the lower primary stage is universalised except in certain pockets of the HK region. The Lambani Thandas and Camps of migrant population do not have adequate schooling facility. There are nearly 500 such thandas/camps which do not have access to schooling. The population of some of these units are not viable for a formal school. Non-formal/evening schools may serve the purpose.

It is at the higher primary stage that there is observed a yawning gap between the State's share of the population (17.89 per cent) and State's share of children at the higher primary stage which is 10.30 per cent. The total share in primary education works out to 16.06 per cent. The shares of scheduled castes and scheduled tribes at lower primary and higher primary stages as well as total primary education, as compared to State's population share of these groups respectively given in brackets, are: 20.44 (22.00), 15.03(29.00), 18.98(22.00), 18.53(29.00), 10.30(22.00) and 16.06 (29.00). Analysis of drop-out rates is, however, not attempted in this paper for want of reliable statistics.

Women's Education

Enrolment of girls is quite low at the lower primary stage and it is lower still at the higher primary stage. In fact, a total absence of sanitary facilities - toilet with water facility, is one of the strong reasons for low enrolment of girls. Low enrolment of girls at lower and higher primary stages of education as well as secondary education has stunted the demand for college education among girls. The demand is abysmally low. There are hardly 12 women's colleges and they are spread across 10 out of 32 taluks in the region. There are no hostels for girl students at taluk/district headquarters. Commuting to college in crowded buses everyday not being a safe proposition, the proportion of girls enrolled in Gulbarga University is hardly 10 per cent. This is the lowest for the State. Karnataka, Mysore and Bangalore Universities have over 35 per cent girls while Mangalore University has 55 per cent share. Nine out of the 12 women's colleges in the region do not have facility for science education.

Another important indicator of educational performance is literacy. There are 20 districts in the State and the ranking of the four districts of the HK region in terms of literacy in the State are 17, 18, 19 and 20 respectively for Bellary, Bidar, Gulbarga and Raichur. As any 21st district is not there in Karnataka State, there is no need for further comments.

Literacy campaigns have been completed in Bidar and Raichur districts. They are in prógress in Bellary and Gulbarga districts. The coverage of illiterates in Bidar and Raichur districts have been 1.55 lakhs and 1.89 lakhs against targetted population in 9 to 35 age-groups of 2.98 lakhs and 5.91 lakhs. These coverages work out to 52.01 per cent and 31.97 percent. To say the least, performance is moderate in Bidar and dismal in Raichur. There is also an opinion that compared to base-level literacy status the performance of these two districts is not 'that bad'; opinions differ. In case of failure/limited success of literacy campaigns, infrastructure/financial support cannot be held responsible. There is a systematised, nation-wide, uniform funding support. A research study by this author has shown cultural constraints and dysfunctionalities in campaign management as the main variable in observed performance.

There is an additional problem in the field of education in the HK region. That is the problem of minorities. There are three major language minorities - Urdu, Marathi and Telugu. Their enrolment in HK region as a proportion of enrolment of children in the whole State (20 districts) for these three minority languages is 25.18, 22.20 and 67.87 per cent, respectively.

Recommendations

The recommendations made here are for the region as a whole some of which can be taken up by HKADB.

(a) HKADB should take interest in literacy campaigns in Gulbarga and Bellary districts as well as Restoration and Post-literacy programmes in Bidar and Raichur districts. Periodical reviews and monitoring this centrally sponsored programme can be taken up by the HKADB in its regular meetings.

(b) An important area that is so far neglected and requiring attention of HKADB is women's education. At the higher primary school stage, it is required to construct sanitary facilities for girls—toilet and water facility - in Bidar, Bellary and Gulbarga districts. Raichur district is not mentioned as such a proposal has already been accepted for the District under the DPEP being operated by the State Government and funded by the World Bank against their credit adjustment social safety net programmes. The HKADB also needs to build girls' hostels for colleges to step up women's participation from the present abysmally low 10 per cent level.

(c) Teachers' training programmes are required to be promoted by HKADB through the Joint Director of Public Instruction and DIET's of the region. They involve marginal expenditures. The subjects for training are: Refresher courses in school subjects; modern techniques of teaching—multiple-grades/use of low cost no cost teaching aids/periodical, objective MLL based evaluation; gender-sensitivity/regional backwardness sensitivity training etc.

(d) Science education has to be given top priority in future educational investments. There is no need for starting colleges afresh. The HKADB Board can construct laboratory buildings and provide capital infrastructure facilities such as equipments, furniture etc, to the existing Arts colleges so that they can start science courses (B.Sc.). Science exhibitions, Science fairs, Science quiz competitions should be held on an inter-district, inter-taluk and inter-school basis at various levels. The Divisional Educational Office can take up planning, organising and guiding this work with the help of the HKADB.

(e) NGO involvement is to be promoted and encouraged by HKADB for running non-formal education programmes for Tandas/ Camps and other needy regions. Illustration of the work of 'SAMOOHA', an NGO funded by ACTION AID, regarding educational support activities in Deodurg taluk of Raichur district is a pointer in this direction.

(f) Periodical and continuous monitoring of educational development is most essential. This is to be taken up by the HKADB in a comparative perspective on several process and output indicators.

(g) Intra-region, inter-taluk disparities in educational development need to be bridged, to tolerable levels, on a top-priority.

13

POPULATION, FAMILY WELFARE AND HEALTH INFRASTRUCTURE

M.R. Narayana and P.H. Rayappa

1. Introduction

This paper aims at (i) explaining the selected population changes, developments in health services and infrastructure in the Hyderabad-Karnataka (H-K) region, and (ii) comparing these changes and developments in the districts with that of the region and in the region with that of the state. These comparisons are intended to unearth the nature of regional backwardness, and intra-regional and inter-regional disparities in the process of regional development as they are related to population and health. Thus, the results of this paper have implications for a strategy of balanced regional development in a sectoral context. Since in every region, the comprising people are bound by the social institutions like the family, a balanced development of the region will ultimately have welfare implications for families as well.

The scope of this study is restricted to examining the contemporary issues in population and health as a demographic phenomenon, mainly within the framework of current population policy. Thus, no attempt will

* Grateful thanks are due to Professor N. Baskara Rao (ISEC, Bangalore) and to the following persons for useful discussions and official cooperation: Mr Umakantaiah (State Demographer); Dr Shivaram [Director (Projects)]; Dr T. Nizamuddin (Divisional Joint Director of Health and Family Welfare Services, Gulbarga); Dr Shamarao (District Health and Family Welfare Officer, Gulbarga); Sri Prabhakara Rao (FPAI, Gulbarga); Medical Officers and health staff at Gabbur PHC, Gulbarga district; and Lady volunteers of the Anganwadi Centre at Gabbur, Gulbarga district. In the same way, the assistance of Mr A. Prakash Rao in data collection is thanked.

be made to (i) examine the sectoral changes from a historical perspective, and (ii) relate population changes either as a determinant or as a consequence of regional economic development.

2. Data Base and Limitations

This study is based on the available (secondary) information on population and health at the district and division levels. The major official sources of this information are the published/unpublished documents of Directorate of Census (Bangalore), Bureau (Directorate) of Economics and Statistics (Bangalore), Directorate of Health and Family Welfare (Bangalore), Office of the Divisional Joint Director of Family Welfare Services (Gulbarga) and Office of the District Health and Family Welfare Officer (Gulbarga). However, due to poor maintenance of old records/publications, certain data could not be traced in time at the District Headquarters or at the State Directorate of Health and Family Welfare. In this paper, such data are classified as data not traced (N.T).

3. Selected Demographic Changes

Table 13.1 summarises the selected demographic characteristics of districts in the H-K region in terms of changes in total population, urbanisation, sex ratio and density of population.

3.1. Population size, growth and distribution

Broadly speaking, total population changes of a region are a function of natural growth (i.e. number of births minus deaths) of population and net migration (i.e. in-migration minus out-migration). If the natural growth and net migration are positive, then the region gains in population size. Or, a region gains in population if the increase in population size due to natural growth (or net migration) is more than the decrease in population due to net migration (or natural growth).

In Table 13.1, the total population size shows an increasing trend from 1971 to 1991 in all districts of the region as well as in the state as a whole. In the same way, the growth of population is positive during 1971-91, although this growth varies across districts and over time in the region. In particular, all the districts have experienced a higher growth of population during 1981-91 as compared to 1971-81 except Bellary; and during 1981-91 all the districts have experienced a higher growth of population than at the state level. Surprisingly, this high growth of population in the region is accompanied by a decline in the growth rate

TABLE 13.1 Selected demographic characteristics of districts in H-K Region: 1971-1991

Indicators	1971						1981						1991					
	Bellary	Bidar	Gulbarga	Raichur	Region	State	Bellary	Bidar	Gulbarga	Raichur	Region	State	Bellary	Bidar	Gulbarga	Raichur	Region	State
1	2	3	4	5	6	7	8	9	10	11	12	13	14	15	16	17	18	19
1. Total population ('00000)	11.22	8.24	17.39	14.15	51.00	292.99	15.89	9.95	20.80	17.84	63.48	371.40	18.90	12.55	25.82	23.10	80.37	449.80
2. Growth of population	1961-71						1971-81						1981-91					
	22.62	24.28	24.3	28.64	25.09	24.2	32.71	20.75	19.61	26.08	24.47	26.76	26.93	26.13	24.13	29.48	26.61	21.11
3. Internal migrants as a percentage of total population	11.48	6.46	6.85	9.37	8.5	10.61	14.5	7.21	8.46	11.6	10.44	11.92	N.A.	N.A.	N.A.	N.A.	N.A.	N.A.
4. Intra-state migrants as a percentage of total population	4.94	1.7	3.63	5.99	4.26	6.66	6.39	2.13	5.04	6.8	5.09	7.53	N.A.	N.A.	N.A.	N.A.	N.A.	N.A.
5. Inter-state migrants as a percentage of total population	6.54	4.76	3.22	3.38	4.25	3.95	8.12	5.08	3.42	4.8	5.35	4.39	N.A.	N.A.	N.A.	N.A.	N.A.	N.A.
6. Distribution of total population:																		
As a per cent of region's total	22.00	16.16	34.10	27.76	-	-	23.46	15.67	32.77	28.10	-	-	23.52	15.62	32.13	28.74	-	-
As a per cent of state's total	3.83	2.81	5.94	4.83	17.41	-	4.01	2.68	5.60	4.80	17.09	-	4.20	2.79	5.74	5.14	17.87	-

(Contd.)

TABLE 13.1 (Contd.)

1	2	3	4	5	6	7	8	9	10	11	12	13	14	15	16	17	18	19
7. Total area in sq.kms ('000)	9898	5451	16224	14005	45578	191773	9885	5448	16224	14017	45574	191791	9885	5448	16224	14017	45574	191791
8. Density of population	113	151	107	101	118	153	151	183	128	127	147	194	191	231	159	165	187	235
9. Sex ratio	967	963	981	981	973	957	973	968	981	988	978	963	965	952	962	978	964	960
10. Percent of urban population	27.15	14.46	17.78	15.36	18.69	24.31	33.05	17.82	22.86	19.27	23.25	27.89	29.86	19.57	23:62	20.79	23.46	30.92

Notes:

1. Growth of population refers to percentage decadal variation in total population.
2. All migration figures refers to migration by the criterion of place of birth.
3. Internal migration refers to the sum of intra-state migration and inter-state migration.
4. Intra-state migration refers to migrants who were born outside the district of enumeration, but within the state.
5. Inter-state migrants refer to migrants who were born outside the state of Karnataka, but within the country.
6. N.A. refers to not available.

Sources: 1. Government of Karnataka (1993); 2. Government of Karnataka (1991); 3. Government of Karnataka (1990); 4. Census of India (1993); 5. Census of India (1986); and 6. Census of India (1977).

of population in the state from 26.76 per cent during 1971-81 to 21.11per cent during 1981-91.

Since the districts of the H-K region are bordered by other districts in the state and by other states, it is exposed to considerable intra-state (or, inter-district) and inter-state migration. For instance, the figures in Table 13.1 show that the internal migration has increased in all districts of the region during 1971-81. Note that the role of internal migration is particularly strong in districts of Bellary and Raichur which have larger component of inter-state migrants. Nevertheless, internal migration has been utmost 15 per cent of the total population in the region. Thus, the high growth of population is mostly contributed by the natural increase in the region.

Unlike the growth of population, the distribution of each district's population in the total population of the region and the state has remained almost the same during 1971-81. For instance, during 1971-81, the share of region's population has remained around 17 per cent of the state's total population; and the share of Bidar in the total population of the region has remained around 16 per cent. However, a marginal increase is evident in these spatial distributive patterns during 1981-91.

3.2. Density of Population

Another interesting aspect of demographic changes in the H-K region is the pattern of density of population. The invariant geographical area of districts over the years and positive growth of population have resulted in continued increase in density of population in all districts of the region. However, the density of population of the region has always remained lower than that of the state. On the other hand, of the four districts, Bidar (Raichur) has the highest (lowest) density in the region. In fact, the density of population of Bidar is higher than the density of population of the region, but closer to the density of population of the state.

3.3. Sex Ratio

The sex ratio (i.e. number of females per 1000 males) in the region shows increasing trend from 1971 to 1991. This trend is moving towards achieving sex parity in the total population. Further, the sex ratio in every district of the region is higher than the sex ratio in the state, except for Bidar in 1991.

3.4. Urbanisation

As a region transforms from a traditional rural set up into a modern industrial set up, the process of urbanisation gains momentum. Thus, urbanisation is a broad indicator of modernisation, industrialisation etc. From a demographic viewpoint, urbanisation is defined as a process in which the per cent of total population which lives in urban areas increases over time. In Table 13.1, it is apparent that the H-K region has a low level of urbanisation as compared to the level of urbanisation in Karnataka state. However, the inter-district variations in the levels of urbanisation is prominent. For instance, Bellary district has maintained a higher/equal level of urbanisation as compared to the level of urbanisation at the region and state level during 1971-91. For other districts in the region, the performance is exactly opposite. In particular, Bidar is the least urbanised district in the region throughout 1971-91.

On the whole, the selected demographic indicators in the region suggest that the region has experienced a higher natural growth of population as compared to the state, especially during 1981-91. This high growth is relevant for all districts and is characterised by considerable inter-district variations. Also, the region is characterised by considerable inter-district variations in sex ratio, density of population and urbanisation.

4. Measures to Contain Population Growth

Consequent upon the continued increase in natural growth of population, several economic problems have been persisting in the region, such as poverty, unemployment etc. In a way, these problems are related to population growth. Hence, a reduction in population growth is considered to be a solution, at least in part, to many other problems as well. Thus, the need to contain the natural growth of population is a policy imperative in the region.

4.1 Policy Measures

An important public policy towards controlling natural population growth in India is the Family Welfare Programme. This policy has two major components. First, it contains measures to reduce fertility. These measures include both terminal (or surgical) methods (e.g. sterilisation: Vasectomy and Tubectomy) and temporary (or spacing) methods (e.g. IUD, Oral Pills and Conventional Contraceptives). Second, it contains measures to reduce maternal and child (i.e. infants and pre-school children) mortality and morbidity by improving their health conditions. These measures are also called Maternal and Child Health (MCH) services, or programmes for Child Survival and Safe Motherhood [CSSM]. These measures/services/programmes mainly include ante-natal, natal and post-natal care such as (i) immunisation programme under which TT, DPT, Polio, Measles, BCG, DT etc vaccines are supplied; and (ii) prophylaxis schemes (i.e. prophylaxis against nutritional anaemia and blindness).

In addition to the direct policy measures stated above, public policy towards controlling population growth has several other indirect measures. First, it is well known that an increase in age at marriage reduces fertility level and raises average age of child bearing. This, in turn, leads to reduction in population growth. In recognition of this relationship between age at marriage and fertility, the government has increased the legal age at marriage from 18 years to 21 years in case of males, and from 15 years to 18 years in case of females in 1978. Second, it is widely recognised that a rise in female literacy may have a negative effect on fertility, since a literate woman can be more responsive to family welfare programme than an illiterate woman. Also, literacy helps in better delivery of IEC (i.e. information, education and communication) activities in regard to family welfare programme. Thus, in the ultimate analysis, a literate woman should motivate herself towards small family norms and better health care. Consequent upon these advantages in the relationship between literacy and fertility, public policy efforts have increased in spreading literacy among the masses, especially in rural areas.

4.2. Performance of policy measures

In what follows, the performance in the H-K region in reducing population growth will be briefly analysed. For analytical simplicity, the performance will be broadly evaluated using two indicators, viz., target-indicators and impact-indicators. Table 13.2 summarises the selected target and impact indicators from 1983-84 to 1993-94 for each district and for the region and the state. In order to understand the path of performance, data on performance for 1988-89 is also given for the indicators above.

4.2.1 Target-indicators

Under the target-indicators, performance is shown for fertility control measures and selected MCH services, where performance is indicated by the achievement as a percentage of the target for each measure.

First of all, it is apparent that as compared to 1983-84, the performance of all fertility control measures during 1993-94 has improved in all the districts or in the region as a whole and in the state. However, the comparison of performance of family planning measures between 1983-84 and 1988-89 and between 1988-89 and 1993-94 indicates that the performance of the region is consistently lower than the State except in regard to Oral Pills. However, this consistency is not evident from the comparison of performance between the districts and the state. For instance, during 1983-84, the performance of all districts or the region in all fertility control measures was clearly below the performance at the state level. During 1988-89, this performance is maintained by all districts except Bidar whose performance was clearly above the state level in all measures. However, this performance is disturbed by Gulbarga in IUD and Bellary in OP during 1993-94.

On the other hand, the performance of the selected MCH services in Table 13.2 shows better performance of the region in 1988-89 as compared to 1993-94 as well as compared to the State, except with regard to immunisation programme for measles. However, as in the case of performance of family planning measures above, the performance path of MCH services of districts is neither time-consistent nor measure-consistent.

4.2.2. Impact-indicators

The numerical target-indicators show the direction of policy changes, but it leaves unexplained the impact of policy changes. In order to capture the impact of policy changes, and to evaluate the performance of a policy measure through its impact, the impact-indicators are analysed below. In Table 13.2, selected indicators of the impact of policy measures outlined in section 4.1 above are listed. A brief discussion of these impact indicators is given below.

(i) Per cent of eligible couples protected by birth control measures: This is an important indicator of the impact of family planning measures. Table 13.2 shows that of the eligible couples, the highest proportion is protected by sterilisation, followed by IUD, Oral Pills (OP) and Conventional Contraceptives (CC). Secondly, it is evident that the proportion of eligible couples protected by all methods has increased from 37.35 per cent (46per cent) in 1988-89 to 40.48 per cent (50.25 per cent) in 1993-94 at the regional (state) level. Note that this increase is largely contributed by an increased proportion of couples protected under spacing methods rather than under the terminal methods of family planning. Thirdly, among the districts in the region, the highest (lowest) number of eligible couples are protected in Bidar (Gulbarga) district with regard to all methods.

Notwithstanding the performance above, the per cent of eligible couples protected by all methods in the region is lower than at the state level.

(ii) Changes in vital rates: In India, vital rates (i.e. birth and death rates) at the state level are regularly available from the Sample Registration System (SRS). And, the district level vital rates are available from demographic surveys or/and from the estimates (using census data) made by demographers.

Table 13.2 provides information on Crude Birth Rate (CBR) and Crude Death Rate (CDR) for three districts of Gulbarga division, as reported in the evaluation study of IPP-III (Karnataka) by Reddy and Gopal (1993). This study gives vital rates for two time periods (1984 and 1992). Hence, comparison of rates in time and space is possible. Accordingly, birth rates have declined in all the districts and in the region in 1992 as compared to 1984, as is the case for the state based on SRS rates. However, the magnitude of this decline is the highest in Gulbarga district (7.1), followed by Raichur (6.1) and Bidar (2.3). For the region (state) as whole, the decline in CBR is 5.7 (2.1). In the same way, the CDR have also declined between 1984 and 1992. The magnitude of this decline is highest in Raichur (5.7), followed by Bidar and Gulbarga (1.3). For the region (state) as a whole, the decline in CDR is 3.0 (1.9).

Although the declines in CBR and CDR are a testimony for the favourable impact of family welfare programme in the region, both the birth and death rates in the region are still higher than at the state level.

(iii) Female literacy: Table 13.2 shows that female literacy is considerably low in all the districts of the H-K region. In fact, the region has always achieved a lower level of literacy than at the state level. Nevertheless, considerable efforts seem to have gone into promoting literacy in the least literate districts of Gulbarga, Bidar and Raichur in recent decades. Consequently, the literacy rates have gone up in these districts in 1991 as compared to previous census years.

(iv) Mean age at marriage: In spite of the enforceable legislation on banning the child marriage and fixing the minimum age at marriage for males and females in the country, the mean age at marriage is considerably low in the region as compared to the state. In Table 13.2, the mean age at marriage of currently married women is as reported in the Reddy and Gopal's (1993) study referred to above. This information shows that the mean age at marriage of currently married women was around 14 years

TABLE 13.2 Selected indicators of maternal health and family welfare performance of districts in H-K Region: 1983-84 to 1993-94

Indicators	1983-84						1988-89						1993-94					
	Bellary	Bidar	Gulbarga	Raichur	Region	State	Bellary	Bidar	Gulbarga	Raichur	Region	State	Bellary	Bidar	Gulbarga	Raichur	Region	State
I. Target-Oriented Approach (i.e. Achievements As a Percentage of Targets):																		
1. Family Planning Performance:																		
Sterilisation (Vasectomy + Tubectomy)	45.01	49.06	31.45	38.96	39.51	57.37	71.11	101.55	60.90	57.34	68.67	92.73	59.60	100.21	73.31	56.37	68.49	93.76
IUD	49.94	25.72	25.16	31.45	33.59	55.30	73.97	111.15	71.08	91.62	83.81	97.47	57.64	97.47	105.54	82.78	84.79	91.67
Oral Pills	52.75	15.76	25.43	51.70	37.78	37.36	109.92	151.26	99.37	105.22	111.62	118.14	80.00	78.73	70.37	71.68	74.12	76.78
Conventional Contraceptives	77.90	49.60	54.86	89.33	69.13	64.62	95.76	100.58	99.55	74.59	91.81	101.70	76.83	80.40	88.98	78.62	82.09	89.03
2. Maternal & Child Health Performance: (Immunisation and Nutritional Programmes)																		
D.P.T.	N.A.	N.A.	N.A.	N.A.	N.A.	N.A.	80.01	103.29	92.42	89.74	90.31	82.99	76.53	99.37	96.86	93.69	91.55	93.54
Polio	N.A.	N.A.	N.A.	N.A.	N.A.	N.A.	70.10	102.58	90.51	89.71	87.18	82.99	75.94	102.36	96.87	93.45	91.82	93.50
B.C.G.	N.A.	N.A.	N.A.	N.A.	N.A.	N.A.	86.21	98.67	92.53	103.16	94.96	82.99	89.89	106.79	108.54	104.39	102.67	101.73
Measels	N.A.	N.A.	N.A.	N.A.	N.A.	N.A.	62.51	49.52	72.16	83.79	69.67	82.99	72.68	97.28	106.40	88.00	91.70	88.89
T.T. (pregnant women)	N.A.	N.A.	N.A.	N.A.	N.A.	N.A.	78.87	87.32	75.47	88.09	88.09	81.67	92.58	92.72	99.57	103.78	103.78	98.09
II. Impact Indicator Approach																		
1. Percent of eligible couples protected by: Sterilisation (Vasectomy + Tubectomy)	N.T.	N.T.	N T.	N.T.	N.T.	N.T.	32.80	35.30	24.30	29.20	30.40	38.00	34.67	38.18	27.36	28.67	32.22	41.23

(Contd.)

TABLE 13.2 (Contd)

IUD	N.T.	N.T.	N.T.	N.T.	N.T.	N.T.	4.10	5.90	3.80	4.60	4.60	5.30	4.33	6.96	5.00	5.24	5.38	6.14
Oral Pills	N.T.	N.T.	N.T.	N.T.	N.T.	N.T.	1.30	1.30	1.40	1.40	1.35	1.60	1.28	1.57	2.10	1.85	1.70	1.79
Conventional Contraceptives	N.T.	N.T.	N.T.	N.T.	N.T.	N.T.	0.90	1.10	0.90	1.10	1.00	1.00	1.05	0.91	1.38	1.37	1.18	1.09
All methods	N.T.	N.T.	N.T.	N.T.	N.T.	N.T.	39.10	43.60	30.40	36.30	37.35	46.00	41.33	47.62	35.84	37.13	40.48	50.25
2. Vital rates (1984: 1992):																		
Crude birth rate	N.A.	35.8	38.4	40	38.4	30.9	N.A.	N.A.	N.A.	N.A.	N.A.	N.A.	N.A.	33.5	31.3	33.9	32.7	28.8
Crude death rate	N.A.	9.8	11.1	12	11.2	10.7	N.A.	N.A.	N.A.	N.A.	N.A.	N.A.	N.A.	8.5	9.8	6.3	8.2	8.8
3. Mean age at marriage (1984: 1992):	N.A.	13.95	13.63	13.66	13.72	N.A.	N.A.	N.A.	N.A.	N.A.	N.A.	N.A.	N.A.	15.36	15.27	15.3	15.31	N.A.
4. Female literacy (1971: 1981: 1991)	14.6	8.69	8.6	9.3	10.3	20.8	19.2	14.4	25.1	13.6	18.08	27.08	26.2	24.8	20.1	17.8	22.23	37.4

Notes: 1. N.A. refers to not available.

2. N.T. refers to data not traced.

3. The figures of 1984 (1992) for vital rates and age at marriage refer to Baseline (Endline) Survey conducted by the Population Centre, Bangalore, during August-October, 1984 (January-March, 1992), in connection with the evaluation of IPP-III (Karnataka) by the Population Centre (Bangalore). For details see Reddy and Gopal (1993).

4. Figures for female literacy refer to respective census years.

Source: 1. Directorate of Health and Family Welfare, Government of Karnataka, Bangalore; 2. Reddy and Gopal (1993); 3. Government of India (1991); 4. Government of Karnataka (1991); and 5. Government of Karnataka (1990).

in 1984 but increased to around 15 in 1992. This is in contrast with the mean female age at marriage of 18 years (1981 census) in the Karnataka state. In a way, this signifies that the mean female age at marriage has remained low and stagnant in the region. This stagnation is supported by the estimates of mean female age at marriage in Goyal (1988; 139-140) for districts in Karnataka for 1971. The estimates were as follows: Bellary 17.11; Bidar 15.96; Gulbarga 15.86; and Raichur 15.9.

On the whole, the analysis above shows that the performance of family welfare programme in the H-K region is relatively poorer in both quantitative and qualitative aspects. In particular, these poor performance are mainly attributable to low female literacy, low female age at marriage and low proportion of eligible couples protected by different methods of family planning.

5. Provision of Health Infrastructure

Family welfare programme in the region is implemented through a network of organised infrastructure (physical and human) in the region. The provision of this infrastructure is guided by the same norms as elsewhere in the state.

Table 13.3 summarises the levels of public health infrastructure in the H-K region for different years. In general, the provision of this infrastructure is guided by the major criterion of population size. That is, higher the population size of a district, higher should be the level of infrastructure and vice versa. Accordingly, the levels of health infrastructure can be related to the distribution of district's population in the region' total and in the state's total.

First of all, there exists a close conformity between the distribution of districts' population as a per cent to region's total and state's total in 1981 (or 1991) census and the distribution of different physical health infrastructure as a per cent to region's total and state's total during 1983-84 and 1988-89 (or 1993-94). This conformity establishes that the provision of physical infrastructure is in tune with the general needs of the region, provided the total population is a measure for health infrastructural needs of the region. It should be emphasised that in recent years the improvement in physical health infrastructure (e.g. hospital buildings) in the region is promoted by special programmes under the India Population Project, the Hyderabad-Karnataka Area Development Board etc.

Another important aspect of health infrastructure is the bed-population ratio. A high (or low) ratio indicates a poorer (or better) provision of health services (e.g. in-patient services). The evidence in Table 13.3 reveals that this ratio is considerably higher in the region as compared to the state. In particular, Raichur district shows the highest bed-population ratio in the region for entire reference period.

In addition, Table 13.3 reports the provision of health staff (i.e. medical doctors and health workers) which is one of the programme inputs (other inputs being transportation, medicine, instruments and equipments etc.) for implementation of health and family welfare programme. Although the number of these staff is sanctioned according to national norms, the number of staff actually working may be different due to vacant positions. Thus, an important indicator of health staff position is the vacant position as a percentage of sanctioned positions. In Table 13.3, this percentage is given for the H-K region for the year 1992-93. This percentage varies across districts and by staff type. In general, the region faces the problem of a large number of vacant positions as compared to the State. This problem is apparent in regard to both male and female Senior Health Assistants. However, the acuteness of the problem varies between the districts in the region. For instance, the vacant position of doctors (or Female Senior Health Assistants) is very acute in Gulbarga (or in Raichur) district. And, the problem of vacant position is very acute in regard to male Senior Health Assistants in Gulbarga district.

6. Summary and Implications

This paper has presented selected basic information on population changes and development of health services and infrastructure in the H-K region of Karnataka state. The major implications of a broad comparative analysis of this information between the region and the state is summarised below:

1. The region has experienced a high natural growth of population, especially during 1981-91. Low female age at marriage, low female literacy and lower proportion of eligible couples protected by different methods of family planning may account for high growth of population in the region. In addition, a strong desire to have a large family (contributed, in part, by a strong son preference) may also be an important factor for high growth of population in the region. These factors imply that the measures to control population growth in the region need to be strengthened for changes in attitude and behaviour towards fertility of all

TABLE 13.3 Selected indicators of health infrastructure in districts of H-K Region: 1983-84 to 1992-93

Indicators	1983-84						1988-89						1993-94					
	Bellary	Bidar	Gulbarga	Raichur	Region	State	Bellary	Bidar	Gulbarga	Raichur	Region	State	Bellary	Bidar	Gulbarga	Raichur	Region	State
1. Number of hospitals:	13.00	5.00	6.00	3.00	27.00	233.00	14.00	7.00	14.00	9.00	44.00	176.00	14.00	6.00	14.00	9.00	43.00	293.00
As a per cent to region's total	48.15	18.52	22.22	11.11	100.00	-	31.82	15.91	31.82	20.45	100.00	-	32.56	13.95	32.56	20.93	100.00	—
As a per cent to state's total	5.58	2.15	2.58	1.29	11.59	100.00	7.95	3.98	7.95	5.11	25.00	100.00	4.78	2.05	4.78	3.07	14.68	100.00
2. Number of dispensaries:	67.00	48.00	92.00	76.00	283.00	1876.00	70.00	46.00	94.00	71.00	281.00	1869.00	11.00	2.00	11.00	6.00	30.00	208.00
As a per cent to region's total	23.67	16.96	32.51	26.86	100.00		24.91	16.37	33.45	25.27	100.00		36.37	6.67	36.37	20.00	100.00	—
As a per cent to state's total	3.57	2.56	4.90	4.05	15.09	100.00	3.75	2.46	5.03	3.80	15.00	100.00	5.29	0.96	5.29	2.88	14.42	100.00
3. Number of Primary Health Centres:	13.00	11.00	22.00	18.00	64.00	328.00	33.00	25.00	50.00	43.00	151.00	836.00	46.00	35.00	74.00	62.00	217.00	1297.00
As a per cent to region's total	20.31	17.19	34.38	28.13	100.00		21.85	16.56	33.11	28.48	100.00		21.20	16.13	34.10	28.57	100.00	—
As a per cent to state's total	3.96	3.35	6.71	5.49	19.51	100.00	3.95	2.99	5.98	5.14	18.06	100.00	3.55	2.70	5.71	4.78	16.73	100.00
4. Number of Primary Health Units:	42.00	32.00	56.00	51.00	181.00	1303.00	37.00	18.00	36.00	21.00	112.00	848.00	28.00	13.00	30.00	9.00	80.00	622.00

(Contd.)

	As a per cent to region's total	23.20	17.68	30.94	28.13	100.00	—	33.04	16.07	32.14	18.75	100.00	—	35.00	16.25	37.50	11.25	100.00	—
	As a per cent to state's total	3.22	2.46	4.30	3.91	13.89	100.00	4.36	2.12	4.25	2.48	13.21	100.00	4.50	2.09	4.82	1.45	12.86	100.00
5.	Number of Family Welfare Centres:	21.00	15.00	30.00	23.00	89.00	516.00	41.00	30.00	63.00	51.00	185.00	1034.00	20.00	14.00	30.00	24.00	88.00	474.00
	As a per cent to region's total	23.60	16.85	33.71	25.84	100.00	—	22.16	16.22	34.05	27.57	100.00	—	22.73	15.91	34.09	27.27	100.00	—
	As a per cent to state's total	4.07	2.91	5.81	4.46	17.25	100.00	3.97	2.90	6.09	4.93	17.89	100.00	4.22	2.95	6.33	5.06	18.57	100.00
6.	Sanctioned number of doctors (MO & AS+LMO):	N.T.	N.T.	N.T.	N.T.	N.T.	N.T.	N.T.	N.T.	N.T.	N.T.	N.T.	N.T.	103.00	91.00	181.00	131.00	506.00	—
	Vacant positions as a per cent of sanctioned posts	N.T.	N.T.	N.T.	N.T.	N.T.	N.T.	N.T.	N.T.	N.T.	N.T.	N.T.	N.T.	11.65	13.19	3 0.39	19.85	20.75	—
7.	Sanctioned number of Junior Health Assts. (Male):	N.T.	N.T.	N.T.	N.T.	N.T.	N.T.	N.T.	N.T.	N.T.	N.T.	N.T.	N.T.	268.00	167.00	438.00	337.00	1210.00	N.T.
	Vacant positions as a per cent of sanctioned posts	N.T.	N.T.	N.T.	N.T.	N.T.	N.T.	N.T.	N.T.	N.T.	N.T.	N.T.	N.T.	42.91	5.39	12.33	8.90	17.19	N.T.

(Contd.)

TABLE 13.3 (Contd.)

8. Sanctioned number of Junior Health Assts. (Female):	N.T.	N.T.	N.T.	N.T.	N.T.	N.T.	N.T.	N.T.	N.T.	N.T.	N.T.	N.T.	380.00	276.00	507.00	375.00	1538.00	9137.00
Vacant positions as a per cent of sanctioned posts	N.T.	N.T.	N.T.	N.T.	N.T.	N.T.	N.T.	N.T.	N.T.	N.T.	N.T.	N.T.	12.63	0.72	15.28	6.67	10.08	—
9. Sanctioned number of Senior Health Assts. (Male):	N.T.	N.T.	N.T.	N.T.	N.T.	N.T.	N.T.	N.T.	N.T.	N.T.	N.T.	N.T.	43.00	19.00	84.00	72.00	218.00	N.T.
Vacant positions as a per cent of sanctioned posts	N.T.	N.T.	N.T.	N.T.	N.T.	N.T.	N.T.	N.T.	N.T.	N.T.	N.T.	N.T.	11.63	0.00	60.71	22.22	33.03	N.T.
10. Sanctioned number of Senior Health Assts. (Female)	N.T.	N.T.	N.T.	N.T.	N.T.	N.T.	N.T.	N.T.	N.T.	N.T.	N.T.	N.T.	53.00	44.00	70.00	74.00	241.00	—
Vacant positions as a per cent of sanctioned posts	N.T.	N.T.	N.T.	N.T.	N.T.	N.T.	N.T.	N.T.	N.T.	N.T.	N.T.	N.T.	16.98	50.00	17.14	75.68	41.08	—
11. Number of beds in hospitals and dispensaries:	1494	519	1312	447	3772	36861	1630	606	1484	610	4330	41259	1738	794	1744	958	5234	49949
Population ('000) per bed	997	1917	1585	3991	1683	1008	1160	2071	1740	3787	1856	1090	1087	1581	1481	2411	1536	901

Notes: 1. N.T. refers to data not traced. 2. MO refers to Medical Officer; AS refers to Assistant Surgeon; and LMO refers to Lady Medical Officer.

Source: 1. Directorate of Health and Family Welfare, Government of Karnataka, Bangalore; 2. Office of the Divisional Joint Director of Health and Family Welfare Services, Gulbarga Division, Gulbarga;

3. Government of Karnataka (1993); 4. Government of Karnataka (1991); and Government of Karnataka (1990).

eligible couples without any gender bias or discrimination.

2. The region lags behind in the development of health services. This does not mean that a mere change in the norms for establishing the primary health care institutions would ensure the required health services. Rather, given the same level of physical infrastructure, health services can make a strong spatial and temporal difference, among others, due to availability of medical staff and health workers. In the H-K region, these differences can be singled out due to high vacant positions. Thus, the health staff position in the region should ensure no vacant positions as a first step towards promoting better health services. In the ultimate analysis, health services are delivered at the inter-personal level. Thus, apart from the on-job-training and education, a strong sense of dedication, commitment, care for the poor and the needy have to be reinforced in the minds of the health staff. It is needless to say that highly dedicated and committed staff should be honoured and provided with sufficient incentives, irrespective of their positions.
3. The provision of health services and infrastructure is not a state monopoly in the region. Thus, private-commercial enterprises (e.g. private hospitals/dispensaries/nursing homes etc.) and private-voluntary organisations (e.g. Family Planning Association of India) are at work in the health care sector of the region. In the same way, publicly-supported, voluntary organisations [e.g. Anganwadi Centres which implement the Integrated Child Development Schemes (ICDS), e.g. prevention of Protein Energy Malnutrition (PEM) among children of 6 months to 6 years] are at work at the grassroots levels of health care delivery. The coexistence of all these institutions is of importance and relevance to the study of regional health care, because their impacts are felt either directly or indirectly in the coverage of health care in the region. Thus, it is important to devise special strategies for promotion of private health sector in the region including measures for promotion of indigenous medicines.
4. The target-oriented approach to family welfare programme has shown that the time-path of performance is quite erratic. This may, in part, be due to the timing of supply and utilisation of different but complementary programme inputs (fixed and variable), such as buildings, medicines, transport, equipment and instruments, staff position etc. In addition, several non-

recordable inputs (e.g. dynamism of DHOs) may also be of importance to the success of the programme in a district. Thus, a detailed analysis of the role of these inputs as determinants of the programme's performance may be undertaken in the region. This analysis, other things being equal, will help in designing a strategy for consistent performance path of family welfare programme as it is related to programme inputs.

5. It is well known that inter-regional disparities are concomitant in the process of regional development. The H-K region is no exception to this in the health sector. In order to make a more realistic assessment of the nature and consequences of these disparities, the unit of region should be as nearer to the people as possible. In the context of the health sector, a realistic assessment of disparities may be attempted at the Sub-centre level in the region.
6. The needs of today and hopes of tomorrow of people in different locations are different. Area development is an important policy attempt to know these felt-needs of the people at the grassroots level. In this regard, the constitution of the Hyderabad-Karnataka Area Development Board in 1991 is the most welcome policy move. The Board has a vital role to play in the development of the region.

REFERENCES

Census of India. (1993). Final Population Totals, Part-I of 1992, Vol.II, Series-1, Census of India 1981, India, Office of the Registrar-General and Census Commissioner, New Delhi.

Census of India. (1986). Migration Tables (D-1), Part-V-A&B, Series-9, Karnataka, Census of India 1981, Directorate of Census Operations (Karnakata), Bangalore.

Census of India. (1977). Migration Tables (D-1), Part II-D, Series-14, Mysore, Census of India 1971, Directorate of Census Operations (Mysore), Bangalore.

Goyal, R.P. (1988). Marriage Age in India, B.R. Publishing Corporation, New Delhi.

Government of Karnataka. (1993). Karnataka at a Glance: 1992-93, Directorate of Economics and Statistics, Bangalore.

Government of Karnataka. (1991). Statistical Abstract of Karnataka: 1988-89, Bureau of Economics and Statistics, Bangalore.

Government of Karnataka. (1990). Statistical Abstract of Karnataka: 1983-84, Bureau of Economics and Statistics, Bangalore.

Government of India. (1991). Analytical Review of Couple Protection Rates (1990), Evaluation and Intelligence Division, Department of Family Welfare, Ministry of Health and Family Welfare, New Delhi.

Reddy, P.H. and Gopal, Y.S. (1993). Trends and Differentials in Fertility, Mortality and Family Planning Practices: An Evaluation of IPP-III (Karnataka), Population Centre, Bangalore.

14

POVERTY ALLEVIATION PROGRAMMES

S. N. Sangita

1. Introduction

The present paper examines the strengths and weaknesses of Poverty Alleviation Programmes (PAPs) implemented in the Hyderabad-Karnataka region with a view to suggesting improvements for their effective implementation. Three important and interrelated issues on which the success of the PAPs depends are discussed here. The first type of issues examined are: whether the existing PAPs in the HK region are adequate to improve the economic status of poor on par with the rest of the state.? Whether the schemes identified under PAPs are relevant to the region? Whether they are integrated with the ongoing spatial and sectoral programmes for effective utilization of resources? Whether the schemes identified under PAPs are viable and sustainable? The second type of issues are : whether the programmes are targeted effectively for the poor? Whether the assets provided under PAPs are of good quality? Whether adequate and timely inputs and services are provided to the beneficiaries? To what extent the beneficiaries have utilised the loans or assets given to them to improve their economic status? The third type of issues are : whether PRIs and NGOs can ensure people's participation for effective formulation and implementation of PAPs?

The study mainly focuses on Integrated Rural Development Programme (IRDP), Training of Rural Youth for Self-Employment (TRYSEM) and Jawahar Rozgar Yojana (JRY), which constitute major share both in terms of resource allocation and coverage of PAPs in the HK region. The study is mainly based on the secondary sources of data. The latter are, however, supplemented by limited field observations and interviews with the officials, non-officials and beneficiaries in Gulbarga district. The paper has four sections. The second section focuses on the nature, coverage and performance of PAPs in the HK vis-a-vis the rest of the State. The third deals with the programme design (identification and formulation of schemes), targeting of the programme (selection of beneficiaries and location of works, supply of credit and other inputs), utilization of the assets and recovery of loans. The last section presents some policy recommendations.

2. Profile of PAPs.

IRDP and TRYSEM were started in 1979 to improve the economic status of people living below the poverty line (Rs.11,000 in 1992-93 as against Rs.3,500 in 1978-79). Rural Poor under IRDP are provided with bank loan (10 per cent interest) and subsidy (25.50 per cent) to secure income generating assets. At least 50 and 40 per cent of IRDP beneficiaries are to be SC/ST and Women respectively. Self-employment ventures are selected on the basis of local demands, resources and infrastructural facilities. Beneficiaries are selected out of the list of eligible families placed in the Grama Sabha meeting, in which officials, bankers and elected representatives are present. The TRYSEM trains rural youth (18-35 age) drawn from the poverty group to develop among them technical and managerial skills or upgrade the existing skills so that they can start self-employment ventures. The selected youth are trained for 3 to 6 months after which they are given financial assistance under IRDP.

The wage-employment providing JRY is the product of the merger of NREP and RLEGP and has been in vogue since April 1989. The expenditure on this programme is shared between the Centre and States on the basis of 80 : 20. The funds of JRY are earmarked 22 per cent for state level schemes and 78 per cent for the district. State level funds in turn are distributed in the following manner: 10 per cent for construction of free houses (Indira Awaas Yojana), 30 per cent for irrigation wells (Million Wells Scheme) and 60 per cent for construction of class rooms under operation black board. 90 per cent of these free houses and irrigation wells are earmarked for SC/ST and freed bonded labourers.

The district retains 20 per cent of JRY funds and the remaining 80 per cent is allocated to Gram Panchayats. There are no restrictions or sectoral earmarking for spending these funds by GPs, except 15 per cent allocation on schemes that benefit SC/ST. However, there is a 30 per cent reservation for women in employment generation. At least 60 per cent of the resources have to be spent on wage component. Wages are paid in foodgrains. Contractors or middlemen are not to be engaged in the execution of JRY works. Works under these schemes are decided by village panchayats in consultation with the Taluk Panchayat.

District Rural Development Agency (DRDA) is mainly responsible for implementing PAPs. Comprehensive plans for these programmes at the Village cluster, Block and District on the basis of local needs, resources and infrastructural facilities are prepared to identify poverty reduction projects. Depending upon the availability of resources under various programmes, annual action or credit plans are prepared and approved by the District level Consultative Committee (DLCC) consisting of government officials, bankers and non-official member. However, in Karnataka, some of these powers have been transferred to the PRIs. They have a major say in selecting the schemes under JRY and IRDP.

3. Performance of PAPs

The available literature suggests that the people below the poverty line were more in the HK region. On the basis of revised poverty line (Rs.11,000), in Gulbarga district, three fourths of persons were below the poverty line. However, it was one fifth in Raichur district on the basis of old poverty line. Though the incidence of poverty is higher, the performance of PAPs in the HK is far from satisfactory when compared to the rest of the state. For instance, on an average in a district 4328 beneficiaries under IRDP were assisted in the HK region as against 5193 in the state in 92-93 (Table 14.1). The corresponding figures for Bidar and Bellary were 2681 and 3018. Similarly, on an average, 575 persons in each district in the HK region were trained as against 670 in the state under TRYSEM. It was 279 in Bidar district.

Same is the case with the implementation of the district credit plans. For instance, in Gulbarga district, 55 to 86 per cent of the district credit plan was implemented during 1991-94 as shown in Table 14.2. In other words, only a little more than half of the total schemes planned in the district in 1992-93 were executed. Low recovery of loans, cautious approach of bankers in the light of economic liberalisation and lack of rapport between district officials and bankers appear to be the major factors for non-achievement of targets under the credit plan.

3.1 Project Design

This section mainly analyses the type of schemes or activities selected under PAPs for the last 5 years with a view to understand their relevance

TABLE 14.1 Performance of PAPs in Hyderabad Karnataka Vis-A-Vis the State (1992 - 93)

	Bellary	Bidar	Gulbarga	Raichur	HK Region	State Average
IRDP	3018	2681	5841	5773	4328	5192
TRYSEM	710	279	640	669	575	670
100 Wells Programme	138	285	167	464	264	313
Mandays Generated (in lakhs)	23	13	33	23	23	21
Foodgrains utilised (in tonnes)	1171	436	–	293	633	854
Bhagya Mandirs	33	21	183	193	108	81
Gober Gas Plants set up	199	58	87	376	180	788
House site allotted	10274	6227	10311	4720	7883	7640
People's Housing Schemes	487	516	1145	508	664	897
Water Supply a. Bore Well	5025	3143	7041	6057	5317	6334
b.Piped water	232	219	457	382	323	369
c.Mini water supply	346	176	425	413	340	308

Source : Karnataka Statistics at a glance 1992-93, Bureau of Economics and Statistics, Government of Karnataka, Bangalore, 1993.

to the region to promote sustainable employment and development. The analysis also covers per capita consumption of subsidy and loan component of IRDP. We are presenting some field level impressions in support of our argument. By way of illustration we are presenting some statistical information with reference to Raichur and Gulbarga districts. We find that milch animals, bullock carts and shops were very popular under IRDP in Raichur district. Of the total number of IRDP schemes during 1989-94 milch animals and sheep accounted for 46 per cent in Raichur and

TABLE 14.2: Percentage of Achievement of the Credit Plan in Gulbarga District (91-94)

	Agriculture	SSI & Rural Artisans	Trade and Services	Total
1991-92	84	89	93	86
1992-93	65	39	45	55
1992-94	58	98	130	76

Source: District Annual Credit Plan.

39 per cent in Gulbarga The corresponding figure for shops was 17.2 and 15.2 respectively. During the same period, bullock and carts accounted 25.64 per cent in Raichur and 16.3 in Gulbarga.

Similar is the case with the schemes identified under TRYSEM and JRY. During our field visit, we were told that trades like tailoring were popular under TRYSEM. We were also told that a large per cent of the schemes identified under RLEGP/NREP/ JRY were roads. Added to this, a substantial portion of available funds under MLA quota is also being spent on roads. This is being done in spite of clear guidelines for spending JRY funds on productive schemes like social forestry.

During our field visits we found that the activities selected under PAPs were not relevant to the area. The following are the reasons for this state of affairs : In the first place, the lower level officials prefer to identify easy trades like tailoring, basket weaving, dairy, poultry and so on, when they are pressurised to fulfil the block targets. In the absence of training facilities, these are easy options for the administrators. Secondly, the bankers normally tend to identify a scheme where the risk of recovery is minimum and the loan component is small. Thirdly, officials and bankers prefer schemes which bring them rents/commissions. Fourthly, the elected representative perceives popular or visible schemes like roads and buildings (rather than productive ones) which would bring him good will and public support. In some cases, such schemes also help him or his supporters to get return benefit in the form of commission. Finally, the beneficiaries also prefer trades or units like milch animals, poultry, since they are quite familiar with them. The necessity of executing a number of schemes under different programmes also leads to wrong identification of schemes and wastage of resources.

In fact, we came across instances where a single individual has been trained under different programmes or members of a single family having been assisted. This is more so in schemes where SC/ST beneficiaries are involved. The extent of wastage due to duplication and other wastages can be known, if one looks at the number of schemes given under PAPs and the resultant increase of goods and services generated out of these schemes in the district. For instance, as we noted above during 1989-94 the milch animals and sheep in Raichur district accounted for 46 per cent of the total schemes identified under IRDP. Similarly, milch animals in Gulbarga Taluk accounted for 26.66 per cent of the total schemes assisted under IRDP (Kallur, 1992 : 340). But there is no substantial increase in their number and products generated out of them as well. The number of she-buffaloes per lakh of human population in Raichur district was 3455, 2756 and 3530 in 1966, 1977 and 1990 respectively. The corresponding number for sheep was 17940, 15924 and 17030. Same is the case with other districts in the HK region. The corresponding number of she-buffaloes for Gulbarga was : 2843, 1810 and 2230. And for the sheep it was 16583, 13020 and 12360.

The other important aspect about the viability of the project is the per capita availability of the subsidy and loan, repayment schedule and incremental capital output ratio. The per capita consumption of subsidy in Raichur had gone up to Rs.1985 in 1993 from Rs.778 in 1985-86. The corresponding increase of per capita credit was Rs.5279 and Rs.248 respectively. However, subsidies are below the state and national average. The per capita consumption of subsidy in 1989 in Raichur was Rs.1337. While it was Rs.1367 in Karnataka and Rs.1466 for the country. On the other hand, the per capita availability of credit in Raichur was Rs.4048 as against Rs.2355 and Rs.2149 respectively for Karnataka and the country as a whole. While incremental capital output ratio for Karnataka and the country in 1989 was 1.8 and 1.76 respectively. However, according to a study it was 0.53 in Gulbarga Taluk in 1990 (Kallur,1992:343). This is a very disturbing feature.

3.2 Implementation

In this section questions of targeting (selection of poor), quality of assets, retention and utilisation of assets, monitoring and recovery of loan are discussed. In Karnataka, in the past a large per cent of non-poor were included as IRDP beneficiaries. In recent times the per cent of non-poor has come down considerably. The lower per cent of non-poor in Karnataka can be attributed to the active involvement of PRIs, selection of beneficiaries in the grama sabha meetings, and better awareness among beneficiaries. In the absence of socio-economic profile of beneficiaries, we could not ascertain the position relating to this aspect in the HK region. However, according to a study carried out in Gulbarga Taluk on IRDP, it was reported that "...Authorities did not hold gram sabha meetings regularly, and further, whenever the meetings were held, the selection of genuine poor was not discussed thoroughly" (Kallur, 1992).

Our field observation also confirms the same. In recent years, there have been complaints about the manner of selection of PAP beneficiaries in the grama sabha meetings. According to a senior level district officer, gram panchayat leaders were not interested in transperant selection through grama sabha meeting. According to him, vested interests and fear of not satisfying every body might be the possible reasons. Lack of publicity about the PAP benefits and grama sabha meeting, failure to display the selected list in the public, alteration of the selected list in the grama sabha, selection of supporters by the political leaders were instances given in this regard. Similar allegations were also made by the elected leaders against the officials and the bankers. They include : the practices of not inviting them to grama sabha meetings, preparation of the list prior to, or outside, the grama sabha meeting, non-inclusion of names suggested by them on one pretext or other, and selection of beneficiaries with the help of middlemen.

Based on the observations of officials, non-officials, bankers and people we list the following as the reasons for misidentification of the beneficiaries. First, political leaders prefer to select their own supporters expecting in turn electoral support. On the other hand, party workers/ supporters avail this opportunity to generate income by getting assets for themselves or taking commission from the beneficiaries. Secondly, in some cases, the political leaders themselves are the main beneficiaries of these programmes. Many instances of misutilisation of JRY funds by Mandal Panchayat members are cited in this regard - some of them having worked as contractors. Thirdly, local officials select non-poor at the instance of political leaders, influential persons and friends. They also prefer to select the non-poor to show them as a success story. The study in Gulbarga Taluk says "four people collided with the field officers to inflate the number of asset, and the difference amount was shared among parties involved on the basis of a pre-determined formula. It further adds, that five beneficiaries were given cash (which according to rules is not allowed) and it was misutilised by them (Kallur, 1990 : 235). On the other hand schemes selected under NREP/JRY appear to be rich biased. Poor-oriented schemes such as development of village common lands with social forestry to meet the fuel and fodder needs of the poor did not find favour.

Another issue relates to the effectiveness of these programmes in generating additional income for the beneficiaries. Misappropriation of funds and selling of assets given to them in a relatively short time for consumption purpose will come in the way of raising additional income. The asset retention position in the HK region appears to be not satisfactory. In a study in Gulbarga district, 221 out of 364 units assisted under the Self-Employment to Educated Unemployed Youth (SEEUY) were intact in 1989 (Chandrakavate, 1990). According to a senior bank officer, the asset retention rate was 4-7 per cent in some of the districts of the HK region. According to him, this fact was known to the officials but they were not willing to share the information. We were also told by the villagers that some of the beneficiaries were not having the assets. According to them, some of them did not buy the asset and the people who bought the assets, sold them subsequently. It appears that some of the benficiaries were intrested more in subsidy of the scheme than income from it. Whenever, we expressed a desire to watch the asset, the beneficiaries evaded the issue. Even they could not produce monitoring card or bank pass book when asked for it. However, some of the beneficiaries gave the following reasons for not retaining the assets: inadequate loan, substandard asset, inadequate income, lack of marketing facilities and consumption expenditure. In other words, monitoring of IRDP assets did not receive adequate attention by the administration. In fact, according to the study in Gulbarga Taluk, monitoring was done partially and officials were visiting villages which happened to be mandal headquarters (Kallur, 1992).

The other important issue relates to the poor recovery of bank loans. The percentage of recovery in Gulbarga district during 1988-93 was around 23 to 43 per cent as shown in Table 14.3. The recovery position has declined substantially. The average recovery for 1991, 1992, 1993 was 36 per cent, 24 per cent and 25 per cent respectively. Misutilisation, consumption expenditure and low income appear to be the main reason for the non-payment of loans. According to a study in Gulbarga district, only one fifth of the 364 units assisted under SEEUY cleared their dues completely. According to it, willful defaulters due to misutilisation of funds accounted for 34.1 per cent. While it was 33.71 per cent and 23 per cent for low income and reinvestment respectively (Chandrakavate, 1990). Yet another sutyd, in the same district found similar results. According to the study, farmers mentioned heavy family expenditure was the main reason for non-payment of the crop loan. While it was 24 per cent due to crop failure and 12 per cent on account of investment on irrigation works (Warda, 1988).

Retention and utilisation of the assets for TRYSEM and JRY have

TABLE 14.3 Sector-wise Percentage of Loan Recovery to the Total Demand in Gulbarga 1988-83.

Year	Agriculture	S S I	Tertiary	Average net recovery
1988	49	30	49	42.67
1989	38	29	42	36.33
1990	25	17	26	22.67
1991	41	28	39	36.00
1992	29	10	32	23.67
1993	33	13	30	25.33

Source: Compiled from District Annual Credit Plan Reports.

not been analysed systematically in the absence of information. However, TRYSEM performance appears to be not satisfactory in Gulbarga district when compared to Raichur and the state average. In Raichur nearly a half (49.24 per cent) of the total trained during 1981-93 were self-employed and another 3.1 per cent were wage-employed (Table 14.4). The corresponding figure for Gulbarga was 11 and 7 per cent respectively. On the other hand, the self-employed at the state level accounted for 41.5 per cent (1989-93). We found the following factors to be mainly responsible for the unsatisfactory performance of TRYSEM. They are: non-identification of relevant trades, selection of non motivated beneficiaries, inadequate development of skill, entrepreneurial and managerial ability among the beneficiaries due to poor quality of training, non-preparation of project report immediately after training and failure to secure various inputs like credit, rawmaterial and marketing. In Gulbarga and Raichur 105 and 126 lakh mandays respectively were generated under JRY during 1989-94. The retention of assets under JRY appears to be better than under IRDP. During our field visits, we saw that houses under Indira Awas Yojana were under construction. Similarly, we observed the completed school buildings under operation black board. Roads laid under NREP/ JRY were also visible, although many irregularities were brought to our attention in this regard. In some of the villages, elected leaders were using these schemes to improve their popularity among the electorate by implementing them efficiently. Another positive aspect of this programme is the creation of additional employment for the poor particularly SC/ST and women during drought. Improvement in food intake, wage rates and mandays are mentioned in this regard. Ineffective maintenance and utilisation of community assets created under this programme and their non-durability and poor quality execution of works by the contractors and misappropriation and misutilisation of funds appear to be the constraints under this programme.

It is evident from the above analysis that the PAPs are inadequate to improve the economic status of poor in the HK region on par with the rest of the state. The performance of PAPs in the HK region is far from satisfactory when compared with rest of the state. The district plan targets were not achieved fully. Economic viability and sustainability of the schemes selected under PAPs did not receive adequate attention. However, no systematic effort was made to estimate schemes available under different programmes to prepare a comprehensive plan and thereby to avoid concentration of certain trades and wastage of resources. In fact, certain schemes like milch animals were over represented and thereby sectoral imbalances were created. The per capita consumption of subsidy

TABLE 14.4: Performance of PAPs in the HK Region

	Bellary	Bidar	Gulbarga	Raichur	HK	Karnataka	All India
IRDP							
No. of beneficiaries							
Per capita subsidy (Rs) 1988-89				1337		1367	1466
Per capita credit (Rs) 1988-89				4048		2355	2149
Capital Investment Ratio 1988-89			0.53	1.8		1.76	
Selected through gram sabha (%)							
Intact of Assets (%) 1988-89						65.27	72.88
People with vikas patrika (%) 1988-89						4.47	38.06
Recovery of loans(%)							
People crossed poverty line (%) 88-89						48.77	64.02
TRYSEM							
Total Trained (since inception) 81-93				5818		52045*	
Self-Employed(%)				49.24		41.5	
Wage Emplolyed(%)							
Expenditure on training (in lakhs)				3.51			
				102.23			
J R Y							
Expenditure (lakhs)							
Mandays generated (lakhs) 89-94			106.6	128.420			
Foodgrains distributed (89-94)			767.23	3632.85			

* 1981 - 89.

and credit and incremental capital input ratios in the HK region were not favourable when compared to the state average. Therefore, these schemes may not be sustainable. In fact, a significant per cent of beneficiaries could not retain assets intact due to faulty design of the project. Similarly, projects created under JRY were not effectively put to use. Very moderate percentage of the trainees were self-employed under TRYSEM. Misidentification of beneficiaries was large. Assets were not fully retained. And loan recovery was poor.

4. Policy Prescriptions

Based on the above review, some policy prescriptions are suggested in this section. Although additional funds for PAPs are desirable to help the region on par with the rest of the state, we are not recommending the same. Instead, the HK Board should allocate resources to improve the performance levels (fulfilment of targets) of PAPs and effective utilisation of available resources under PAPs. As a first step in this direction, the data base of PAPs in particular and other welfare and development programmes in general should be strengthened. At least, progress regarding block and sector wise performance of welfare and development programmes of the last 10 years (in terms of money spent, people benefited and schemes selected) should be prepared. This would help to assess the impact of programmes and to take corrective measures. Besides, the planning and monitoring function of the HK Board should be strengthened.

The present system of selection of schemes on the basis of political populism and interest, administrative convenience and target fulfilment, and the risk aversion nature of bankers should be replaced by scientific selection based on merit. While formulating the schemes/projects, effective spatial and sectoral linkages should be established. As a first step in this direction, linkages among PAPs and departments should be strengthened to minimise leakages. At the second level, their integration with development activities particularly land resource, rural eco-system and industry-based activities (soil conservation including afforestation, water harvesting, construction of field channels drainage, desiltion of irrigation tanks and so on) along with other non-crop and non-agriculture sector activities should be ensured for sustainable employment and development. Third, they can be integrated with the social development programmes such as health and family planning, education, drinking water and so on for the overall development of the HK region. Besides economic viability and preference of the beneficiary/community should be considered while selecting the schemes.

The third type of policy prescriptions relate to improvement in the implementation process of PAPs. Two types of recommendation are identified in this regard. The first one suggests that people's participation through NGOs and PRIs in both plan formulation and implementation is the best institutional mechanism for strengthening PAPs. Genuine NGOs have certain advantages over PRIs. But such NGOs in the HK region are few in number. Under the circumstance, PRIs are the second best alternatives provided they fulfill the following conditions: Selection of schemes and beneficiaries in the grama sabha should be done in the presence of elected representatives; and officials, bankers and NGOs should ensure transparency in selecting beneficiaries, locations and schemes. Secondly, clear guidelines, sectoral allocation and set procedures for execution as well regular supervision and audit can check the PRI officials and non-officials from misutilisation and misappropriation of resources. Maintenance (under JRY) and monitoring of the assets (under IRDP) and recovery of loan by PRIs can be tried in select GPs. The villages which fail to recover loans should be denied future development projects. At the same time, the PRIs (GPs, Taluk Panchayats and ZPs) should be provided incentives in the form of awards and prizes by the HK Board on the basis of their performance with regard to implementation of PAPs.

The second set of policies under institutional mechanism are aimed at changing the orientation of actors - official, non-officials, bankers and beneficiaries through training. The beneficiaries should be trained for a short duration (3-4 days) to improve their skills, and organisational and entrepreneurial ability to handle the assets. Organisation of beneficiaries by NGOs and other agencies improves their articulative capacity. PR leaders and other functionaries particularly at the village level should be trained not only in state craft but also on philosophy and procedures of PAPs. In this regard, the HK Board should synchronise its efforts with the on-going training programmes for PR functionaries at the instance of Government of India. The HK Board also should provide dynamic leadership to bring rapport between officials and bankers by activating consultative committee meetings at the district and taluk levels (DLCCs and TLCCs) for effective planning, monitoring of PAPs and recovery of loans.

REFERENCES

Chandakavate, M. S., *Scheme to provide Self-Employment to Educated Unemployed Youth,* Ph D thesis, Department of Economics, Gulbarga University, Gulbarga, 1990.

Hanumantha Rao, "Integrating Poverty Alleviation Programmes with Development Strategies", *Economic and Political Weekly,* November 28, 1992.

Kallur, M S, "Income and Employment Generation Through IRDP for Poor in India", *Asian*

Economic Review, 34 (2), August 92 : 340 - 347.

Michael, Bamberger and Abdul Aziz (Eds), *The Design and Management of Sustainable Poverty Alleviation Projects : The South Asian Experience,* The EDI of World Bank, Washington D C, 1993.

Montek, S. Ahluwalia, "Policies for Poverty Alleviation", Asian Development Review, *Studies of Asian and Pacific Economic Issues,* 8(1), 1990 : 111-132.

Rao, V. M. and Abdul Aziz (Eds), *Poverty Alleviation in India : Programmes and Actions,* Ashish, New Delhi, 1989.

Sangita, S. N., "Self Employment Programmes for Rural Youth : The Role of Non-Governmental Organisations (NGOs)", *Management Review,* 5(2), July-Dec. 1990 : 1-30.

Sangita, S. N., et.al., "Training of Rural Youth for Self-Employment in Karnataka : Policy Perspectives", *Man and Development,* Vol.12(1), March 1990.

Sangita, S. N., Institutional Arrangement for Controlling Corruption in Public Life : Karnataka Experience. *Indian Journal of Public Administration,* 41 (1) Jan-Mar, 1995: 45-67

Sangita, S. N., Panchayati Raj System in AP and Karnataka : A Comparative Perspective, Monographed, ISEC, 1993.

Warda, V. S., *Commercial Banks and Agricultural Credit,* Ph D thesis, Department of Economics, Gulbarga University, Gulbarga, 1988.

INDEX